Thurman Munson

For Herbie Wilson
and his three most loved —
for their footprints left behind

Thurman Munson

A BASEBALL BIOGRAPHY

by Christopher Devine

McFarland & Company, Inc., Publishers
Jefferson, North Carolina, and London

Library of Congress Cataloguing-in-Publication Data

Devine, Christopher
  Thurman Munson : a baseball biography / by Christopher
Devine.
      p.   cm.
  Includes bibliographical references and index.
  ISBN 0-7864-1089-2 (softcover : 50# alkaline paper) ∞
  1. Munson, Thurman, 1947–1979.   2. Baseball players—
United States— Biography.   I. Title.

  GV865.M78 D48 2001
  796.357'092 — dc21   2001020240
  [B]

British Library cataloguing data are available

Manufactured in the United States of America

On the cover: Thurman Munson *(courtesy Louis Requena)*

McFarland & Company, Inc., Publishers
  Box 611, Jefferson, North Carolina 28640
    www.mcfarlandpub.com

ACKNOWLEDGMENTS

The reader might notice that under the title of this book is a line that reads, "by Christopher Devine." That's a trick I use to save space and keep the reader's attention. The truth is, I couldn't have come this far on my own.

If I weren't so sly, the byline would look something like the following, which includes the thoughts that register in my mind at the sight of these names:

First, those who shaped the writer...

I thank Donna Devine most of all not just for being interested in this project but for being active by reading, giving, and believing. I thank God for blessing me with this experience and all of its byproducts. I thank Edith Wilson for love, guidance, righteousness, and wisdom; Michael A. Devine, whose hard work has opened many doors; Evie Schmidt for being her helpful self; Rich Foley for cultivating my interest in the pastime of baseball; Jenn and Mike Devine for familiarizing me with life and then making it more interesting; Z, for bringing out the best in me; and P squared (aka Pete Costella and Ryan Puza) because you'd bug me if I left you out.

And then those who shaped the writing...

I thank Bill Ryczek and Bill Hageman, my advisors, both of whom were unfailingly generous with their time and their insight. They walked me through this entire process, and I will remember their help. I thank Frank Devine for giving me a very important book: the autobiography of his childhood icon, Thurman Munson; the involved faculty of Westfield High School: Barbara Chiampa, Madeline Warner, and Julie Schlobohm; the workers at the Westfield Atheneum, who dug under the dust to uncover those heavy old newspapers; Roseanne Casale and the *Westfield Evening News* for letting people know about their hometown boy; John Daly for being a more resourceful researcher than me, and a helpful one, at that;

Bobby Plapinger for being a friend and a good businessman; Tim Lewis for helpful remembrances; Guy Waterman for generosity when it was inconvenient; all the authors who regarded my letters with respect and provided useful advice: Mark Alvarez, Evelyn Begley, Bryan DiSalvatore, Fred Stein, and Irving M. Stein; and finally, the Society for American Baseball Research for providing a quality forum that both appreciates the richness of baseball and enhances it.

CONTENTS

PREFACE

The life of a soul on earth lasts longer than his departure.
— Angelo Patri, quoted by Bobby Murcer
at Thurman Munson's funeral.[1]

Thurman Munson's life was lived in the shadows.

This was natural for a man of his position. One of Thurm's backstop brethren, Johnny Bench, once said, "A catcher and his body are like an outlaw and a horse. He's got to ride that nag until it drops."[2] That was quite clearly true of Munson. He was a player who dedicated himself completely while on the field, absorbing the punishing blows that are the catcher's badges of honor. That was Thurm's signature on the game: his devotion every day, not a single vivid moment that could be pinpointed, like Hartnett's "homer in the gloamin'," Thomson's "shot heard round the world," Larsen's perfect game, or Reggie Jackson's three-clout classic at the Bronx's Yankee Stadium on an unforgettable October night in 1977.

Thurm was there for that game. If one looks closely at the tape, scouring the video for the thick, bushy mustache, the dusty Yankee cap jammed on backwards, the conspicuous orange chest protector against the pinstriped number 15 jersey, one will see. Munson's there, slashing a forgotten single and hobbling home as one of Jackson's ribbies on the initial four-bagger. He slaps his teammate's hands and leads the charge to the dugout. He's the one rising from the dugout bench, shouting in Reggie's ear on number two, and whacking the frame of his thick shoulders. He's a little farther away for the final blast. A little farther from Jackson's ear and from the arms that are about to lift the Yankee helmet to an electrified throng of awestruck rooters. And each time, Thurm fades away just a little more.

1

That night, the New York Yankees' fans were fortunate enough to witness history. They saw a moment that epitomized the dominance of Reggie Jackson. They also saw a night that epitomized Thurm Munson.

While watching a tape of this game the other night, listening to the crowd's thunderous chant of "REG-gie! REG-gie! REG-gie!" I realized that only once had Yankee Stadium, or any other place for that matter, rung with chants of "Thurman ... Thurman ... Thurman." That time, the chant was low and somber, not electric or celebratory. It was August 3, 1979, the day after Munson died in a plane crash — a death so dramatic that it overshadowed his life to become his defining moment.

It is unfortunate that Munson's legacy does not lie in his baseball career. Munson was respected for his will to play the game the way it should be played, with the consuming hunger and vigor of a passionate professional. While it may seem that he is being lauded excessively here, his story will justify my enthusiasm. He suffered broken hands, separated shoulders, and blows that left him unconscious, but his perseverance made them all seem harmless. It was no mistake that he earned the reputation of the toughest man in the league.

Yet Munson's reputation transcended pure grit. He was renowned as his era's supreme defensive catcher (three consecutive Gold Gloves), clutch hitter (.373 cumulative World Series batting average), and leader (World Series berths in each of the three full seasons of his Yankee captaincy). Additionally, in seven of Munson's nine full seasons, he captured either the Rookie of the Year, Gold Glove, Most Valuable Player, or the world championship.

Although Munson operated in the shadows, he deserves to be brought to the light. A thorough search through Thurm's life brings the truth of his life into the foreground, which has been occupied by his dramatic passing for far too long.

Thurman Munson was a vital part of the success of baseball's most storied ballclub. I hope that Munson's story will impress the reader and inspire a true appreciation for his years of service and dedication on the ballfield, his leadership as a teammate, and his loyalty as a friend, husband, and father. If that comes to be his legacy, then all work was leisure, all reaction will be reward, and each day lived was investment in the future.

It's all the breath he has left.

Christopher Devine
Westfield, Massachusetts

1

MUNSON V. STATE OF MIND

Omnia vincit veritas (Truth conquers all).
— Munson family motto

How is it that a man could be dethroned during the completion of his crowning achievement?

Thurm Munson sat in the clubhouse absorbing the mortifying defeat of his New York Yankees in the 1976 World Series with the balancing knowledge of the season that had been put to rest with the night's final out. The Bicentennial had yielded a fine campaign for the rugged backstop: a new title as captain of the Yanks, a World Series berth, a Most Valuable Player honor. For number 15, that invincibility was not diminished once the crisp breeze of October rolled around.

Munson had set the ballparks afire in the playoffs and made history doing so. He had destroyed the Kansas City Royals in the American League Championship series with ten hits, three RBI, and a .435 average. The Yanks overall racked up eight runs, one homer, and a .222 batting average in the World Series. Thurm had collected eight of their 30 hits, over a quarter of the team output. With two runs and two RBI to his credit, he outpaced all series participants but Johnny Bench with a .529 clip (.004 shy of his Cincinnati counterpart). A 4–4 performance in the final game tied a World Series record, as did a string of six consecutive hits. Of course, that did not provide enough consolation.

While awaiting the sting's dissolution, Munson was approached by American League official Bob Fishel, who proposed that he represent the junior circuit in postgame interviews. As Thurm reached the stage, Cincinnati Reds manager Sparky Anderson was delivering a victorious oration in

praise of his men, one narrowed down into petty comparisons. "Munson
is an outstanding ballplayer and he would hit .300 in the National League,
but don't embarrass nobody by comparing them to Johnny Bench."[1]

Munson had readily conceded that Bench was his superior on the
field, however he would not allow himself to be *told* to accept that. Later
he wrote:

> I couldn't believe what I was hearing — I don't know if he was aware
> I was standing there. I'd read a lot about the class Anderson was
> supposed to have. This is how he behaved after winning a world
> championship? I didn't want to get into a hassle with him, but I
> was really mad about what I'd just heard.[2]

Disgusted, Munson shot back upon his turn at the microphone. "For
me to be belittled after the season I had and after the game I had ... it's
bad enough to lose, but worse to be belittled like that."

With the sarcasm that had made him infamous, Munson left no room
for misunderstanding. "To win four in a row and rub it in my face, that's
class. I never compared myself to Johnny Bench, but if I played in the
National League, I might be the best offensive player in the League." Thurm
then turned to Bench, who had since entered. "Nice going, J. B. Super."[3]
There's class.

The factor of character may seem irrelevant in evaluating the legacy
of a baseball player. After all, what difference does it make to a man's batting average if he has a sunny disposition? Well, "Sunny Jim" Bottomley
has a plaque in the Hall of Fame and "Sad Sam" Jones doesn't. Then again,
Ty Cobb was a charter member of the Cooperstown boys, so forget that
theory. But while the pastime is regarded as a game of numbers it is quite
obviously a game of character as well. Whether a positive or negative image
prevails, it is that impression that carries on in the memories of fans
throughout the years. They don't remember Munson for his looks, now,
do they? No, without that brash and genuine spirit, his stamp would not
have been so heavily imprinted on the game. So as the ink runs dry on
that stamp, it is time to refresh memories and challenge the accepted por-
trayal of one of the most misunderstood figures to ever cross the diamond.

The way the media presents Munson today, one would think their
relationship had been rosy all along. It wasn't. Their current sentimental-
ism is out of solemn sympathy and respect but is not a genuine represen-
tation of the ire directed at him while he lived. The rift between the two
factions grew so irreparable that Thurm cut off contact with the press during the famous, forgettable beard saga of August 1977. Yet they kept trying.

In May 1978, Sparky Lyle was approached by a woman writing an article on Munson. Her main topic was "Why is Thurman so mean?"

Lyle was sick of hearing writers' synopses of his teammate. Sparky boomed:

> Just leave the guy alone. Thurman just wants to be left alone. He knows how good he is. Quit writing about why he's so mean. Just accept the fact he has an off day like everybody else, except he has more of them.... Maybe the guy doesn't like to talk to strangers. Did you ever think of that?[4]

Actually, Lyle was right. According to other teammates and his wife, Diane Munson, that was exactly Thurm's problem with the media and many other people. He was a shy man who had a fear of revealing his true self to someone who might not respond with sensitivity. (The reasons for that will be spelled out in chapter 2.) To those who didn't understand the reasons for this behavior he came off as grumpy or surly. The more reporters pried for a glimpse into his psyche, the more Munson resisted. And with that, the negative image grew. As his attorney, Bob Woolf, explained, "The public image of him was all wrong. Thurman was really a pussycat."[5]

Woolf's thought was seconded by Yankee manager Billy Martin. "For the people who never knew him, didn't like him, I feel sorry for them. [He was] not only ... a great competitor but a leader and a husband and a devoted family man. He was a close friend. I really loved him."[6]

Many others did as well, even opponents. "He has always had a warm word for everybody," Orioles ace Jim Palmer remembered. "There aren't too many people who really care about other people, but he would always ask you how you felt and how your family was. I know that sounds like a cliche, but he knew my wife, and I felt he truly meant it."[7]

The genuineness of his actions provided yet another component for trouble with the writers. The media wanted a showman on hand to perpetuate the rowdiness of the "Bronx Zoo" image. That might have been fine for someone like Sparky Lyle or Reggie Jackson, but it was against Munson's character to give in to that. Instead, he opted to speak softly and carry a big glove. Of course, the sober, quiet nature of a demure defensive king didn't sell papers. Criticisms of him did. Yet Munson stuck to his guns and operated as he felt was true and right. Many teammates could attest to that.

Catcher Rick Dempsey recalled his first day with the Yankees in 1973. He was a touted prospect who had been back and forth in the majors since his debut on September 23, 1969. Four years later, when he walked into the Yankee locker room, Munson was the first to greet him. "You're the kid who's gonna try to take my job, aren't you?" Thurm asked.

"Yeah, if I can," replied Dempsey.

"Well, nice to have you around."

"From that day on, Thurman was my idol," said Dempsey years later, trembling to fight back tears. "He was always reassuring me, telling me that someday I would get my chance. He was never afraid to tell me how I could go about taking his job."[8]

Of course, swiping Munson's job was *not* apple pie. Whether it was known on the outside or not, Thurm was one of the most respected men in the game. In the words of Bob Woolf, "He was a throwback to the old days of baseball."[9] Whitey Herzog, who managed against the Yankees in multiple American League Championship series, was highly critical of the club's big payroll and big names. Yet he deeply respected number 15. "If I could have had my choice of players on [the Yankees], I would have taken Thurman Munson, the catcher," Herzog wrote in his autobiography, *White Rat*. "He could throw, he could hit, he was aggressive, took charge of the game the way a catcher should.... I haven't seen many catchers who do the job offensively and defensively as he could."[10]

Bill Virdon, Yankee manager during 1974 and '75, developed a notably similar view to Herzog's. The skipper once raved, "If I had 25 guys like Thurman Munson, I wouldn't even have to manage this team. He does everything well. He's aggressive. He's not as big as some good ones I've seen, but he's strong and quick. There's a lot of enthusiasm in him."[11]

Enthusiasm was a necessity in Munson's line of work. The catcher is recognized as the general of the field, the hardest working, most tireless, grittiest soldier that baseball can produce. There is virtually no point in a game when he is not on the move and putting his health on the line for his team's benefit. The position takes heart; not everyone can do it. Rocky Marciano, the acclaimed boxing champion, was a catcher as a kid due to his stocky, resilient build. When he reached a crossroads in his life where he had to decide between boxing and baseball, he chose the former. Contrary to expectation, his mother exhaled with relief. "I didn't raise my son to be a catcher!" she exclaimed.[12]

The position of catcher perfectly suited Munson, though. George Steinbrenner summed that up eloquently. "Hurt is in direct relation to character," he once said. "I can remember Thurman Munson playing with all of his body black and blue."[13]

In 1978, the controversies, traveling, and especially injuries had weighed Munson down to where he did not think he could continue. Nevertheless,

he persevered through a
costly but successful season. While playing in an
unfathomable 154 games
and logging 617 at-bats, he
hit .297, six homers and 27
doubles, rapped out 187
hits, and scored 73 runs.
His teammate and friend
Graig Nettles was asked at
the end of September by
Phil Pepe of the *Daily News*
who baseball's Comeback
Player of the Year was. Nettles barely paused. "Thurman had that won the first
day of the season."

"Why?"

"Thurman said he was
never coming back, and he
came back, so he's gotta win
it."[14]

A week or so earlier,
Munson had dislocated his
right shoulder in an
important home series
versus Boston. After the
season he would undergo
surgery back in his home-
town of Canton, Ohio, to

Munson rears back and guns for a potential base
thief in a game at Yankee Stadium. Munson was
heralded for his strong arm. (Courtesy Louis
Requena)

relieve pressure in the acromioclavicular joint. He hardly told anyone
about his suffering. Manager Bob Lemon, however, knew and wanted to
play backup Mike Heath behind the plate. Thurm's injury was so bad that
the joint could be physically moved by another's hand.

But Munson didn't hit well as a designated hitter, so he opted to continue uninterrupted as the everyday catcher.

Through all the trials, Thurm consistently found the strength of character to have fun at what he did. Jim Palmer knew this firsthand: "I can
remember tense, critical games when I'd strike him out, and I'd see him
give me a grin. I think that was his way of telling me that striking out
wasn't the end of the world."[15]

Thurman Munson was certainly not a perfect person. And some of the negative impressions of him were accurate. He was said to have spit on the shoes of autograph seekers and to have an obsession with material objects ranging from guns to cars to planes, all of which either sealed his fate or came close to it, as will be explained later. But he had reasons for certain behaviors and was a truly great man in the final analysis. In the arms of his family or in the dust behind home plate, he was a man that knew his duty and loved doing it well. After all of his efforts in baseball, he was remembered as the only man never booed at Yankee Stadium, and that vivid impression is all that was ever needed to be said to the general public about Thurman Munson. Perhaps he was not surprised by their appreciation. Thurm believed that the Yankee fans knew him well, much better than they thought they did, for after all those years and the scores of games the patrons witnessed, they saw the true emotion, intensity, and heart that drove him.

But today, right now, what does he have to show for it? To the modern mind, Munson was a man who died instead of a man who lived. Yet there is so much to remember of him, the rabble-rousing pack with which he became a champion, and the rowdy atmosphere in which their greatness was accomplished, one in which charisma overshadowed leadership and controversy spat at winning streaks. Against the odds, how did a grumbling warrior of heart ever capture reverence? And why did it stop?

It's odd to see the way Munson is represented in Cooperstown today. In nearly every shop one can find apparel, statues, or memorabilia bearing his mustachioed chipmunk image. Above the slick hardwood floors of a bat shop are found the T-shirts of but five heroes. Alongside such greats as Mickey Mantle and Babe Ruth is Thurman Munson. In one window, a large painting of him stares out prominently at the crowded street. A beautiful display it is, featuring action shots of Thurm catching, scurrying along the base paths, and slashing a hit safely, all surrounding a gleaming face-front portrait. Thinking what a great token of respect it would be to own such a prize, I asked the price. The store owner, as though he'd been through this many times before, deadpanned, "Fifteen hundred dollars." Perhaps this was an overzealous gesture of tribute to Thurm's uniform number. I laughed incredulously as I walked out the door.

There seemed to be no building that had forgotten him. Except perhaps one.

The disparity between Munson's standing in these places and his standing *within* the neighboring Hall of Fame is dramatic. No other man denied by the Hall of Fame carries such high regard in the community. He is renowned and revered as a legend inside nearly every shop and exhibit, and yet he's just another "what if" to the greatest show in town. What is it that has so polarized the perspectives of these two groups? Could it be that Munson just doesn't deserve induction? If the rest of this chapter does not clarify that, surely the next nine will. This book's goal is to educate against misconceptions, for misconceptions have dogged the legacy of Thurman Munson to this day.

Perhaps the saddest misconception about Thurman Munson is that had he not passed on, had he played longer, he would have made the Hall of Fame. Contrary to popular belief, it is quite doubtful that Munson planned to continue playing for much longer. "Thurman had talked about retiring after this season," Yankee catcher Jerry Narron said in August 1979. "He talked to me and told me that I would have to do most of the catching this year, and that if he did come back next season, he would probably play a different position and definitely not catch as many games as he had."[16]

But first Thurm would have to fulfill his contractual obligations, which ran through 1981, as he told teammate Bobby Murcer in '79. "I can't afford to quit now. I have to play another three years. Then I'll be set. Then I'll have enough money to quit."[17]

Because of his injuries, Munson would have been forced to leave behind the catching position for either first base or designated hitter. But how long would that have lasted? Playing for the Yankees was a demanding job. Eventually, lingering in the clubhouse under the leader label would have worn itself thin as his family and lucrative business ventures remained planted in Canton. And with the benefit of the latter, he certainly would not have needed to play for the money. Had God altered the path, it is clear that Munson would have retired after the 1981 season, if not before.

When Munson died in 1979, there was much talk of early admission into Cooperstown, as had been allotted to Lou Gehrig and Roberto Clemente. The prospects seemed bright.

Munson's accolades and the records of ten seasons' time are impressive.

He was 1970 American League Rookie of the Year; 1976 American League Most Valuable Player; winner of three consecutive Gold Gloves, 1973–75; and a seven-time All Star. He received Most Valuable Player votes in seven seasons; was captain of three consecutive pennant-winning ballclubs and two straight world champions (in each of Munson's full seasons as captain, the Yankees reached the World Series); and was the eighth Yankee to have his uniform number retired.

Munson batted over .300 in five seasons; in 1977 became the first American Leaguer in 23 years to bat over .300 and drive in 100 runs for three straight seasons; had a .339 lifetime American League Championship series batting average and a .373 lifetime World Series batting average; set a World Series record in 1976–77 with seven consecutive base hits in the World Series; and was one of the finest clutch hitters of all time.

The catcher committed just one error in the 1971 season, on a play in which he was knocked unconscious; had a .998 1971 fielding percentage; caught three different first-time 20-game winners; and was widely considered the best defensive catcher and handler of pitchers of the 1970s.

Thurm's career stats seem low until one compares him to other Hall of Fame catchers (as originally compiled in Phil Pepe's column "Baseball Spotlight" according to Linkugel and Pappas, p. 88). Despite the brevity of his career, Munson collected more games than Roger Bresnahan, Buck Ewing, or Roy Campanella, while only 59 fewer than Mickey Cochrane; had more hits than Bresnahan, Campanella, or Ray Schalk; had more seasons of .300 or better in batting average than Bresnahan, Yogi Berra, Schalk, Rick Ferrell, Johnny Bench, Campanella, or Carlton Fisk; and had more 100 RBI seasons than Bresnahan, Ewing, Schalk, Ernie Lombardi, Gabby Hartnett, Cochrane, or Ferrell. Plus, Munson logged a career average 25 points higher than Bench and 21 points higher than Fisk, who substantiated Munson's theory by slowing dramatically after leaving cozy Fenway Park in 1981.

Finally, Bill Dickey is considered by many to be the best catcher of all time. He averaged 120 games a season. Munson? 128. His 1,278 games caught is more than numerous heralded catchers whose careers spanned far longer than his did.

The yardstick by which all Hall of Fame candidates are measured is a determination of whether the player has dominated the game over the course of ten seasons. Period. When Munson's achievements are examined both as an individual and in comparison, a voter would be hard-pressed, almost ignorant, to answer that Munson does not belong. Yet, so far, he has been refused. Since his death, such players as Jim Bunning, Phil Rizzuto, Richie Ashburn, Don Sutton, and Tony Perez have been inducted. Among the men who received more votes than Munson in given years were Joe Torre, Bill Mazeroski, Vada Pinson, Luis Tiant, Bobby Bonds, Dave Concepcion, Lew Burdette, Mickey Lolich, and Don Larsen. By this ranking, the writers have voiced a collective opinion that these players dominated baseball more than Thurm Munson did.

The tallies speak for themselves. In 1981, the Hall of Fame voting began for Munson. His 62 votes fell 239 ballots short of selection. The rest of the decade was similar: 26, 18, 29, 32, 35, 28, and so on. The 1990s continued in this way:

1990 — 33 votes; 1991 — 28 votes; 1992 — 32 votes; 1993 — 40 votes; 1994 — 31 votes; 1995 — 30 votes

A recreation of Munson's locker — including his spikes and glove — stood on the first floor of the Hall of Fame for several years. It has since been removed. His plaque is missing, too.

2

EDUCATION OF THE OHIO SON

*You've got to be a man to play baseball, but you've got to
have a lot of little boy in you, too.*
— Roy Campanella

At the time, the kid was clean-cut, an All-American catcher from
nearby Kent State, and the number one draftee of the New York Yankees.
His mother labored all day to make the house shine with beauty and the
children were dressed in their finest formal clothing. New York general
manager Lee MacPhail and scout Gene Woodling soon arrived, and with
that, negotiations began. A lone man chose to ride the sofa decked out in
work pants and an undershirt. Uttered Darrell Munson loudly, "He ain't
too good on pop fouls, ya' know." The Bombers inked Thurm anyway.

Despite his undying pride for Canton, Ohio, Thurman Lee Munson
was born in neighboring Akron — 21 years before the aforementioned
scene — on June 7, 1947. He was fourth in the Munson lineage, following
siblings Darla, Janice, and Duane. Few of Thurman's childhood photos are
in public circulation save a joyful, winking portrait of the hefty infant
published in his 1978 autobiography, *Thurman Munson* (written with
coauthor Martin Appel), and a hazy front yard snapshot. In that one, young
Munson fashions his batting stance for the camera, his baggily uniformed
left leg crooked slightly forward, a smooth, ash baseball club slumped
upon his nine-year-old shoulder.

The name of Thurman Lee was chosen in honor of some obscure former athlete, according to father Darrell, a long-haul truck driver with an
acid tongue. His labor provided the Munsons with sufficient support, but
nothing in excess of necessity. "Truck drivers didn't make much money

12

then," Thurm explained to a writer years later, "and it was really tough for him supporting a family of four kids. Yeah, we had food and clothing, all right, but not a dime over that."[1]

Economics, however, were not the derivation of the family discontent. Darrell, who as Thurman put it, "wasn't around a lot," appeared friendly and supportive in public, but his intimidation at home was disheartening. Mother Ruth's primary purpose was to keep the children in line, lest they be reprimanded. From the beginning, Thurm was an unusually sensitive person, and the experiences undoubtedly shaped a great deal of his character and subsequently his image.

When he was four years old, Thurm and the family moved to a country town by the name of Randolph. Since the new home was a farm, Thurman now had a vast, open course on which to pursue the sport of baseball. Utilizing this ocean for education, Duane and Darrell schooled Thurm on the game, as the three partook in frequent fielding sessions. Sometimes one of the boys caught one for a bloody nose, but Darrell kept on swinging. Likewise, Thurm continued pounding his Hutch model glove, deftly mastering the trade.

After a few years in Randolph, the Munsons moved once more, this time to Canton, Ohio. The family acquired a small residence bordering the more opulent sector of town, impressive enough to cost a cool $30,000 on the market.

Though Thurm had just stepped into the football mecca of the nation, it was here that his baseball skills would be honed. At the farm in Randolph, if either Darrell, Duane, or Thurman were absent for their grounder practices, none could play at all, whereas in Canton the ballplaying corps was large and active enough to maintain a consistent schedule. Thurm participated often in pickup games, and through the quality sports program offered in Canton, he and Duane soon became recognizable local names. The latter apparently did not invest much interest in his athletic career. "Duane was a great athlete, but he didn't care that much whether he won or lost," Thurm lamented in a small biographical segment of a 1978 juvenile book named *At Bat*. "I never could play that way."[2]

The distinction of local fame was not lost on Thurman, who took great civic pride in lore citing Canton as the city in which Denton True Young earned the moniker "Cy." The legend held that Young's pitches were so vicious that they tore up a nearby fence like a cyclone, and thus he was named. Of course, if one were to incline his ear to legend he'd pick up a half dozen other reasons why the moundsman was crowned Cy.

Being in the vicinity of major league baseball — near Cleveland Municipal Stadium — Thurman couldn't escape the desire to play in the majors. The desire to witness the event was quenched one young afternoon when Darrell bought tickets for an Indians game. Once he reached the park, Thurm excitedly grabbed his seat in the leftfield bleachers. As game time approached, his oak-brown eyes caught a glimpse of star pitcher Mike Garcia crossing by the section, and the boy called down to Garcia. The Indians pitcher stopped between strides to sign a ball and loft it back up to Munson. It was his first catch of a big league pitcher's throw. Reveling in the moment, Thurm tucked himself back in his seat to watch the professionals toil.

At the age of 12, there was a different love in his life. While a member of Worley School's Junior Patrol, a program in which he aided children in crossing the street, he worked alongside a young girl who gladly returned his affectionate feelings. Soon this genial, engaging friend followed along by bicycle as Thurman made his rounds delivering the *Canton Repository* and purchased assorted candies for him with her 30 cents of lunch money. Thurm was in awe of her affluence; after all, his midday allowance was three dimes shy of that. Diane Dominick was his first girlfriend. She was his only girlfriend.

Their relationship grew swiftly. Within a year, the two spoke with naivete of marriage, for they were the perfect match. Diane acted as a buffer against the darker side of Thurman's life, as did her parents, chiefly father Tony Dominick. Thurman became like their own son, though the Munson parents were not as amiable toward Diane.

It was a tough time for Munson, who was — as any such youth — still forging his character. As Diane explained to sportswriter Armen Keteyian in 1987:

> Thurman was basically an insecure person. It stems from his childhood. He had a tough one. His dad ... was a real tough cookie. He was real hard. So Thurman had some real problems growing up, and I think he kept a lot of his insecurities inside. He had the kind of personality that he never wanted to talk about them, never wanted to show the hurt. He developed an exterior that was gruff, or whatever people wanted to call it.[3]

Munson himself later conceded that the absence of his father was hurtful and that his reaction came in almost subconscious emotions.

Thurman's public sentiments on Darrell wavered between explanatory truthfulness and respectful dishonesty. With any in-depth knowledge, one must presume that this qualifies as the latter: "My father was a go-getter," he was quoted in *At Bat:*

I think he's the one who always made me want to play hard. He always wanted me to do better. I remember once he came to see me play in the minors. I had a great day at the plate —five for five, I think, with a couple of home runs. After the game what does my father tell me? He tells me I looked bad behind the plate. That's the way he was. He wanted me to improve, so to my face he'd often criticize me, but to everybody else he'd say, "Hey, that's my son." So I always knew he was proud.[4]

Even after Thurman's death, that concluding statement was forever in question.

In 1960, Munson entered Lehman High School. A decent student with respectable grades, he described his behavior in the presence of education as "a little mischievous." Thurman did, however, admit some liking for school, especially in the subjects of English and history. Surprisingly, he was not fond of mathematics and business courses at this point, though his skill for the subjects was a profitable and well-enjoyed feature of post-graduate life. As far as extracurricular activity, Thurman Munson was, believe it or not, a poet. Actually, it is no great revelation for someone of such rich emotionality, for a young man who consistently bottled up his deep and numerous impulses. The topics were not atypical for an adolescent, ranging from God to children to miscellaneous subjects.

For the Polar Bears of Lehman High, Munson was an undeniable superstar: wingback on offense and linebacker on defense for the local love, football; a fleet-footed guard who averaged 20 points per game on the basketball court; All-City and All-State in both sports. And then, of course, baseball. He earned three letters in each sport, and, most impressively, captained all three squads by his senior year. Of most significance to Thurman was that the fielded teams were quality ones that could rack up wins.

A savvy varsity baseball coach by the name of Don Eddins instilled his renowned work ethic into Munson, who was then a slender shortstop who also pitched and caught a few games. Thurm was not stationed behind the plate due to some unavoidable amount of talent but out of pure fearlessness, for he was the only one brave enough to catch a young fireballer on the high school squad. His play at the position was not of any notable consistency until Munson's senior year, when the desperate question of who would labor behind the plate regularly arose. To the surprise of all, Thurm took over and blossomed in the ever-demanding post.

Not one to sit on his hands, Munson dutifully kept in shape. As a sophomore the kid was a light 125 pounds, no small feat in the presence of Ruth Munson's home cooking. In keeping with baseball training, he would sprint a full mile to Diane's house, deposit a kiss, and then run the mile home.

After school finished in June, life centered around the Canton City Baseball League, with its well-organized schedule of 40 or more games. While Canton also offered Little League and Pony League, Thurm chose this group and there he excelled. As the team's starting shortstop (though he did make occasional battery appearances), he tore up the league batting in the number three slot for the Seran Agency club, where his averages climbed annually: .372, .381, and .441. His team perennially advanced to the American Amateur Baseball Congress national tournament, played in Battle Creek, Michigan. Thurm enjoyed the opportunity to gauge the area talent, and, summarily, his confidence seemed to increase with every passing year.

In 1964, Munson graduated high school holding numerous options in his hands. Not attempting the majors was seemingly a sage decision, for, as Lee MacPhail put it, "He wasn't an attractive catcher then, I guess."[5] Based on the opinion of a council of family and friends, he chose college instead. Higher education was a costly endeavor, and unless supplemented by a scholarship, there would be no such endeavor at all. Letters flooded in from Michigan to Syracuse, yet only three of the 80 baseball offers volunteered economic aid.

Had he chosen to venture into football, scholarships would have hardly been an issue. Countless schools vied for his services on the gridiron, but Thurman wisely shied away. "I knew baseball was my sport, and wanted to continue at it," he reasoned a decade later. "Even if I played college football and did well, I knew I'd never play in the pros. But I needed a scholarship to attend college, and I kept waiting."[6]

Those particular offers were slow in coming. One from Arizona State, quite possibly the most outstanding baseball school at the time, held the stipulation that Munson would only receive the benefits of a scholarship if he made their university nine. Deeming that offer too risky, Munson turned instead to an unrestricted offer from local Kent State University.

Kent had a quiet campus, for the time being at least, despite the size of the student body. Of the 10,000 students enrolled there, most were already residents of the Buckeye State. Not far from Canton, there was still enough distance to make Thurman feel guilty about leaving Diane behind, but the two managed to meet often enough to make the discomfort subside.

On the other hand, Thurm was thrilled to get away from home and start on his own. This was his first extended sojourn, and thus he did feel some uneasiness. He reacted very well to it all, taking delight in the added responsibilities. It was vital to his character to face the inevitable problems involved in growing up and living on one's own. Munson quickly got to work after arriving at Kent State. First he designated business as his major, an area in which he progressed with unfortunate lethargy. Next, Thurm pledged to the fraternity of Delta Upsilon. He also joined both the basketball and baseball teams. While the former was nothing of note, the latter's season was a turning point in Munson's career. At the time, freshmen were not allowed on the varsity team (the NCAA changed the rule a few years later), so he cracked a more flexible lineup than would have been faced in varsity as a shortstop.

Apparently, the coaches couldn't stand to see Munson's 195-pound frame lumbering about the mid-infield dirt instead of behind the plate. The change worked out well, but Thurman's mentality was a surprising sticking point; while his defense was no travesty, it was his offense to which he paid most mind. He opined frankly that defense was tedious, and offense the refreshing opposite. Though coaching for his new position was often lacking, he acquired the necessary knowledge easily. As an athlete of fine reflexes with a sweet swing, Munson picked the job up quickly.

However, the showcase didn't last long that freshman campaign. Scheduled for a meager 11 games, the season was cut by wet and erratic weather to only three. Thurman played each one behind the plate and compiled a .416 batting average in the abbreviated span. Thurm was thoroughly disappointed by the shortage of activity, for he wanted to enjoy the season longer. By the time he left for the Canton City Baseball League (CCBL) that summer, the name of Thurman Munson was not one without a ring of familiarity.

Upon returning for his sophomore year, Thurman made some major changes. Cutting out basketball was a simple switch, as he could now concentrate all of his energies on baseball (and studies, of course). Thurm made the transition from a business major to health education, seeking a teaching degree. It may have seemed like a wise career choice, but in fact the transfer cost him so many credits that by the time he dropped out of college, Thurm was 30 shy of graduation.

In athletics, under the tutelage of Dick "Moose" Paskert, a reputable veteran of 19 seasons (most notably in the Mid-Atlantic Conference), Munson got the nod as catcher on the varsity version of the Kent Flashes. Paskert's opinions were valuable, for he had coached such men as Minnesota Twins third baseman Rich Rollins and the future Yankee player, manager, general manager, and scout extraordinare, Gene "Stick" Michael. Moose was exceedingly proud of the graduated pros, and he ensured that Rollins and Michael model bats were in constant supply for the Kent players' use. Thurman loved playing for Paskert, a man he saw as an apt and knowledgeable coach, not to mention a personable and funny fellow.

As the team's starting backstop, Munson caught the likes of future Cy Young Award winner Steve Stone. But the chemistry hardly resulted in much; the team did not win a title during Munson's tenure.

Thurman remained industrious during the summer, returning to the CCBL and working as a house painter. But it wasn't until the next summer that he truly went to work. His junior season service on the Kent State baseball team merited significant attention, and that year the rewards came through. In June 1967, the Chatham, Massachusetts, club of the famed Cape Cod League lost its catcher to an injury. Acting on rave reviews, manager Joe "Skippy" Lewis recruited Thurm with a requisite side offer of $75 per week for a job in the Chatham Parks Department. The package was a certain blowout on the pro/con scale — the CCL was a well-known eight-team showcase of talent, one of six leagues in the country funded by Major League Baseball and an outstanding program for collegiates. The decision wasn't difficult.

The CCL has been responsible for a mass of professional talent in its rich history, and in an organization such as the New York Yankees, talent was also needed in scouting. Once the mightiest titan in all of sports, the Yankees had fallen sharply by this time after being purchased by a CBS syndicate only a few years before. With the organization in need of skilled young men, the judge sent forth was Harry Hesse, an old-time New Yorker now transplanted to eastern Massachusetts. According to Thurman, Hesse had the appearance of a scout. Fortunately, he had brains too, though one didn't require much to know this kid Munson had some fire. He excelled, sporting a .420 clip, enough to outrank his nearest competitor by an astounding 65 points. His defense was also noteworthy; in one game, he picked off three base runners. In addition, the Chatham club went 30–9 to rank atop the league. Munson's numbers were too outstanding for the MVP voters to ignore. Once more, the decision wasn't difficult.

Personally, the trip east was a lot of fun for Thurm. Playing for Skippy Lewis, he learned a great deal and genuinely appreciated the instruction. Not that he didn't return the favor. As Skippy's son, Tim Lewis, recalled in 1999, "Though I vaguely remember it as I was five years old, he was my babysitter a few times. My mom would have to scold him about teasing her children to the point of tears."[7] It may sound harsh, but Thurman — often affectionately described as a big child — would reputedly only kid someone he liked.

Skippy must have forgiven Thurm's treatment of his children, for in his "thirty years of coaching high school, college, and in the minors for the Tigers," Tim recounted, "Munson was his favorite."[8] Thurm and manager Lewis kept up a correspondence through the years, a grateful pupil keeping up with the sources of his success. And success was right around the corner.

Hesse's report back to New York was emphatic; the kid was golden. He wanted Munson signed immediately. However, that was an impossibility, for a rule was in effect at the time prohibiting any player with at least two years of college experience from being inked until he reached 21 years of age. So the Yanks did the next best thing; they sent a reliable scout to monitor Kent State for its 1968 season.

The man was Gene Woodling, and this was not to be the first time he helped build a dynasty. The fellow Akron, Ohio, native had established a reputation with the bat by capturing four minor league batting titles by the time he finally won a platoon role with the 1949 Yankees. While alternating with knuckle-faced Hank Bauer, Woodling managed to prove himself the finest defensive left fielder in baseball in the eyes of skipper Casey Stengel as well as a sterling performer in the clutch, as shown by his string of solo homers in each World Series between 1951 and 1953. A season later, he was dealt to the Baltimore Orioles in a record 17-player exchange. Just short of his 40th birthday, Woodling's contract was purchased by the hapless New York Mets. Casey Stengel, now reunited with his old soldier, groaned in reference to Woodling's complaints of old, "Now he can play all he wants."

While hovering quietly over Munson all year Woodling had become comfortable with being silent, for he refused to say a word or make his presence known. "I'd rather not let a boy know I'm there watching him," explained Woodling. "That way, he'll just play naturally."[9] Thurm had no trouble finding him, though; Moose would point the old fellow out nearly every game.

Many scouts tracked Munson that season, and most reports were favorable. One, however, was not. A scout for the Cleveland Indians emphatically discounted the young man for his slow wheels. ("I don't know who he was looking at," Thurm snarled, "because I could run in high school. I was fast."[10]) On the other hand, Woodling — a major league veteran of 17 seasons and seven clubs— was so high on his prospect that he brimmed with excitement at the thought of Thurman's speed. The scout once said that he could not "get over the way Munson could run for a guy built like that. He had the quickest release throwing the ball of any catcher I've ever seen."[11] These sentiments were clear in Woodling's scouting report. The entire document was crossed out and in its place was scrawled two words: GET HIM.

Sure, Woodling could have submitted an all-encompassing assessment, but apparently his two-disyllabie critique sufficed. A decade later, he expounded on those opinions left beneath the scribble. "As I watched him ... I could see that he already had outstanding ability as a catcher. In other words, defensively, he was major league caliber. He stood out like a light bulb with those guys he was playing with."[12] To stand out against his bigger, stronger, flashier counterparts was not easy. But Woodling just shrugged:

> Some [scouts] ... look at size. I don't. A kid of 5'8" or 5'9" [Thurm was 5'11"] can certainly play big league ball....
> His hitting was just so-so. In fact, I had some reservations about it, but ... that's the last thing I worry about. In fact, I'll admit now that Thurm's hit a lot better than I thought he would ... Anyway, it didn't take long for me to decide he was the real goods.[13]

In Munson's senior year of college in 1968, his baseball line proved Woodling's assessment correct. Over 25 league games he amassed a .314 average with 30 RBI, 19 extra-base hits, 24 runs, 9 stolen bases, and, in a remarkable show of patience, 24 walks against merely 3 strikeouts. That was enough to convince Woodling to introduce himself as the season drew to a close. Thurm acted calmly, as though he hadn't been aware of Woodling's presence. But there was no room for tip-toeing by that time, for Thurman's greatness was confirmed when, out of 5,000-plus national collegiate catchers, he was designated superior and named the All-American at the position. By no means was this a minor achievement, it meant more to him than the Rookie of the Year, MVP, or Gold Glove honors. The ratios between the college award and those of the major leagues were far different: the eligible class for the latter was a fraction of the candidates up for the collegiate award.

Munson sought to continue his college education though his four years were up and he expected to be drafted by a major league club. The senior experience was a successful one. His grades were improved, even though his thoughts focused almost exclusively on baseball. Thurman would later fondly recall the college years he left behind as the best of his life.

Shortly after school ended, he made the trek back to Canton. The stay home wasn't expected to be long, as he prepared to leave for the Cape Cod League on June 6. With future Red Sox pitcher John Curtis, Munson headed east that day. Upon his arrival, the telephone rang; it was Thurman's sister. Though Thurm was rather nonchalant about it ("I had no preconceived notions, and just waited to see what happened," he wrote in his autobiography), it just so happened that the major league baseball draft was that day, and Munson had been selected fourth overall by the New York Yankees. The earlier selections read like a laundry list of regrets: Tim Foli, Pete Broberg, and Martin Cott. Number four didn't feel slighted. It was hard to believe he had made it. With his bags already packed — or, more accurately, not yet unpacked — he took a plane back to Canton to be with his family and the Dominicks. Thurm had initially planned to play at Cape Cod and then sign with New York, but the excitement was too much to put off, and so he nixed that idea.

The selection of Munson was quite definitely by design. The Yankees had boasted a prodigious history of legendary catchers, but the team was faltering by 1968. The tradition had started 40 years earlier, when a young man by the name of Bill Dickey took over as the receiver. The previous season's famed Murderers Row had actually thrived without a stable catching corps, instead enduring a merry-go-round platoon of Benny Bengough, Pat Collins, and Johnny Grabowski. When Dickey assumed the role, there was no halting his greatness, which catapulted him to a status as the sport's best-ever catcher by the time he retired in 1946. Waiting in the wings was a 21-year-old Italian kid from the famed "Hill" in St. Louis. Lawrence Peter "Yogi" Berra, whether remembered for his comedic shtick or golden baseball ability, became one of the game's most recognizable faces, especially in October. He appeared in a record 14 World Series, and even managed the Yanks to one in 1964, four years after the task of receiver was passed to Elston Howard. Ellie was stellar on defense and a force with the bat. The first black man to ever play in a Yankee uniform (1955), he was also the only black Yankee to ever capture the American League MVP, which he was awarded in 1963. When Howard was dealt to Boston three and a half seasons later, New York was left to count on a fledgling bonus baby: Jake Gibbs. He was a solid player and a terrific guy, but the Yanks demanded better. They felt that was taken care of with the drafting of Thurman Munson on June 6, 1968.

The next day was Munson's 21st birthday, and he was finally allowed to be signed. MacPhail and Woodling visited the house, as described earlier, and after brief negotiations, Thurm settled happily for $75,000 in bonuses and payment for the remainder of his education. "I was always interested in money," he later conceded of the contract agreement. "But when I first signed, got my bonus, and saw how much tax they took out of it, I said 'My God, if they're gonna do this to me — if I ever really start making some money, I'm gonna be in trouble'."[14] Munson generally liked MacPhail and found him easy to discuss the matter with. Thurman handled the situation calmly and effectively, asking little but gaining much.

The bonus arrived in two installments, and Munson "took the little money I had left after taxes and put it into real estate"—an acre and a quarter of Canton land. Some believed he had lost his sanity, but Thurm was vindicated within the year after peddling it for a tidy $12,000 profit.

His assignment was to the Double-A Eastern League team in Binghamton. He packed, made his farewells, and left to make $500 per month playing ball in upstate New York. Woodling predicted Munson would be on a major league roster by 1970. As far as the kid from Ohio was concerned, it was the destination that he coveted, not the number of steps along the trail.

Standing between Munson and those glorious emerald blades of the professional ball fields was a rotten, broken-down clubhouse with holes in the floor. His teammates on the Binghamton Triplets had a good humor about it, though. Including by such players as Frank Tepedino, Gary Jones, and Steve Kline, the team was a formidable one skippered by Cloyd "C. B." Boyer. A former pitcher and brother of big league stars Clete and Ken Boyer, C. B. was basically the minor league pitching coach for the Yankees, stationed that season at Binghamton awaiting advancement. Clever, helpful, and supportive, he was a great manager for Thurman, who truly respected him.

C. B. took a good long look at Munson and agreed with MacPhail that he would be in the big leagues by 1970. Thurm, however, did his best to prove precocious. Though he kept reserved on the prospect of being a major league prospect, Thurman immediately got in a groove against the Double-A pitchers. He was surprised to find that the pitching in his Kent State and Cape Cod days was not all that inferior to the minor league variety. The only real difference was the *number* of good arms; in that, the pros were far supreme. Thurm jumped off to a good start against the pitching, although hitting remained his favorite side of the game. But he knew that to get further in the organization, he would have to become stellar on the defensive end.

Munson practiced catching more throws and got in some throwing of his own. He began relishing the opportunity to fire a strike to the fielder's mitt and nail a potential thief. It was a challenge. And Thurm was game. Even when he lost the handle on a ball, he considered the chance not wasted and tried to peg the runner out. Constantly he practiced, for Thurman was no fool—he may have been praised often for having a rifle-like arm, but the young man knew the gun was no good without a marksman.

His practice was so relentless that it became possibly his only deficiency on the diamond. "There's a lot of enthusiasm in him," Yankee manager Bill Virdon commented in *At Bat*. "His only defect might be that sometimes he throws a little too enthusiastically."[15]

Bill White, a former first baseman and broadcaster, seconded that opinion late in Munson's career:

> Sometimes it seems that Thurm wants to gun that guy down at second by fifteen yards instead of getting him by three or four feet. When that happens, he ends up throwing the ball into center field. But as for the strength of his arm, let's face it, to be a catcher you don't have to have that much of a gun. Thurm is quick. I've been in baseball a long time, and I have yet to see anybody outrun a baseball.[16]

From the figurative to the literal, gun-toting lingered as a possibility that haunted Munson in 1968. The war in Vietnam was raging, and he was a healthy young man. So at about midseason, the Yanks took matters into their own hands. After being flown down to Fort Lauderdale, Florida, Thurman met Ed Bastian, general manager of one of the franchise farm clubs. Thurm was ushered into an army post neighboring the Bombers' spring training facility and given a physical. It seemed that he would be enrolled in the army reserve very soon, but the physical forced an unexpected change of plans. A bone spur was detected in Munson's right ankle, which was enough to keep him from the reserves.

But life habitually moves toward balance. In the few days missed for the physical, Thurman was deprived of too many at-bats to qualify for the batting championship with his .301 average. His 226 at-bats were short by about ten.

The stadium paint shone, reflecting the busy August scene outside. Within its walls, the pros were too annoyed to care, for today they faced an exhibition against one of their subsidiary clubs making a stop on its way from Waterbury, Connecticut, to Binghamton. The minor leaguers didn't have time for sight-seeing in New York due to tight scheduling. Instead, the men made their way through the park, some taking in the beautiful spectacle of the outfield's monuments, while others lumbered through the stands, soaking in the view.

The man on the bench wasn't impressed. He appreciated the tradition, sure, but had seen it all for years. Ravaged by injuries, it was his pleasure to rest that aching body, so broken after years of service, in the dugout. Despite his pains, he still managed to lead the team in home runs. The young man approaching, however, saw him as a mythical figure. Trembling, he approached the dugout. The kid faked some coolness and stuck out his hand. "Mickey, I'm Thurman Munson."

Surely, Mickey Mantle didn't care. He'd seen these guys come and go. With little interest in his eyes, Mantle smiled politely, "How ya' doin'?"

Perhaps this was Munson's only moment as a hero worshipper, but it was worth the concession. He had long looked up to "The Mick," and now they were on a level playing field.

The Binghamton Triplets and New York Yankees played to a compact crowd that day. After all, who cared about the outcome besides the bush leaguers on the field? Thurman took the game as a special thrill, and he was uncharacteristically impressed. Before a mighty legion that included Mantle, Mel Stottlemyre, Jake Gibbs, Fritz Peterson, and Rocky "The Rock" Colavito, Thurm doubled.

The Munson line for 1968 was impressive, especially for a number one pick of whom there were so many expectations: 78 games, 68 hits, 12 doubles, 6 home runs, 37 RBI, and a .301 average. He stood proudly as the only batter in the league to crack .300.

Soon after the exhibition, Munson's draft number came up. He did not try to fool himself; he knew no matter what the technicalities were of his condition, he'd soon be in the military. Sure enough, despite the bone spur, Thurman passed the physical. Now it was just a waiting game.

But happier times were upon him. On a weekend in Binghamton, Diane and her mother dropped by for a short stay. It was on that visit that Thurman and Diane decided to get married on September 21, shortly after the season's end.

Amid the dwindling days of summer, Thurman Munson and Diane Dominick were married at a traditional ceremony in Canton. Their families were there, as were several of Thurm's buddies, including Binghamton friend Tim O'Connell, who served as usher. The newlyweds left shortly after for their honeymoon in Hawaii.

Upon his return, Thurman sought to straighten out a few matters. After moving in with the Dominicks, he attempted to rectify his credit shortage at Kent State, but couldn't handle the schedule with baseball in the picture later that spring. He reluctantly gave up on the idea. Meanwhile, the prospect of military service hung overhead.

When the dust of January's intense pension negotiations between major league baseball players and owners had cleared, an agreement stood among the former not to sign contracts until demands were met. Some players, namely those not yet member's of the Players' Union, were not granted the benefit of this information. "Thurman Who?" read the caption in the *New York Times*. A non-roster invitee, Munson was reporting early, as catchers do. At the Fort Lauderdale training site, the young man stood baffled with his face pressed against the locked gate. The place was empty. Munson had no idea what was happening.

Despite the embarrassment, it was good to be back. The winter months had been painfully long. With a new wife and a baby on the way, he knew that, if fate so pleased, the call could come to begin service in the army reserve. Yet to his surprise, another call to duty was phoned in.

By the time the owners capitulated and brought the players back to the field before spring training began, Munson had realized his value. The New York Yankees didn't have many live arms in 1969, but they at least had a lot of arms. And naturally, there were bodies needed to catch them. Thurm arrived in Lauderdale fully aware that there was no shot at making the team. He was there to catch pitchers. Nevertheless, Thurman gave it his full effort, and that was not easy.

The training camp was a good one, but oppressively tiring. At ten in the morning, the players took a lap around the field and then proceeded to 15 minutes of exercise under rookie coach Elston Howard. After this, the players split into groups to work on fundamentals. While his Yankees next took their swings, manager Ralph Houk eyed them from his customary perch: planted in the dugout, constantly pestered by sportswriters and organization men.

Houk was a tough military hero (awarded a Silver Star for gallantry during the battle of the Bulge) nicknamed "The Major," who Munson had first met at the Yankee Stadium exhibition game. Described as sensitive and understanding, he crossed all barriers with the players due to his ability to pleasantly coexist with anyone. Using subtlety and intelligence, he would deal with each player individually; if one made a mistake during the game, Houk would hold off until the next day and then discuss it with the culprit behind closed doors. The media was not as sensitive to Houk during times of disappointment. He was criticized heavily by the press for the Yankee shortcomings, but he withstood the blame in putting the franchise in the foreground. He was a strong role model for Munson both in character and ability. Thurman would later call him the best manager in baseball. Houk was also optimistic nearly to a fault.[17]

Optimism was greatly needed for the Yankees in those days. When Houk began his second stint as manager of the Yankees, they finished a lowly tenth in the league race. The year was 1966, and at the end of it Lee MacPhail arrived as general manager and executive vice president. An honest man of great integrity, MacPhail debuted in the position with a gutsy vow. "It will take a minimum of five years to put the Yankees back in contention," he conceded. The sentence was received roughly by New Yorkers, yet better than was to be expected. The son of former New York co-owner Larry MacPhail, Lee was a former GM and president in the Orioles organization, the disheveled godchild of St. Louis's pathetic old Browns. By the time he finished, the O's had initiated a two-decade run of success. Having served as farm director and director of player development, MacPhail felt the only way to win was to build from the bottom up.

Quickly he acted, securing young, skilled prospects like Lindy McDaniel, Jack Aker, Ron Klimkowski, Danny Cater, Curt Blefary, and Ron Woods. Through strengthened scouting and, most of all, patience, the "five-year plan" was a promise fulfilled. Though the Yankees became a star-filled success under later management, it would not have been possible without the farm system built up under Lee MacPhail. Consequently, they picked the pace up slowly with a rise to ninth place in 1967 and fifth in '68. The youth movement was a growing success, which didn't hurt the progression of Thurman Munson.

Without the services of army reservists Frank Fernandez and Jake Gibbs, Munson took the job of catcher in early spring training. Here was a man who was not supposed to play at all, not in late innings, not to pinch-hit, not to pinch-run. Yet he caught in each of the first six games that spring, handling all nine innings in two. Both were wins. It was a great break for Thurm and a great sight for the expectant eyes waiting to view New York's premier selection.

Catching the Yankee staff instilled confidence in Munson, while he also developed a respectful appreciation for the position and its rigorous requirements. Thurman tried tirelessly to produce, which he knew he could do if just given a fair chance. The same thought must have clicked in one of the Yankee heads, for Thurm was sticking around awfully long for someone who had no chance. The cuts came for non-roster backstop's John Ellis and Charlie Sands, and Munson was consistently assured that he'd be turned over to Triple-A Syracuse. The season drew nigh, camp neared dissolution, and finally Thurman was cut from the roster.

Munson still had some training to do. He was going to Hollywood, Florida, to join Syracuse, a team primarily composed of the '68 Binghamtons. There he would truly make his mark with 37 hits, a couple of homers, 17 RBI, and a .363 batting mark.

Munson did not spend the entire 1969 season with Syracuse. In early April, Frank Fernandez withdrew from the Yankee lineup when he was called for an army reserve meeting. The front pages neglected it, but to a kid in Richmond it was everything. Thurm Munson was preparing for an exhibition game there when he received the call that the Yankees were in need of a bullpen and emergency catcher. There wasn't any grand story to tell from the call-up: no game appearances, no headlines, just a weekend of observation. But his experience justified the inconvenience.

Later that month, Munson was notified of his military duty. His orders were for Fort Dix, New Jersey, where he would go for a four-month stint in the army reserve.

Army life was tolerable for Thurman. He served as a clerk, which, despite its simplistic ring, turned out to be a difficult task. It entailed a great deal of hard labor but was mixed with a fair amount of amusement, such as baseball, or at least forms of the game. It was reminiscent of games played during the Civil War when rowdy contests were conducted with captives and officials at Union or Confederate prisons. Through this, the young pastime was passed on to sporting men across the nation. A century later at Fort Dix, it was Munson's enthusiasm being spread. During softball games at the base, his fellow soldiers were compelled by Thurman's competitiveness to actually put together some quality games.

On the professional side, 1968 Rookie of the Year and fellow Yankee Stan Bahnsen served weekend duty at Fort Dix, and it was he who kept Thurm up to date on club affairs. Munson, unlike his informant, was given occasional weekend passes so he could play for the Syracuse Chiefs, provided they were at home. If they were on the road, Thurm instead took batting practice at Yankee Stadium.

With 88 games and 290 at-bats in the minors under his belt, Thurm reluctantly saw the 1969 season as over, and his big league days on hold until the next year. But in early August Frank Fernandez once again was obligated to attend to his army reserve duty. Munson was called up and this time placed on the 25-man roster. The road taken to earn the call-up had been a difficult one, but as he explained in consummate Munsonesque eloquence, "You don't get rich playing in Syracuse."

The headlines of the day read, "Saigon School Blast Kills, Wounds Scores," "Evidence of Gas Hints Crude Form of Life on Mars," and "Pentagon Target of ABM Foes." It was Friday, August 8, 1969. Man had first landed on the moon just 19 days prior. Back in New York, the Yankees were 22 games shy of the Baltimore Orioles, in next-to-last place with a .491 winning percentage. At only .009 better was Catfish Hunter, who, along with his Oakland Athletics, opposed the Bombers in a twi-night doubleheader. The Yanks were riding a five-game winning streak after a day off, and in the players' lounge slept their future.

Shortly after arriving in New York that afternoon, Thurman Munson sought some much-needed rest. While he was lying on a couch in the lounge, Ralph Houk interrupted. "Don't get too comfortable," the Major warned, "you're going to be playing this time."[18] Thurm had been through this drama in April, but it seemed that this time he'd get his chance to play.

Tom Tresh had captured the 1962 Rookie of the Year award and was a staple at shortstop for the Yankees for most of the decade, but in June of '69 he was dealt to the Detroit Tigers. With Tresh having left behind his number 15, Munson was ready to fill the shoes (or uniform) two months later. "It was a nice low number to pick up in the middle of the season," Thurm noted in his book.[19] He was given it before the August 8 game, and no Yankee would ever again don that numeral.

Thurman watched the first game from the bullpen. While spending time warming up relief pitchers, he witnessed Larry Haney drive in two with a double to elevate the As to 5–3 in the top of the tenth. Fernandez had one last shot before he departed, in the form of a home run. Then Thurman received the order from Houk to pinch-hit. It seemed his time had come as he waited in the on-deck circle with two outs in the bottom of the tenth, but the man at the plate was retired, leaving Munson a few more hours to wait until he could lay claim to the status of a major leaguer.

Due to the delay from extra innings, the second contest was put off until eight o'clock in order to take the primetime spot on television. Thurman knew he'd be starting the nightcap as catcher, so he took the time to discuss the game with pitcher Al Downing. Downing was a veteran pitcher of varied success who was hailed early in his career as the "black Sandy Koufax," but in the game he'll forever be the humble answer to a trivia question. He was the only man in uniform for both Roger Maris's 61st homer of the 1961 season and Hank Aaron's 715th in April 1974. Of course in the latter, he conceded "Bad Henry's" shot, while the former saw him in the pen. Back on August 8, 1969, it was Maris's record that was on their minds, as Downing and Munson discussed how especially to throw to Reggie Jackson, an exemplary athlete with 37 round-trippers at the All-Star break. The conversation went easily given the familiarity of the two, as Downing had endured a spell rehabbing an injury at Binghamton in 1968. It still seemed to be causing him trouble in '69, given his 2–3 mark before taking on Oakland.

Those who have never heard the dignified, grandfatherly tone of Bob Sheppard on the Yankee Stadium public address system cannot understand. One comes to feel that each word spoken is a throwback to the old days; it is a contribution of class to the game. Surely Munson must have felt chills as Sheppard introduced him to New York. "Batting eighth, the catcher, number 15, Thurman Munson, number 15." The kid was warming up in front of the dugout at the time. He received a rather impressive response given the meager crowd in attendance and the fact that this was a man they had probably either never heard of or only skimmed over in the sports section. Perhaps the fans thought Tresh had bulked up and returned.

As the eighth batter in the Yankee lineup, Thurm stepped into the box versus James Augustus "Catfish" Hunter, a calm, cool owner of a perfect game who was said around the league to know how to win. He was a personable and humble man, a potato farmer from Hertford, North Carolina. Of this, future teammate Lou Piniella would kid, "When I take my wife out to dinner, I take her in my Cadillac. When you take your wife, you take her in a John Deere tractor."[20] He didn't have his noted mustache at the time, but Cat did have a grand reputation and an even better repertoire. In the first plate appearance of Munson's major league career, it was him versus Hunter. Munson stood in the righthander's box with an assassinlike focus, positioned and await-

Munson poses at Comiskey Park in Chicago, wearing his game face. (Courtesy Brace Photos)

ing the pitch. He sported a timid, stiff, awkward stance, knees bent slightly forward, bat erect. Thurm dug in and drew a walk.

Despite a ground out in the fifth inning, Munson was enjoying an impressive debut. He and Downing were cruising along with but a few shakeoffs from the pitcher's mound. The game was scoreless going into the bottom of the seventh, when Thurm came up again, with Gene Michael on base. Cat's throw came in a bit high, but Munson uncoiled, extended, and drove a liner to center field. Reaching first base without incident, he had major league hit number one. But it was not over yet. On the play, Michael continued on to third and Thurman to second. Coach Elston Howard retrieved the ball and the game continued. Downing flied out before Horace Clarke singled to drive in Michael and Munson.

Downing retired the As easily in the eighth, and in the bottom of that frame, with the bases loaded and the infield drawn in, Munson lined a single to right field, scoring two Yankee runs for a 5–0 lead. The second tally was able to be made because by knocking it to right, when the catcher received the throw he would have to catch, turn, and tag, whereas if he directed a drive to left, the backstop would simply have to catch and bend. Over the years, Munson often employed the system of making a clean connection and knocking the ball to the opposite field.

Downing went on for a complete game shutout, his first of the year in either department. The triumph added to the winning ways the Yanks had experienced of late, which helped to boost their morale. Consequently, Thurm felt more comfortable, and he spent the night as a guest at Gene Michael's home. This was a reunion for the two, who had met and grown close during Michael's stops at Kent State during Munson's tenure there.

When he woke up at Michael's house the next morning, it was time for the Yankees' Old-Timers Day. Munson posed for pictures with Gene Woodling and then spent the game watching from the bullpen as ace Mel Stottlemyre took the As down by a 2–1 score.

On the last day of Thurman's weekend pass, the matchup was Oakland's Lew Krausse versus Fritz Peterson, a fast worker and merciless joker. Munson desperately desired to play, so when he walked into the dugout it was a great relief to see the lineup card bearing his name taped to the wall.

The contest began rather violently when a Peterson pitch struck Athletic's outfielder Rick Monday. It broke the metacarpal bone in his hand, sidelining him for four to six weeks. Peterson was known as a pitcher with precise control, and a slew of varying pitches, so much so that Thurm would have needed more than his allotted number of fingers on his signal hand to keep up. Yet Peterson gave up a hit in the third to pitcher Krausse for the third time in 1969. Munson did manage to avenge the battery.

Late in the game, Bobby Murcer knocked a home run. Thurm was up next, and he took a Krausse offering to left for another yard job. Incredibly, Gene Michael homered next for a back-to-back-to-back triumvirate. After the fact, the press memorialized the old combination of Mickey Mantle and Roger Maris, predicting a new "M&M Boys," despite the extra member now involved. While the media overemphasized the feat, it was only one short of the record held at the time by the 1963 Cleveland Indians and '64 Minnesota Twins of four consecutive home runs. Coincidentally, Oakland's Ted Kubiak, Reggie Jackson, and Sal Bando had matched the Yankee achievement of three earlier in 1969.

The offensive output evened Peterson's record at 12–12. It also balanced the Yankee record at 57–57, their first time at the .500 mark since the eighth of June.

Munson knew that the party was over — for the time being. Right after the game, he packed his bags for Fort Dix. As he recounted in his autobiography, "I remember going to sleep that night wondering if it was really possible that only a few hours ago I was hitting a home run at Yankee Stadium."[21]

Munson headed back to Fort Dix after the Sunday game, but received a leave in midweek. He scored once on Tuesday, August 12, part of a Yankee eight-run inning, a tally which was the club's greatest single-frame showing since July 2, 1965. Within the week, New York won their 11th of 13 games, moving to fourth place for the first time in two months.

Back in the army, Munson was miserable, his mind engrossed in the pride of being a Yankee. Fortunately, on August 30 the reserve stint had run its four-month course, and Munson was relieved of duty. Thurman was undoubtedly pleased to be cut free, but to his disappointment the Yankees assigned him to Syracuse. Between the games he played in during the next week and those spent with the Chiefs on weekend passes, Thurm added 11 games and 38 at-bats to his total. Though Syracuse was in the midst of the International League playoffs, their catcher had larger conquests on his mind, confident that he was destined to become a legitimate major leaguer. After he caught a couple of games against Louisville, the call arrived on the first of September for Munson to join the Yankees in Cleveland. He would never revisit the minors.

By the time Munson returned to the Yankee corps, it looked more like a corpse. The team was hovering lethargically at 20 games shy of Baltimore's mighty first-place Orioles, a famed powerhouse that would go on to shock the globe in the World Series— by losing to the Mets. Those Mets were taking over New York as the unquestionable apple of the Big Apple's eye. For the first time in decades the Bombers were a second-rate show in Gotham. Yet on September 2, the contracts of Ralph Houk and Lee MacPhail were extended for three years. Commented Yankee president Michael Burke, "We have boys now — at the major and minor league level — who will write the next chapter of greatness in Yankee history.... The extension of Ralph and Lee's contracts is part of a considered plan to build another winner."[22]

Burke had seen enough days without a winner; it was a sad blemish on the story of an American classic. An intelligent and masterful man from the Northeast, Burke starred in baseball, basketball, and football at the University of Pennsylvania. During World War II, he undertook legendary missions, most notably a highly dangerous one in Italy as a member of the secretive OSS. The tour was death-defying to the definition's core; Burke was deservedly awarded both a Silver Star and Navy Cross; and his exploits were portrayed in the movie *Cloak and Dagger* by "Pride of the Yankees" icon Gary Cooper. After the war he returned to America and assumed a post as general manager for Ringling Brothers, Barnum and Bailey.

But on a gray day in September 1966, Burke took over as president (or as some sarcastically insisted, owner) of the New York Yankees. He had done other work as a CBS executive, but they thought it was time he made his mark with the Yankees. That didn't work out well. Frankly, the year was miserable. In one of the darkest moments in club history, they drew only 413 attendees to a weekday makeup game. But Burke was determined to attain growth and help where he could during his tenure. He was a man who easily connected with the community, and he ensured that Yankee players visited schools in impoverished areas, discouraging children from dropping out of school and various other missteps. Burke also distributed, according to the Yankees, hundreds of thousands of free tickets to young Yankee fans just to let them know they were cared for. It was said that he was the only likable asset of the franchise in days when the crowd came out for no other reason than to root against them. Yet only pleasantries were exchanged between him and a bull of a young catcher who came up in 1969.

On September 5, Munson enjoyed a homecoming. The game was a twi-night doubleheader in Cleveland before Diane and countless relatives. Frank Fernandez was shifted to right, and Thurman was inserted as catcher while manning the lineup's five spot. While standing on the field at Municipal Stadium and looking at the sizable crowd on hand, he must have been reminded of the far-off afternoon when Mike Garcia stopped to sign an autograph. Now Thurman himself walked the same field.

The Indians had lost eight in a row at that point. Realistically, they were the only team worse than the Yankees. With fireballer Sam McDowell sent out to face Mel Stottlemyre, Thurm managed a single in four at-bats, but Cleveland pulled off a win in the bottom of the ninth inning.

The second game was a memorable one, a pitcher's duel between Peterson and Dick Ellsworth. Fernandez homered to put the Yanks ahead, and Munson, on a 2–4 day, drove in a run to make the score 2–0. There it stood in the bottom of the ninth with two out. Peering at first base, Houk noticed Chuck Hinton, the once-fleet 35-year-old outfielder in his second hitch as a Tribesman, straying from the bag. The signal for a pickoff was for the first baseman, in this case the fiery Joe Pepitone, to touch his belt buckle, and this he did. But the kid catcher didn't throw. Pepi tried again before the next pitch, yet Munson still held, either because he forgot the sign or didn't notice. Pepitone wasn't interested in excuses. Flailing his arms to be granted a time out, the wild Italian strolled halfway down the line, calling, "Hey, Thurman." Pepitone reached for his belt buckle and pulled the strap out a full foot. On the subsequent pitch Munson reared back and gunned Hinton down. The runner somehow hadn't caught on at first base, and his error ended the game.

Attaining an everyday position was nothing automatic for Munson, despite the dramatics. Houk, with whom Thurm anxiously desired to forge a good rapport, stressed the importance of becoming familiar with the tendencies of rival hitters. Houk put Munson on notice that in order to be a regular in 1970, he would have to know how to have the hitters pitched to, for he would be calling the pitches. This developed into one of the greatest strengths in his game, as he was later reputed to handle a pitching staff with the greatest wisdom and aptitude in the league, exactly the mastery that Munson had of the categories in baseball that could not be recognized by statistics. At one point in his career, the Yanks would note that he was an unquestioned field leader and the best in the league at calling a ballgame. Thurm was elevated in his craft via the tutelage of catching legend Elston Howard and bullpen coach Jim Hegan. Of course, Munson knew he would also have to get inside the pitchers' head's to call their games, so he sought the help of Hall of Famer and special instructor Whitey Ford. It would all pay off. Using his new training and lightning-quick release, Thurm shot down 7 of 12 runners trying to steal in 1969. Not bad for a rookie.

In his hasty tour of the major leagues, Munson had managed to make a significant impression. Stated one unidentified veteran in *At Bat*, "He gives you a lot of confidence out there. You start pitching to him, and you forget he's just 23 years old."[23]

"I remember reading stories about [Cincinnati's Johnny] Bench, how he bawled veteran pitchers out his first year," echoed another. "This kid is the same way. If he feels you're not putting out, or not doing something right, he lets you know about it in no uncertain terms. He's not afraid to speak out."[24]

After a day of batting third, Thurm dropped to sixth on September 14. The Yanks were leading Boston by a run going into the top of the ninth, but with two outs and the game so close, future Kansas City Royals' manager Tony Muser slapped his first major league hit to tie it up at 2–2. Bobby Murcer led off the New York half with a single before being advanced by Ron Woods. Now Munson came to bat, proposing to reimburse the Yankees and the home fans for an earlier error. Facing Sparky Lyle, he singled to left, and Murcer came racing home, trying for the game. With a head-first slide, he registered as safe for a thrilling 3–2 win.

On the 18th, Munson's double and a game-winning John Ellis single defeated the Senators 4–3, establishing the Yanks at .500, 28 back of Baltimore. To be that far back and even in wins and losses was no fault of New York's. In fact, Detroit was then in second place by 18½, despite a .567 winning percentage. With the Miracle Mets the talk of the sports world, the Yankees were pushed to the back seat, to the back pages.

Michael Burke assured all concerned that the Yankees were alive and well in a September interview. "I suppose you could say we're in a battle with the Mets for the baseball dollar, but we're not really competing on the same basis.... I don't think we have to usurp any of their popularity.... I don't think you can say the Yankees are unpopular when we draw over a million fans."[25] This was the Bronxmen's 24th consecutive season of greater than one million customers, while the Mets cracked two million on the weekend of Burke's comments.

The Yankees closed the 1969 season with a 79–81 fifth-place record, finishing 28½ games behind the Orioles. "You can learn very little from victory," Hall of Fame ace Christy Mathewson once said. "You can learn everything from defeat."[26]

3

FRESHMAN IN THE
OLD SCHOOL

I want to thank the good Lord for making me a Yankee.
— Joe DiMaggio

As dawn cracked on the 1970s, Thurman Munson was cruising the Caribbean. For the most part, the idea of playing baseball during the winter was an effort to make up for time lost due to military service and to get back in shape for the upcoming season. He had proposed the idea to an unreceptive Yankee brass that fall. They had argued, but it was soon arranged for the 22 year old to take the field for San Juan, Puerto Rico.

Thurman and Diane had flown down to San Juan as 1969 drew to a close. Munson was actually rather fortunate to play, as the number of major leaguers allotted to the league was restricted, and slots were reserved most for young ones under 20 years of age.

The San Juan team was an impressive one, managed by former Yankee pitching coach Cot Deal and including Lee May, Willie Crawford, Sid O'Brien, Jose Cardenal, and a man who was not only the king of Puerto Rican baseball but a regal member of the American version. Roberto Walker Clemente, an icon of Ruthian proportions, was expected to play in his native country, as were most players whose country of origin was included in the circuit. Clemente was a legendary right fielder for the Pittsburgh Pirates with a gun of an arm and 3,000 hits at bat. It was one of the highest compliments that could be paid when he told Munson that if the catcher ever hit .280 in the majors, he should call it a bad season. If so, Thurm's winter ball season was a triumphant success, as he placed second in the

35

league with a .333 batting percentage. He did much of it without Diane, who returned home to Canton early to be with her parents during her pregnancy.

Munson rejoined his wife at Canton after the winter ball schedule concluded, with little time to spare before spring training. To his surprise, he worked out a contract with the Yanks for $15,000, one third above the minimum of $10,000 but another ten grand below the league average. He was coming off a 26-game, 86 at-bat stint in the majors for 1969, a .256 average with a homer and nine runs batted in. However limited his experience, Munson was not concerned.

"I don't see why I shouldn't have a good year," he told skeptics that spring. "I've been preparing for this for a long time, working hard toward it, and I feel I'm ready. I know there are people who don't agree with me."[1] Yet most, in fact, did agree. Many of the critics, experts, and assorted clairvoyants predicted he would earn the Rookie of the Year award and be a vital cog in the Yankee engine, taking over for Jake Gibbs.

As spring training approached and the reporting time for catchers and pitchers came quickly, Munson tested the waters again at Kent State. Soon he found that there was no viable way to handle both college and baseball, and he headed off instead to Fort Lauderdale.

The Yankees had changed over the winter, which was no big surprise. Al Downing was ushered off to Oakland in exchange for established infielder Danny Cater. Also acquired were former Rookies of the Year Ron Hansen and Curt Blefary. While Hansen was a low-key utility man, Blefary was a grand New York headliner.

The Yanks had gotten rid of one problem child and adopted another. An arrogant and contemptible man in the eyes of his teammates, Blefary made public vows concerning his production that would not see fruition (.212, 9 homers, 37 RBI), and subsequently he blamed Houk as the scapegoat for not using him properly. Munson kept a sagacious reserve on his opinion of Blefary until they had the chance to talk, but he did at least respect his fellow Yankee.

New York was far from a favorite coming into the 1970 season. Listed in Las Vegas at 30–1 odds just before the season started, they were tied with Washington for last in the East. As for the chances at a pennant, they were seen at 50–1; at least that bested expansion franchises Seattle and Kansas City at 250–1. Munson, whose Rookie of the Year honor was a consensus choice, was cited as an irreplaceable fortification to the Yankees with his added strength up the middle. Strength up the middle is a fabled necessity for a quality team, and so the scribes invested their trust in Munson and the magic that young blood can often kick into a ballclub. As far as the midfield line, the press was confident in Munson and center fielder Bobby Murcer, but the double play combination of Gene Michael and second baseman Horace Clarke was shelled under frequent scrutiny.

Stick Michael was a fine veteran shortstop whose noble and nimble presence had solidly replaced Tom Tresh with a .272 average. Ironically, it was not he — the fellow Moose Paskert graduate — but Horace Clarke who made a deep impression on Munson. A polite and humble native of the Virgin Islands, Clarke was a hard-running, hard-working family man and the last club member, according to Thurman, to make his residence in the direct vicinity of Yankee Stadium. Yet, for whatever reason, he bore much of the criticism during New York's failure-plagued run of the 1960s.

Clarke had a specific way of dealing with this. With his quiet nature, he rarely responded to or recognized the opinions of the press. The beating of Clarke's reputation thoroughly soured impressionable young Thurman Munson toward the writers. He denied them both cooperation and attention, which — though costly — was his only dignified recourse.

On the positive side, Thurm enjoyed a splendid spring training, including an April 1 exhibition which pitted the Yanks against Kansas City's Royals in Fort Lauderdale. While snow covered the stadium back home, Munson shot a home run in Florida, but then, so did someone else.

Thurman's batting average rounded off to .360 by the warm-up's conclusion and set him in competition for the James P. Dawson Award, which honors the most outstanding rookie in the camp. Someone else did better.

The man in concert each step of the way was a husky, spry catcher out of the California League. Though many eyes were on Munson with high expectations, it was John Ellis who most everyone was talking about. Ellis was a highly touted young native of New London, Connecticut, close enough to Yankee Stadium to bask in the glow of a hometown boy. Filling in often when Munson and Frank Fernandez — now gone to Oakland — were away on military duty, the righty legged out a triple in his initial appearance. He put on quite a show in the 1970 spring training, enough to spark a great on-field rivalry, and Thurman loved competition. Though the struggle between the Yankees' adamant claim that Munson would be the everyday catcher and the pull of the city pens lobbing for Ellis was intense at points, the two catchers managed to get along well in spite of the heat. Despite Munson's spring average, he finished a lowly third in the Dawson voting, behind Ron Klimkowski and the predicted winner, John Ellis. The victor received a beautiful watch for his achievement, with which to monitor his 15 minutes of fame as they swiftly ticked away.

The 1970 season opener was set for Tuesday, April 7, at Yankee Stadium against the nemesis Boston Red Sox. Munson was burdened with a world of pressure that day. As the season stared him blankly in the face, he knew he would be trying to take over the storied lineage of the Yankee catcher. The man most recently cast aside in that role was Jake Gibbs. Gibbs, assured that he would have security with the Yanks, turned down a golden opportunity as a football coach at his alma mater, the University of Mississippi. He was a fine defensive catcher, adept at calling the game, with a penchant for clutch hitting. Ironically, Gibbs enjoyed his finest season in 1970, a .301 average and eight home runs (including two in one game) over 49 contests.

On top of that, Ellis—originally a catcher, but playing first base that day—had fate all but writing his itinerary. He turned heads in the press box and elsewhere by arriving at the clubhouse at 7:35 that morning. Before the game, Ellis received a letter from Mrs. Eleanor Gehrig. "I've waited all these years for Lou's successor," she wrote, "and now he's here."[2] Beside the fact that his father's ticket reservations were lost, it was one fine day.

After five and a half innings of Boston domination, the Sox had built a 4–0 lead. But then it became New York's turn to strike. After Boston pitcher Gary Peters pegged Ellis in the foot and Cater earned a walk, Bobby Murcer lumbered to the plate. A solid all-around ballplayer out of Oklahoma, Bobby had been hailed as the reincarnation of Mickey Mantle, despite his protest of "I'm no muscle hitter" in his southern banjo twang. The 19-year-old rookie had failed to justify the public's high expectations during brief trials in 1965 and '66, largely due to his inability to hit southpaws. After two valuable maturing years in the army, he had returned in 1969 with the opportunity to create his own image by activity instead of reputation. In this at-bat, he produced a run with his single off Peters. It was a make-or-break time for the pitcher—and he broke. Curt Blefary sailed a pitch to left that bounded into the stands for a two-run ground rule double.

That was enough to cause Peters's exit. Called in to relieve was 23-year-old Bill "Spaceman" Lee. As Lee rode out of the bullpen on the famous Yankee golf cart driven by Frankie Albano, a fan's beer bottle caromed off his chest. Wrote Spaceman in his autobiography, *The Wrong Stuff*:

> I thought New York should have signed up the fan who tossed it. He didn't have overwhelming velocity, but he threw a heavy, sinking bottle for a strike. The guys had warned me about Yankee rooters, so I wasn't amazed when I got hit by an object. I was surprised that the fan had such good control on the first day of the season, though.[3]

The effect of the incident was apparently minimal, for Lee was golden in shutting the Yankees down despite an initial faltering. The story of that inning was much like the season of his new mound opponent, Jack Aker. Aker was a crack pen man with a jet black mane who was acquired the year before. He had back problems in 1970 — which created a slow start — but he pulled it together toward the end and compiled sixteen saves. He shut Boston down in the top of the ninth to bring the Yanks into the bottom of the inning with their one, two, and three hitters due. Clarke, Munson, and White all succumbed to Bill Lee's wrathful speed by way of strikeouts, and the game was over. Four to three was the final score. Thurman had committed an error in the game and attained but a sacrifice in three official at-bats. He had no hits to his credit, nor would he until two days later.

To follow Thurm's life solely based on hits, errors, and victories would be ignorant, for if anyone knowledgeable on the subject were to be asked of Thurman's character, his dedication as a family man would be invariably injected into the dialogue. At six pounds, 14 ounces, his daughter Tracy Lynn was born on Friday, April 10. The delivery took place at Canton's Timken Mercy Hospital, but — much to Thurm's regret — the father couldn't be there. He was playing at home, beginning a three-game series versus the Indians; he must have wished it was a road matchup in Cleveland, but he celebrated nonetheless. The night was spent handing out cigars and acting as the resident proud papa. This was a landmark event in Munson's life; he was to be a spectacular father who took special delight in watching the children as they grew. From then on, baseball took an obvious backseat to family. He stressed that the game was a vehicle to support the family, as much as he thoroughly loved to play ball.

Life in baseball continued that Sunday with a truly beautiful occasion, when legends Joe DiMaggio and Mickey Mantle had their center field plaques at Yankee Stadium unveiled. No matter how affected Munson must have been, it proved to be of no divine inspiration. The slumping catcher logged a combined 0–7. He had been hitless the whole series. In the first game of a doubleheader, he and Clarke were hit by the lightning-bolt fastballs of Sam McDowell, who the Yankees beat for their only win out of three. Thurm was adamant that the slump had nothing to do with Diane and the baby, but after the Sunday twin bill, he hopped a plane back to Canton and saw his daughter for the first time. It was the single happiest moment of his life, he noted.

Monday was an off day, which Thurm spent with the family. But the next afternoon, it was back to business. As the Apollo 13 astronauts headed back to earth that day in grave danger, Munson's career did not appear much safer. He was competing with John Ellis, who was staggering just as badly. Having been hyped to a greater extent, Ellis fell a good deal more heavily. The press placed their focus on him, which took a large weight off Munson's shoulders. Ellis went 1–4 as New York lost 8–3.

On April 16, Thurman was back in the lineup but remained hitless in a three-game set against Boston. Another three games followed in Baltimore and still no hits. He was 1–30 for the season, and now the usually calm, confident Munson was second-guessing himself. One writer bravely confronted him amidst the initial fear of his unsavory demeanor with a question about Thurm's ability to overcome the early slip. "Don't worry about me" came the stern reply. "When this year is over I'll be hitting .300."[4] The truth is he didn't sleep some nights. He wondered about his capability of handling the majors, if he truly belonged. Most disturbing was the Yankee's, record at that point, 4–8, caused largely by their catcher's offensive and defensive deficiencies.

The scribes of New York scoffed at his .033 average. "He could get 25 hits in his next 70 at-bats," wrote one, "and that's a .357 clip in itself. Yet it would just give him a .260 mark for his first 100 at-bats of the season. It's a long way to come."[5]

After the failed Baltimore series, Houk beckoned Munson to his office. "Thurman, I told you you'd win more games for this club catching than you would hitting," he admonished. "You've just got to relax. You're my regular catcher, and no one is sending you down or sitting you down. Just get out there and play the way I know you can."[6]

This was not the first time Houk had received acclaim for his handling of such a situation. "On some clubs all you need is a couple of bad days and the manager starts experimenting," said Danny Cater in 1971. "Houk isn't like that."[7]

The conversation served to cool down Munson, who at that stage was zero for his last 24. In the fall, he recounted, "On our first home stand in Yankee Stadium I couldn't even see the ball. But I knew I could hit and Ralph Houk assured me he had confidence in me and that it was only a matter of time."[8]

Despite Diane's golden locks of shining blonde hair, on April the 20th, in Washington, D.C., Thurm had a thing for Brunets. Munson opened the game with his pitiful .033 clip but, courtesy of George Brunet, raised it to .118 by night's end.

Trouble should have been apparent before the Senators' pitcher even logged a third of an inning. After a single, a double, and a pitcher's error, Cater slammed a three-run homer to distance the Yanks at 5–0 before the first out was even recorded. Two innings later, Cater and Ron Woods singled and then, with the weight of failure sagging on his shoulder, Thurman Munson lumbered plateward to shoot a point-scoring double off of Brunet. With a sigh of relief in between, he singled twice more in the game for two RBI altogether in Stan Bahnsen's 11–2 win. Having suffered his only slump of 1970, Munson tore along from there at a .322 pace.

Ralph Houk could be a brilliant man. Once, when pitcher Mike Kekich complained about the Major's treatment, the manager called him in the office, slid the door shut, and threw up his fists. There the issue died out. He wasn't one to allow problems to fester and hurt the team. So Munson knew to trust him when he was benched the day after rocking Brunet. "I just wanted you to think about those three hits a little longer," Houk explained. "Otherwise you might go hitless tonight and start worrying all over again."[9] Though he did not start, Thurman managed to appear late in the game. Most painful to him must have been the 7–5 loss to lowly Washington.

The New Yorkers finished April at 9–12, but they were a scrappy team soon to emerge. Several hitters (Gibbs, Hansen, Frank Tepedino, Jim Lyttle, Cater, and Roy White) would flirt with or attain the treasured benchmark of .300. The rotation was sturdy behind the capable arms of Mel Stottlemyre, Fritz Peterson, and Stan Bahnsen. But the bullpen was the real story, consisting of Steve Hamilton, Jack Aker, and Lindy McDaniel, the latter two with 16 and 29 saves, respectively. McDaniel was star of the pen, a hard-working, hard-throwing, genuinely good guy. He would go on to pile up nine wins and a 2.01 ERA, quite an outstanding season.

The Yanks opened up May successfully, with a 7–1 record. In the May 10 contest in Anaheim, they set off to a 3–0 lead, courtesy of Clarke, Murcer, White, and Cater. Angel pitcher Rudy May issued a leadoff walk to White and retired two batters before a hitless Thurman Munson came to bat. With a misaimed swing, he blooped a lazy hit to right. As weak as it was, White came around to score and Munson stood on second with a double. The safety made the score 4–3, and there it stayed. Five days later Thurm contributed a sac fly that proved to be the winning run. As much copy as he was gradually attaining with his slew of decisive ribbies, the papers would stubbornly misspell his name as "Thurmon."

John Ellis at this point was mired in a nasty 0–20 slump, while Munson was slowly gaining respect. With quiet stats and ways, his name often popped up, and the fans were taking notice. After years of disappointment — virtually no contention since 1964 — they were joyous to see the success of the individual players and the team, which on May 16 stood at 19–16, a half dozen games behind Baltimore.

Those kingly Orioles were the only significant obstacle between New

York and their successful aspirations. The Mets were still most popular in New York, though they couldn't capture a pennant. (It would be a few years before winning would help the fans to grade their affection.) On the 18th of May, in the city of New York, the Baltimore baseball club arrived for an all-important series.

The Yankees were on the offensive in the third frame, starting with Fritz Peterson. The pitcher stroked a home run that wrapped around the foul pole in left field that, with Gene Michael on board, scored two. After four singles, pinch hitter Curt Blefary was intentionally walked. With the bases drunk, Munson saw a single through for a couple of runs batted in. It should be noted that with Thurman's RBI, he once again drove in the winning run.

Munson went on in the next few weeks to enjoy a combined 6–10 doubleheader; the participation itself was noteworthy, for throughout his career, Thurman almost never played both ends of a twin bill. On his 23rd birthday, the Red Sox came to Yankee Stadium, as did 66,000 fans. That was the largest major league crowd in half a decade. Thurm managed to show a single and a run for the home folks, but Boston doused the Yankee flames, 4–3.

A week later, the Yanks were emerging as a serious threat. Jake Gibbs was in as catcher in Kansas City to offer his block of home plate in the third that stopped Pat Kelly dead on the base path. As mentioned before, Gibbs was an excellent catcher. He had his reputation, people knew he was good, but Gibbs felt no need to push this. Nobly putting the team first, he coached Munson in an effort to spark improvement, all the while knowing the starting job had slipped from his hands (similar to the modern Joe Girardi/Jorge Posada Yankee connection). He would retire after the next season and be honored with Jake Gibbs Day, an unbelievable achievement for a man of no real notable statistics.

In the Royals game Ellis was pinch-hit for in the ninth by Munson, with the score deadlocked at 2–2. With White and Woods on base, Thurm slapped a single to right field, drawing the former in for a 3–2 lead. The Yanks shut Kansas City down in the bottom of the ninth, and Munson's RBI once again proved the decisive one. This was the tenth win in New York's last 11 games, raising the Yanks to a .600 winning percentage at 36–24, only three games shy of Baltimore.

On June 21 the Yanks were at Fenway for another wild one. Munson compiled a trio of hits, ribbies, and a run, which swung the series in New York's favor 3–1, 7–2 on their road trip. Adding to the positives was the fact that 31,073 were on hand for the game and 120,478 for the series. Things were looking up on the Yankee end. The scrappy, long-dethroned, under-achieving club was putting themselves once again into the top rank. Ralph Houk spoke after the Red Sox game. "The kids have done it for us.... Our kids have turned this club around. Roy White and Danny Cater are the big hitters for us but it's those kids who make the difference." Proceeding to name Munson, Ellis, and Murcer, he concluded, "These kids give us speed....

"These kids will be tougher in the second half of the season because they'll make fewer mistakes as they get more experience. This has showed in the last three weeks. We made fewer mistakes in those three weeks than we used to make in one week."[10]

The kids were sure in for an experience during a doubleheader versus Cleveland on June 24. The Yanks took both games, but as it turns out, the victor hardly bends history's ear.

Fireworks, both figurative and literal highlighted the fifth inning of the second game. Out of the Yankee Stadium assemblage of 31,925, a New Yorker threw a firecracker from the upper deck that landed and exploded at Indians catcher Ray Fosse's feet. Fosse was a promising catcher who in that season hit for a .307 mark. A very popular man, he could easily have overshadowed Munson — by way of press or talent — if not for the famed All-Star game collision with Cincinnati's Pete Rose about a month afterward. In the top of that fifth inning in New York, Cleveland was leading 2–1 when Stan Bahnsen uncorked a wild pitch, prompting outfielder Vada Pinson to come charging in from third base to score. In Pinson's opinion, the pitcher's tag was overzealous, and so in response he rose and knocked Bahnsen out with a hard left. Elston Howard rushed out to hold Pinson back as the benches cleared, while Munson stood right in the thick of it all. A Cleveland player sprang onto Thurm's back in what look's from the newspaper photo to be either a hug or some strange fighting technique, arms wrapped around the catcher's shoulders, feet off the ground.

A 210-pound man stepped into the batters' box in the ninth inning. His name was Tony Horton, and he faced New York reliever Steve Hamilton. Hamilton enjoyed short-lived fame for his high-arcing, hard-to-hit "folly floater," and, besides Boston's Rico Petrocelli, Horton was the only one to hit that pitch up to that point in 1970. At this point, the game stood, at 7–1, it had been a long day, and a little fun wasn't going to hurt. "He let me know about it," Hamilton explained following the game, "after he got a single off the pitch in Cleveland earlier this year. When he came up there he was nodding his head at me, so I winked at him and threw it."[11]

The first one Horton only nicked for a foul. The crowd was surprised he even made contact, and they roared. Jokingly, the Cleveland batter wagged his finger moundward, and Hamilton obliged. He quickly slipped into the awkward windup; set on the rubber, he began as usual before clamping his foot to the ground suddenly and thrusting his left arm loosely to the air. The ball swooped skyward and eventually reached the batters' box. This time, Horton connected for another blooping pop foul, and Munson raced after it. Running toward the backstop, he lunged forward and caught the ball with a theatrical lunge. In what seemed to be an effort to play to the crowd, Horton flung his bat to the ground and his helmet in the other direction, and after a well-timed stroll of suspense, dropped down on his hands and knees in surrender. He crawled a few steps into the dugout, as the park roared with laughter. Said Hamilton afterward, "When he did that, he fractured me. I wasn't embarrassed; I just went along with the gag. I was laughing at myself and the whole situation. You can have a lot of fun in a game when you're ahead."[12]

Laughed opposing pitcher Sam McDowell, on deck at the time of the incident:

> If I had gotten the chance to hit, I would have gone up there righthanded for the first time in my life. He doesn't throw the thing to lefthanded hitters because he gets them out too easy without it.
> But I would have gone righthanded, then jumped over to the left side while he was throwing it and taken my shot. When it gets up in the air, you have enough time to pack a lunch.[13]

He continued, moving on to Thurman's final inning at-bat, "There's no use fooling around when you're ahead, but if Munson hadn't hit a 3–1 pitch and it had been strike two, I'd have thrown it on the next pitch. But I don't know where it would have gone."

Asked if there was any place for such a pitch, "Sudden Sam" deadpanned, "Yes, I'd say there's a place for it — in softball."

While the sports world howled, Tony Horton was falling apart. Veteran manager Alvin Dark reflected upon the spectacle as "the most sorrowful incident I was ever involved in my baseball career." Shortly after the doubleheader on June 24, 1970, Horton dropped baseball and checked into a mental hospital.

Baseball and the general public ignored the pain and weaknesses of Horton and other brethren, and even 30 years later the scene plays as an ESPN network commercial for the crowds to laugh again.

July opened in Detroit, Michigan. Denny McLain, winner of the two previous Cy Young Awards, was returning that day from his much-hyped suspension for "admissions related to his involvement in purported bookmaking activities in 1967 and his associations at that time," according to Commissioner Bowie Kuhn. After a hiatus dating back to the early part of the year, not everyone was sure if he was truly ready to come back. When Ralph Houk was asked the lineup before the day's game, he admitted, "I can't tell you until I know who's pitching for Detroit." A crowd of 53, 863 showed up at Tiger Stadium because they had a good idea who was.

McLain received a mixed reception, but his Tigers lost the game 5–3; it was the last Yankee win for four more games. That would be snapped on the Fourth of July when Jake Gibbs, the catcher that day, hit a triple and two RBI before tagging up and scoring on Munson's pinch-hit sacrifice.

Another day, another loss, in fact two the next evening to the Senators. Many professed that the Yankees were slipping, but Houk — ever the optimist — combated the sentiment. "Things aren't as bad as they seem.... We haven't even completed half the season yet. It's a long year and leads can dissipate fast. I'd like to take the Baltimore series [to start two days later], but you can't say it's an important series.... We'd like to get our feet back on the ground."[14]

Entering the Baltimore set, the Yanks were on a ten-game slide in which Munson hit merely .227. Said Houk, "This is a young club and they don't get down even when they're losing. But when they lose they start trying too hard. You know, everything comes easier when you win."[15]

Sure enough, the Yanks were playing the Os hard in a game on July 8th. Munson's three-run homer tied it at 3–3, but New York ended up dropping the decision by a run. They would enter the All-Star break with a 46–39 record, a single game back of second-place Detroit, but a full seven short of Baltimore.

As of July 11, Thurm's stats were looking decent: 3 homers, 28 RBI, and 64 hits in 238 at-bats to constitute a .269 average. He did not make the cut for the All-Star squad, but showed no disappointment. According to Munson, he saw it as a great chance to spend time with Diane and Tracy, and this seems to be so. Often he complained of his dislike for being away during important moments in the children's lives, or of having to comfort them in times of trouble with an assurance over the phone that Daddy would be home in a few days. He also took the time to find perspective for the second half of the season. With a .348 mark after the break, it must have worked.

Thurman continued his success by celebrating the retiring of Casey Stengel's number 37 with a 4–5 game, though the Yanks lost 4–2 to the Orioles. The next day, however, a new hero was consecrated in the annals of Yankee history.

Munson had just been notified of a two-week stint he would serve at Fort Dix in early August when New York played a doubleheader at Yankee

Stadium. As the Bombers swiped the first game of that Sunday, August 9, twin bill, Thurm was serving weekend duty, and it looked as though there was no chance of reaching the stadium in time to battle the Orioles. Leaving the base at five o'clock, he hurried furiously across the roads to the Bronx.

It was a silent arrival. No one really knew Munson was there as he dressed quickly and slipped into the dugout at midgame. After a short time unnoticed, Houk called over. "Grab a bat and pinch-hit," he was ordered. As the game progressed, number 15 stepped onto the field and into the on-deck circle. Close to the dugout, a few heads snapped over and saw him. Immediately they erupted into a frenzy. Sweeping over the park, the ripples of applause rapidly amassed into one collective ovation. On their feet, the 42,000 stood for the virtually unknown rookie as "number 15, Thurman Munson" was announced over the public address system. Frank Robinson, a veteran of 586 home runs, a Rookie of the Year, dual MVPs, and managerial stints, looked over at the 23-year-old coming to bat. "That boy will lead the A. L. in hitting one day," he praised. "He'll be a good one."[16]

Batting against Pete Richert, Munson fouled off a half dozen or so pitches, stepped in the box again, and shot a hard liner at Brooks Robinson. Needless to say, the ball was caught.

Of the 23 Bombers used in that August doubleheader, there was only one taking over a legacy. Bill Dickey, Yogi Berra, Elston Howard, Thurman Munson — the great Yankee catchers. From decade to decade, with spellbinding symmetry, each excelled. For Thurman, it was something to shrug off and downplay, but internally he was full of pride. In a time when heroes were crippled with age or just had not measured up, there was the sense of a fresh era. Wrote Munson in reflection, "It was as though, at that very moment, I had become appreciated by the New York fans. I had, in a sense, arrived."[17]

From there, Munson began his fortnight in the army reserve. On August 15, he had a 2–4 day in a win against the Royals, and the next day, along with Bahnsen, he rushed from Fort Dix to collect a double and a run. The victory in that contest made for four in a row and 15 in the last 21. But for the most part in the two-week stretch, Thurman was not there. Unfortunately, neither were his Yankees. Hovering either eight or nine games behind Baltimore, New York seemed to be perfectly happy battling for second place.

On September 8, the Yanks finished putting together a five-game winning streak, and then went straight to a losing skid of four. The fourth one could not be salvaged despite Thurman's sixth and final home run of the year. Nevertheless, New York went up by six games on Boston and Detroit in the race for second place. Two days later, Munson pocketed a couple of base knocks, but New York was felled 5–4 by the Red Sox, and thus the Baltimore Orioles, long considered well out of reach, clinched that day.

As the season was disappearing into the crispness of October, Munson aided his club in their ambitious quest by driving in Peterson as the game-winning RBI in a 2–1 victory. But in the next contest Fritz's pitching would prove more dramatic.

It was a good way to end the season, with Peterson 19–11 going into the final game of 1970. Noticing beforehand that his hotel room number of 1219 would be his record backwards if he lost, the wacky blond twirler had his room switched. He was truly hungry for the 20th victory and pleased to be winning 4–3 entering the ninth. Despite his eagerness to finish the game, Houk called for McDaniel to relieve. Fritz couldn't stand it. The dugout was too close, the radio too harrowing; he just could not know what was going on. Taking a spot under the manager's desk, he waited until his teammates began to file in. "Who won??" he begged frantically. Of course, Peterson had earned his 20th, and the flake was thrilled.

The Yanks then departed for the winter.

Munson opted not to play winter ball in 1970, instead spending time getting to know daughter Tracy. He stuck around most of the time, spoke often with Diane, and in their discussions decided to build a house. In the meantime, Thurman sought to keep in shape by frequenting the local YMCA and developing his new love: golf. Though resistant to indulge himself in the sport as much as many athletes traditionally do (from Babe Ruth and Ty Cobb to Michael Jordan and the Atlanta Braves' pitching staff), he did not make himself look stupid either. It's doubtful he would have cared though. He was a man of humility, often pointing himself out as a bad dresser or simply unattractive. In later years, teammates referred to him jokingly as "Squatty Body." Thurm didn't care; he'd rib them right back.

Munson noted that he was very tired by season's end. Though he missed ample time because of the reserve duty, he had still logged 125 games in 1970. Obviously, this must have been taxing on the knees (as proven later), but this was a small matter to Thurman — he couldn't stand being a bench warmer.

Munson professed to have little use for statistics, as they can often be misleading. How can one ignore 1970, though? Eighty assists led the league, and he threw out 40 of 69 potential base thieves. In Thurm's opinion, the true measure of a catcher's greatness was not how many base runners were taken down but rather how many thought twice and neglected to run.

Back in Pompano Beach, Florida, an old army man was receiving some good news. Ralph Houk had led the New York Yankees to a 93–69 record, better than any franchise collection since 1964. At 24 games over the median mark of .500, they still trailed Baltimore by 15. Thus the Major expected Oriole skipper Earl Weaver to win that year's Manager of the Year. Weaver had 73 points in the voting; the oldest manager in the league, Houk, won it with 118. It was his second, (the first was the historic championship year of 1961). His control of the bullpen, and manipulation of the rotation and the scrappy young club of colts all helped win the award.

Another vote came in that November. By a 23–1 margin, Munson took the Rookie of the Year in a landslide. It's a joke really that it was not unanimous; Cleveland's Roy Foster was granted one vote by the local scribe. (It's ironic that his choice was a regional boy. Perhaps this writer needed some Ohio background.) Munson was only the second catcher (after Johnny Bench) in the award's history of 23 seasons at that time, and he was the first American League catcher. He was also the second AL victor since 1953 to bat over .300, accomplished previously by Tony Oliva (.323). Thurman led the successful Yankee club with a .302 mark, not to mention 6 homers and 53 RBI over 132 games. According to Houk, getting the call in Florida from Lee MacPhail, he was most amazed with his catcher's minimal minor league experience of only 99 contests.

From his Canton residence, Munson spoke to reporters on November 24 at Yankee Stadium via an amplified phone connection. Asked if he had confidence that an award such as Rookie of the Year was attainable after his 1–30 start, Munson answered flatly, "No. But I didn't because my manager didn't lose his [confidence] in me. When I was going so badly, he called me in and told me I was the regular catcher, no matter what I hit."[18]

At this point, MacPhail — present at the stadium — picked up the phone to jokingly ask Thurm if he foresaw a small raise. "I expect a raise will be coming along," he responded. "But I hope it won't be too small."[19]

Munson was a man with little use for accolades in comparison to respect from the league players. But he couldn't deny the pride of placing with all the other great players who had won the award. Among those were five Yankees: Gil McDougald, Bob Grim, Tony Kubek, Tom Tresh, and Stan Bahnsen. With Munson added as number six, New York trailed only their old local foe, the Dodgers.

That autumn, despite all, his name still appeared in the newspapers as "Thurmon."

4

PAYING DUES

Without the catchers, you have all passed balls.
— Casey Stengel

There was something different about the image of Munson as he cracked the nucleus of the 1971 New York Yankees. The sense of a green rookie scrapping to stand atop the heap had disappeared with his November award, and the Yankees had showcased him proudly upon their mantelpiece. One fine example is the annual yearbook. He grace's the cover with bat flung forward in midstride, amidst a half dozen teammates in separate shots. Flipping to the contents page, there he loom's again as the microcosm of the club's vigor, kneeling with ball clenched in mitt, supported by his free hand. As a grimace creases his face, the smoldering dust shoots upward, the cloud trailing a presumably safe Oakland Athletic.

For those familiar with the 1970 team, it would not be difficult to recognize the '71 version. The only significant changes since the opening of the previous year were that Jim Lyttle was the new regular in right, Cater shifted to first to allow Jerry Kinney in at third, and Stick Michael (who had manned three different positions) was platooned with Frank Baker at short.

As the season neared, Houk was confident in his new team, stagnant or not. "We haven't made many changes," he explained. "Instead we're counting upon the additional year's experience our younger players acquired last season."[1]

Apparently, Houk's infectious optimism had been contracted by Munson. "Everyone knows what a young club we have, but they don't realize how good we can be. I'm going to hit more and we'll have more pitching, so I think we could win it all. Don't forget," Thurman admonished, "we have the best manager in baseball."[2]

Munson's confidence had to be strong that spring training, even though reporters hounded him incessantly about the legendary "sophomore jinx," the decline of a young player after a sensational rookie performance. Thurm saw it as pure stupidity, but history tends to suggest otherwise. Most familiar to him was the rise and fall of Stan Bahnsen, whose 1969 campaign fell severely short of the preceding one. Nevertheless, Munson was not scared nor deterred by such theories, for they were mere matters of the mind. To him, defensively and offensively, prospects were bright.

In the spring exhibitions, New York won only about a third of its games. The preseason predictions were hopeful, as was the Yankee attitude entering the year. They opened in Boston on Tuesday, April 6, for an afternoon matchup with Ray Culp. Thirty thousand were expected, but the figure turned out to be 34,517, part of a record-breaking major league total of 401,310 that opening day.

The Red Sox jumped out early against Bahnsen, who was making his first opening Day start. It appeared that the Yanks might contest the 2–0 lead when Horace Clarke lined an RBI single. After Cater scored on the play, Lyttle attempted to follow, but Boston catcher Duane Josephson stonewalled him at the plate. Said Josephson, "I didn't know whether he was going to slide or come crashing in, but those are the chances a catcher has to take. The next time I may get run over and get creamed."[3]

With the score 3–1 Boston, the Yanks needed an offensive eruption. Munson led off the inning with a hit. True to his expectation, he was christening the season successfully with a 2–4 day and a stolen base. Not everyone was as blessed; White, Murcer, and Cater were put down in succession.

Two days later, New York suffered a 5–4 loss at the hands of Washington. Thurman failed to get a hit, though he did reach base and score. The next day he dropped to third in the lineup and went 0–5 in a win. That was followed by an 0–3 showing in the first game of a split doubleheader. While he sat out the second as usual, Munson had a lot to dwell on.

On April 11, 34,745 came out to see the Yankee home opener for the best showing since 1966. With new breath in the Bomber lungs, the New York fans took prime interest in their titans again, especially since the Mets were falling off from those "amazin'" championship days.

Though his team won decisively, Munson stumbled to a hitless three at-bat performance. From there on, he went 0–4, 0–2, 0–5. It was a horrible streak, a 2–30 start. In fact, excluding opening day, he was on an

0–27 run, and had a .067 batting average. It seemed there was little difference between that and the nearly identical initiation of his Rookie of the Year season. There were a few reasons for the slow start. First, as he lost confidence, Munson altered his batting stance but still failed to get comfortable. Additionally, the army reserve duty continued, now for one weekend a month, which usually equated to three or four games. What this did more than anything was break any streaks he may have had going, or any flow to his play. Of course, in all fairness, only one weekend had been lost during that dirty little early spell.

Houk attempted to remind Thurman of the previous season's struggle. "Don't worry," Ralph consoled, "you started like this last year and hit three hundred."[4] But he just couldn't come around. The indestructible confidence of Thurman Munson was being pummeled, and he was letting the idea of the sophomore jinx go to his head. The press addressed the issue so often that it finally permeated his psyche to where the thought obstructed his play. Thurm was miserable. He knew he was better. He had just been given a 100 percent raise by the club to $30,000 before the season, and contrary to his adamant belief in earning a paycheck to the fullest satisfaction, here he was showing little in return. Thoughts of the future bred fear, for as sportswriter Jim Murray once penned, "A king may be a king because his father was, but a ballplayer is a major leaguer only so long as his average shows he is."[5]

If there was any consolation it was the knowledge that, after all, his most valuable role was as a catcher, and though the other end of the battery was struggling mightily, he was yet to err that season. Through such diligence, a leaguewide consideration was beginning to take hold that here roamed the premier defensive catcher in baseball.

Finally, on April 18, Munson went 2–4 while batting out of the two spot. A 2–3 game the next afternoon was sufficient for a day off, courtesy of Houk. The team, however, was 5–8 at that early point in the season, well back of Baltimore. From there, Thurm maintained a steady pace. And the team responded in kind. In early May, New York was victorious in five games consecutively, but this was done partially minus Munson's services as he attended to army duty. In fact, he was absent for an extended period of time before a return on May 15. He stole a base, slapped a hit, watched the Yanks be done in by crumbling defense, and disappeared once more. That game was on a Friday; he would not reenter until Tuesday. His consistent offense couldn't save the Bombers, though; they seemed to be heading downhill again.

By June, Munson was responding healthily to the second spot in the lineup, and he smacked a home run in a game at Yankee Stadium. When

Munson had come to the Yankees, Lee MacPhail knew he'd have trouble establishing a reputation as a slugger, given the park's unfriendly configurations from the perspective of a righthander. The dimensions were a definite obstacle, reading 301 in left, and 296 in right; and center field — toward the tortured "Death Valley" sector — was a nearly unreachable 461 feet! Altogether, it was a good reason for Munson to have a mere two home runs by June 5, to go with a .244 batting average and a sickening amount of ten RBI. Reaching back in history for an intriguing juxtaposition, "Sunny Jim" Bottomley and the well-traveled Mark Whiten have each racked up a dozen in a single game. Surely Thurm was not pleased.

Nor could Thurm have been pleased with his Yankee club. For a team that had impressively claimed a stake to second place the prior year and was predicted to do similarly in the season at hand, it must have dented the Yankee pride to look up on June 16 at Baltimore, Detroit, and Boston in the Eastern Division. A 3–2 edging by the Royals that afternoon put New York ten games back of first and four behind the third-place Red Sox. But if that honor was diminished, two days later there was no denying the core of pride in the Yankees.

There are many awards, accolades, and descriptions by which Munson has been remembered. But if there is one instance by which he is to be defined, one all-encompassing measure of his character, drive, ability, and devotion, perhaps it is the story of June 18, 1971.

Forty thousand crowded Baltimore's Memorial Stadium. It was an important series for the Yankees, imperative if they proposed to stay in contention. At fourth place and 11 games out, New York threw Fritz Peterson against Cy Young Award holder Mike Cuellar in the night game. During the third inning the Orioles staged a three-run rally during which Andy Etchebarren defied the laws of the catcher and bunted his way on for a single. Innocent enough. Next came Paul Blair, a fleet center fielder who on the previous year's May 31 was the recipient of one of the most vile beanings in baseball history, a vicious offering straight to the cranium. By the time of the Yankee game, Blair had regrouped to the point where he shot a double to the outfield, imploring the runner on first to take off. After being waved in at third, he rounded the bag and raced home. The throw came in, and Thurm marched forward to catch it. The three forces merged at once: Etchebarren, the baseball, Munson. The runner blasted Thurm with the impact, knocking him back and the ball loose.

Despite the run scored, the park's attention focused on the fallen receiver, who lay in the dirt, unconscious. Unconsciousness is what it took for him to make an error that season. Out of 614 chances in 1971, the Etchebarren play produced Munson's sole error, for a .998 fielding percentage. Immediately after the collision he was ushered to Union Memorial Hospital to be checked out by a neurosurgeon. Thurm was told that he was okay, but had to be held overnight for observation.

He played the next day.

Munson held nothing against Etchebarren. The two would joke often about the play afterward, but it was apparent that Andy had done no wrong. Thurm understood that if it were to be considered anyone's fault, it was his own, the green sophomore still developing his handling of the trade. Just in case he did harbor resentment, the opportunity to slide into Etchebarren came a few weeks later, and he was safe.

In the game of the injury, Munson's early single put the Yanks ahead 4–0, but they managed to be crippled in the end by an Oriole rally. Thurman's subsequent appearance on June 19 saw him as a pinch-hitter for Lindy McDaniel. Though he did not make a hit, that hardly diminishes the act of regrouping so quickly from the previous day's blow. As Gibbs caught in his place, New York took this one by the same score as Baltimore had posted on the 18th, 6–4. The Yanks were now tied with the Cleveland Indians for fourth place at 11 games back.

On the second of July, it was a rematch of that season's opener, Culp versus Bahnsen. Bahnsen's stretch of seven wins in his previous 14 starts was the most hopeful omen against the Yankee record of 1–4 against Boston over the pair's last five meetings. In the sixth inning, a promising young powerhouse named Ron Blomberg singled for New York before Munson doubled him in. Cater plated him with another double, and the score read three to nothing. And there it stood with two outs in the top of the ninth. With two runners on, Munson stepped to the plate facing Ken Brett, and he unleashed a three-run homer to add three points to the final score. The win, part of a split four–game series, catapulted (or obscurely sneaked) the Yankees into fourth place at 13½ back. They would not really budge for the rest of the season.

Entering the All-Star break, the Yankees were three games under .500 and in fourth by seven games. There wasn't much to believe in. Munson's lone light that summer was the All-Star game. Fosse led the voting for catcher with 645,966, and the Tigers' Bill Freehan trailed at 570,199. Munson ran well behind at 336,602, though he did outdistance the next contender, Ellie Hendricks, by 160,000. When Fosse bowed out with an injury, manager Earl Weaver appointed Munson as the backup catcher. The game was a memorable classic, a Hall of Fame hitting clinic highlighted by Reggie Jackson's shot to the transformer high above Tiger Stadium's roof. Thurm watched for seven innings as Freehan caught, and by Weaver's prolonged neglect of Munson on the bench, he failed to garner an at-bat.

When Thurm finally entered the game, Detroit's hometown hero Mickey Lolich was on the mound. Soon Johnny Bench came to the plate. Digging in, he asked Munson how he was doing, instinctively sensing the young man's uneasiness. "Why am I so nervous?" he begged of the Cincinnati prodigy.

Bench laughed a little and responded plainly, "Because you're supposed to."[6]

It was quite atypical for Munson to be so unnerved behind the plate. Chattiness was a trait he was begrudgingly loved for throughout the league. Rod Carew told in his autobiography of how when playing the Yankees, he would have dirt cast into his shoes from behind while batting. "Rod, what am I doing wrong at bat?" Thurm would implore throughout Carew's ups. "Am I lunging at the ball? Am I too slow? Am I not attacking the ball?"[7]

At the end of the ninth, Munson ran out to congratulate Lolich and the AL crew as they had snapped an elongated losing streak via a 6–4 score. Upon return to the regular season, there remained a sense of victory, albeit a moral one, when the Yankees swept the Milwaukee Brewers by a combined 17–11 score. This qualified New York for its fifth straight win and 13 of 17 to finally position them at the .500 mark.

After an embarrassing first half, they were optimistic after catching a glimpse of play reminiscent of their 47–30 second half run the year before. Said MacPhail, "Let's just say we're a little disappointed about the way the team got off, but we're far from discouraged. The difference between winning and losing games seems to be getting less and less nowadays. Please don't construe that as an alibi but it's a matter of fact."[8]

Munson needed no alibi that season. By the time July closed, his season was looking hopeful. With steady progression his average was raised up to .266 plus six yard jobs and a much-improved tally of 31 runs batted in. Sure, these are low, but compare them with the stats of Ray Fosse — voted by the fans as the starting All-Star catcher — compared at .264, 4, and 32 in only two more at-bats. Given Munson's nearly unblemished defense that season, he was quite clearly Fosse's superior.

Three weeks later Thurman plunged to .254 and for understandable reasons. Diane, carrying their second child, was having a difficult pregnancy, while their house — in the New York suburb of Norwood, New Jersey — was in the process of being built. Most harrowing, his mother, Ruth, suffered a stroke at the end of the summer, and Darrell promptly decided to leave her and the family. The collective incidents weighed heavily on Thurman's mind, and he flew to Canton whenever possible. Like a replayed trauma, it was all merging and hitting him at once. Mental, physical, emotional — the forces rendered him unconscious to the pillars of routine in his life.

But he played on.

Surprisingly, Munson opened August swinging, and swinging well; settled comfortably in the two spot, he stroked a homer to begin the month. He continued on that pace, but it was hardly enough. The team was floundering hopelessly, and within the week they stumbled to virtual elimination at 18 back.

As time marched on, Munson was not into the games either. Throughout mid- to late September, he was often absent from the lineup, either for military or personal reasons. When he was present, though, not much came to fruition, merely a series of 0-fers.

On the last night of the season, the Yankees were at RFK Stadium facing the Senators, where much more than a simple game was on the line. After more than a century of baseball as a Washington staple dating back to historic pickup games on the White House grounds, their club was being transferred to Texas by enigmatic owner Bob Short. Fuses were short during the final game, fans — all 20,000 present — buzzing with anger throughout until finally in the ninth they showed Short what they thought. The Senators were leading 7–5 with one out left to be recorded in the game. New York desperately wanted the win, for they had entered at 81–80, and a loss would throw their season back to a sub–.500 embarrassment. The Yankees got their wish, for with two already retired, the fans stormed the field, ripping out home plate, the pitching rubber, and the bases. It was destruction so complete that the umpires were left with no choice but to forfeit the game to the 82–80 Yankees, a 9–0 victory as recorded in the books.

This ended a season that Munson was more than happy to set in the past tense. He logged a .251 batting mark — significantly less than his team-high .302 of 1970 — with a respectable ten home runs but a miserable 42 RBI. Defensively, the run was unforgettable. Along with the lone error, Thurman threw out 23 of 38 potential base stealers and was accepted across the board as the best defensive catcher in all of the big leagues. But, as he wrote, "It was a most unsatisfying season ... and I was glad to put it behind me."[9]

Thurman said he was on the verge of giving up, but that would not have been wise with a family to support. As much as he loved baseball, the family came first, and the game's main purpose was to allow him to take care of them. In order to supplement his overall resources, Munson was becoming increasingly involved in business. He took on real estate, restaurants, shopping centers, banks, commercial land, and work with stocks and figures, all within a few years. Such endeavors allowed him to live atypically well for a man of relatively low salary. He taught himself and developed his own success almost strictly by self-design, which proved to be of immeasurable pride. A consuming vehicle of financial security and stability, business became his hobby. On road trips, when family life was not available, he would spend most of the free day conducting business, balancing his day healthily between the physicality of baseball and the financial side of life. There's a lot of time to kill in the athletic life, and business served to keep Thurman's mind busy in such times.

He often phoned business associates in Cleveland, where the great majority of his dealings took place. Adept at the trade, he was a quick learner with an easy manner, which is ironic considering his gruff reputation. Munson would deal with insurance and real estate men, just as one experienced in the industries as a profession. During frequent discussions of the topic with teammates, they would joke that he owned half of Ohio.

Psychologically, Munson's business was significant. He was a proud man who felt the dealings proved that he was not just another "dumb jock," but one who ordinary businessmen consulted for advice. Most important to him was the cherished feeling of ownership. For the kid who didn't have a penny of lunch money, it was quite a thrilling reimbursement for years of lost privileges. With a taste for sleek cars and fancy possessions, Munson — judging by later comments by teammates — had an obsession for material objects.

He gained much more on December 20, 1971, however, when daughter Kelly was born. Though the labor was difficult, she was a welcome addition and Tracy's new best friend. Their father spent as much time as he could with them, lest he miss a moment. Thurman was, in some ways, the happiest he had ever been.

Near the end of spring training 1972, the realization that the Yankees had no intention of sitting on their hands came full circle. Sparky Lyle of Boston came to New York in exchange for Danny Cater in one of the most famous deals of the time (or infamous, depending on where one lived). Sparky was an original who had no substitute. A flaky relief pitcher with an internal competitive fire, he was a 27-year-old lefty standing 6'1" and 208 pounds, a weight primarily composed of his overwhelming humor and his penchant for practical jokes. That kind of man was the type who sustained a ballclub, and sometimes they broke it apart. Lyle's case was the latter. He had been dealt by the Sox after a nasty shouting match with manager Eddie Kasko.

Houk showed little recognition of Boston's ulterior motives. "A trade can only be made when two clubs need something. The Red Sox needed a good hitter and we needed relief pitching."[10] New York did need help there, as Lyle entered a relief corps depleted by the eventual losses of Jack Aker and Gary Waslewski.

Arriving for spring training — a period Lyle thoroughly detested and often procrastinated to attend — he pleaded with Houk to let him pitch with liberation instead of regimentation. "Give me the chance for a couple of weeks. If I don't do the job, you can do whatever you want with me." The Major ended up more than obliged to consent. Sparky turned out a 9–5 record, 1.92 earned-run average, and 35 saves in 59 appearances for 1972.

Lyle was a welcome addition, even if the team did miss Danny Cater. It was not the only deal before the season, nor would it be the most debated. With high expectations, the Yankees approached the 1972 schedule sporting Stottlemyre, Kline, Peterson, and Bahnsen as the starting rotation. But, seeking to answer a burning question born in 1966 with the departure of Clete Boyer, they traded Bahnsen for third baseman Rich McKinney. The exchange was quite a dominating topic in which McKinney was criticized heatedly and doubted by the press. They were right this time. The McKinney trade was a failure from the start.

The loss of Cater cleared the way at first base for a young slugger named Ron Blomberg. "Ron has taken longer than we originally expected," Houk commented later that season, "but he still could be one of our most exciting ballplayers. He has some of the qualifications of a superstar. The great thing about him is his enthusiasm and competitiveness. That's something no one can teach." Blomberg filled in the rest of the information. "I'm still a growing boy," the Atlanta native said. "When I signed with the Yankees in 1967 I was only about 5'10" and 175 pounds. Now I am 6'2" and 200 pounds."

The Yanks held high hopes for Blomberg, the kid who did "everything left-handed except throw a baseball.... I bat left-handed and kick a football left-handed. Oops— make it left-footed."[11] From whatever side, he put together a substantially productive season.

Tom Seaver established a new major league record when he signed a contract for $122,000 with the New York Mets prior to the 1972 season. It may not have been in bold print in the record books, but on the first day of spring training, Munson finally signed his playing contract for the price of $37,500. Since his stats were down heavily from the previous year, it is quite surprising that he got a raise at all, let alone a 25% hike. Unfortunately, though, on March 31 the pay stopped coming. For the first time in baseball history, the players went on strike.

"As of midnight, the players are on their own," a Red Sox official spat.

"The motel rooms of the players are paid through tonight. That's it."[12] One of those affected players, new team member Danny Cater, summed up the feelings of many a striker. "I can't believe it. I never thought it would come to this."[13] Teammate Carlton Fisk simply shook his head in disgust.

"Obviously, the losers in the strike action are the sports fans of America," lamented Commissioner Bowie Kuhn. "Beyond that, I have no statement at this time."[14] Others elected not to hold their tongues. Sixty-four-year-old former ballplayer Rip Sewell exemplified the old-timer consensus. "I think it's ridiculous to even think about a strike," he complained to reporters at the time.

> First [the players] wanted a hamburger and [the owners] gave them a hamburger. Then they wanted a filet mignon and they gave them a filet mignon. Then they wanted the whole cow and now that they got the cow, they want a pasture to put him in. You just can't satisfy them and I have no sympathy for any of them.[15]

The scoreboard in Pittsburgh, accurately or inaccurately by determination of the hot stove league, read in a diagonal cascade, "Money, Money, Money."

By Thursday, April 13, the strike of 13 days was over. Eighty-six games were lost, not to be made up. The Yankees felt the effects badly — in the wallet. Attendance fell below the million mark that season to 966,328, most definitely as a result of the seven games lost and dissipated interest due to the strike. For a club in contention for the majority of the year, the fan total was expected to be significantly higher; to the contrary, the figures proved the lowest since the war year of 1945.

The Yankees began their 1972 season with an adjusted rotation of Kline, Stottlemyre, Peterson, and Mike Kekich. That four spot, left vacant by the departure of Bahnsen, was the key to competitiveness that season. Fortunately, Kekich won ten before he found his way out, making room for minor league veteran Rob Gardner, who himself was credited with eight. Altogether, 18 victories came out of the fourth slot in the rotation, and that was as key of an assist as could have been granted.

New York, which was picked to place third in the East, opened its season in Baltimore where the great Jim Palmer was set to square off against Stottlemyre. Against the kingly Orioles the game looked to be quite a challenge for the Yanks, but Palmer managed to alleviate some of the pressure with his comments the day before. "I felt readier before the strike," he revealed. "I don't think I'll injure my arm but I might not go nine innings. Most spring games, I pitched six innings, but I feel in pretty good shape."[16] At least the Yankees didn't lose to him. The game was rained out.

A doubleheader was already scheduled for the next day, so the post-ponement would have to wait. But the Yankees utilized their ace, Stott, while Baltimore opted to throw Pat Dobson. The year before, Palmer, Mike Cuellar, Dave McNally, and Dobson all put forth 20-win seasons, so facing the fourth pitcher was not exactly a picnic.

Munson hit seventh and caught that day, but Dobson allowed minimal competition — only four hits. Thurm got one of those, a single, in a couple of at-bats. In the shadow of a nearly perfect defensive 1971, he erred in this first game, already equaling the golden season's total. After the seventh inning, rain once again forced them to wait until the open Monday date, when the Yanks were shut down by McNally 4–0. It was Baltimore's 13th straight regular season victory.

New York played their home opener against Milwaukee on April 18. Munson walked in the third and scored on Clarke's single, helping the club to its first win of the season. Lyle, a man who seemed genetically superior to most humans in the clutch, grabbed the save and exemplified his great effect on the team's play, for when he took control the collection felt a lift.

The Yankees then took to Boston where the Red Sox were boasting their annual early season prospective elation, confident that this would be the year they exploded the "curse of the bambino." The curse is a Bean-town legend that originated with the 1920 sale of Babe Ruth to the New York Yankees. After three championships during Ruth's tenure, once Ruth departed, the team never again took the World Series, while the Yankees set on a path to eternal supremacy. And so the curse had been born, a plague that to this day has tripped the Sox in every futile attempt at elitism. But 1972 seemed to be *the* year in which they would give the Ruthian folklore a run for its mammoth money. In fact, April 20, 1972, was the start.

In the bottom of the second frame Reggie Smith singled and on one of the next pitches ran for second base. Munson fired to the bag but instead nailed center field. Smith was credited with a stolen base, though his advancement to third was accounted for with an E-2. While the grand myth of baseball's "junior jinx" was not a topic on the docket, it was becoming grimly apparent that near-perfection — in this case pertaining to defensive excellence — is *not* easy to repeat. A muff by McKinney, duly nicknamed "Orbit" for his aloof ways, set the stage for a ribbie by Cater. McKinney was just not working out. He would soon be demoted to Syracuse in favor of Celerino Sanchez, but the position remained wide open.

The Yankees picked up a little ground in their half of the fifth when, with Munson on base, Murcer — in the midst of a remarkable season — landed a 380-foot home run in Fenway's right field stands well over the bullpen. Yet this still only made it 4–3 Boston. In the seventh, Carlton Fisk tripled to left field and scored on a Tommy Harper single. With John Ellis's ribbie the next inning, the final score stood 5–4 Red Sox. The Fisk run had proved decisive.

The man who unanimously captured the Rookie of the Year honor that season was one known to Thurman simply as "Fisk" and nothing else. Fisk, beneath the terse label, was a 6'2", 200-pound hard-nosed and aggressive young catcher, but more important, a constant thorn in Munson's side. The two developed a well-publicized feud which exploded in 1973 when Fisk was elected to the All-Star team over his Yankee counterpart by over a half million votes. When reporters pressed, Munson could not keep the fuse unlit for long. "I'm not taking anything away from Fisk," he reasoned, "but get him away from Fenway Park and that easy wall in left field and see how many home runs he hits."[17]

Fisk—cocky, brash, antagonistic, loquacious—wouldn't dare let that slide. "I don't want to bad-mouth Munson, but he is jealous of me. He wants to be the American League All-Star catcher, but I took it away from him. He always wants to talk when he comes to bat. He must think he's another Yogi Berra, which he isn't."[18]

In fact, they did have civil exchanges during their encounters at the plate, but — bottom line — they really didn't like one another. Though the two persistently denied any feud to the press, actions do speak louder than words. Thurman would frequently check his rival's statistics in the newspaper, while Fisk was infuriated at the mention of Munson's name. Fisk later remembered one instance in which Munson found out in the morning paper that he was losing to Fisk in the assist department during one year late in Thurm's career. With Ron Guidry on the mound sporting a masterful ten-strikeout game, Thurman purposely dropped about a half dozen balls and threw them to first to edge Fisk out for the title.

Munson accused Fisk of "grabbing credit" and lacking "class." He alleged that "Pudge," as the Bostonian was called, was fooled by hyperbolic media hype and escalated harmless situations into high-tempered flareups. Fisk's track record speaks for itself; this accusation is apparently true.

The tension didn't pass away, but thrived. A few years into it, Munson was still granting spirited orations of his views to those who inquired. "Compared to him, why should I be so overlooked?" he begged after another All-Star snub:

> He's a good ballplayer, but I don't think he's much of a threat in
> other parks as he is in Boston; he might be a better ballplayer than
> I am, but he has never done the things I've done — set a defensive

Munson tags rival Carlton Fisk at Yankee Stadium in a move that earned Munson his only well known baseball nickname, "The Wall." (Courtesy Louis Requena)

> record for catchers, set a record for assists, hit .300 twice. And in
> six and a half years in the big leagues, how many games have I
> missed?[19]

Not many, Thurman.

Perhaps the whole melee boils down to a couple of bullheaded and proud men, like two Little League coaches battling for the strike call against an eight-year-old. Both offered faults: Fisk's pugnacious brewing of controversy; Munson's rueful scorn about which "Marty Appel said flatly, "Thurman was probably jealous."[20]

One would tend to disagree with the latter — not completely, but in principle. Perhaps Munson was jealous, but was it because Fisk simply garnered attention or because he had not earned all of it? This quote is particularly telling in its plastic give-and-take:

I know I run better than [Fisk], and I know nobody plays harder than I do. Now Johnny Bench is different. I've never hit forty home runs or driven in 120 runs. I haven't done those things. So I can't talk about me being as good as Bench because I haven't done what he's done.

Sometimes I wonder why playing hard hasn't helped my image. But it hasn't. Pete Rose plays that way. Charlie Hustle they call him. He gets more recognition for hustling than he does for playing the game, and he's a great player. I've always played hard. I thought that's the way you were supposed to play.[21]

The game of May 21 was ominous from the start for the Yankees when Boston shuffled through its first ten batters in the opening frame. New York mounted a sixth-inning rally, though, by new member Johnny Callison, Clarke, a Munson single (to apologize for an earlier passed ball), and Murcer, which somehow produced but a single run. Admitted Eddie Kasko, "We made as many mistakes as the Yankees, but we got more runs out of it."[22] The subsequent evening's rainout was beautiful compared to this game's four-error, 11–7 loss. The Yankees were drowning in the AL East cellar, tied with Milwaukee, yet with only a 3½ game deficit from first-place Detroit.

Munson's defensive struggles were building to an uncharacteristic frequency, with errors on the 7th and 16th of May. But he was not about to use an error as an excuse for failure. Had the problems been all his own, that would be one thing. But the Yanks as a team were suffering from his defense.

Fortunately, when its catcher's bat picked up, so did the team. By at-bat number 100, Munson had raised his clip to .290, and New York was clawing its way back. The team's standing ascended rapidly; it was courting .500, only four games behind the Baltimore Orioles. June 3 was a great help, when Munson broke a 10–10 deadlock in the top of the tenth at Comiskey Park in Chicago with a three-run homer off of White Sox moundsman Bart Johnson. Murcer added a three-run bomb of his own, and Lyle spent five innings icing the 18–10 win.

Due to losses to Texas and various other league inferiors, the Yanks were unceremoniously dropped to seven games behind, narrowly escaping the lowest standing in the East. Munson stumbled as well, below his class of talent to .262, a sharp decrease over only a couple of weeks. Fortunately, the team pulled up to third place amidst abundant rumors that Houk was headed for Boston. In response, Mike Burke held an extensive interview to discuss the club's future:

It's been a very tough row these past five years. We thought this year would be it, the year the club would be in contention, and maybe it will. But so far it's been a disappointment.

> Actually, Ralph hasn't said anything about the [Boston] rumors.... I guess it came up in passing. I was in his office in the clubhouse and he kidded about the Boston thing. He said "You don't take that seriously, do you?" and I said "no."[23]

Burke knew the bottom line and addressed it clearly. "We have had enough time to deliver."

In the more obscure spaces of the sports pages, beneath the box scores, Sparky Lyle was running a want ad. It seems he had lost his sole game-time glove, his only one since 1970. The mitt, which had, according to his superstition, helped him to 55 saves, was of deep value to Sparky. In return for its recovery he offered a new model to its finder.

The glove must have been working, for at the beginning of July, Lyle had saved 16 ("real saves," Houk called them) on an 0.98 earned-run average. Generally, everything was kept low on the Yankee club, especially the winning percentage. As word of Lyle's loss went forth, the Yankees felt the sting of a four-game sweep by Oakland. Yet as quickly as they failed, the Bronx men rebounded with that same speed. Five of seven wins immediately following the Oakland series were still only good enough for fourth place. The seven games by which they trailed Detroit were about as severe as the deficit dipped to that season, which is surprising for such a lack-luster output.

Before the Yankees were to seriously compete, they would at least have to rule third place. But even making it to that position was difficult. Their prime obstacle for the slot was Boston. Sox field general Eddie Kasko did not seem too concerned with the teams trailing him. "The important thing," he said at the end of July, "is that we are keeping pace with [Detroit and Baltimore] in the loss column. It all boils down to a head-and-head, and we have plenty of games left with both of them."[24] Like a silent assassin, though, the Yankees lay in wait. On the day of Kasko's comment, New York beat the Sox and the next day beat them again. Boston was splitting apart at its neatly stitched seams.

At an autograph signing in Springfield, Massachusetts, catcher Carlton Fisk openly criticized the lack of leadership from Red Sox stars Carl Yastrzemski and Reggie Smith. The comments echoed eastward across the state, not to mention nationally, and — to find the silver lining — as Boston disintegrated angrily, third place was looking a lot better than fourth in New York.

Munson and the Yankees had a chance to revel in the quaint village of Cooperstown, New York, for the Hall of Fame game on August 7, 1972. Amidst the excitement for the long-overdue first induction of Negro Leaguers into the Hall of Fame, the Yanks took on the Los Angeles Dodgers on the fabled Doubleday Field. Munson was placed in left field, a move strange yet consistent, for regulars were rarely given their routine work upon these occasions in place of reserves. As a testament to that statement, Bernie Allen of the Yankees was inserted into the lineup to clear the Little League-distance fences thrice to spur an 8–3 win.

New York had been enjoying habitual winning ways at the time, placing third via a sweep of Baltimore, two wins over Boston, and three of four over Milwaukee. The lead of Detroit over the Yanks was decreased to four. In the middle game of the Baltimore broom-stoke, Munson avenged the previous year's collision when he steamed home and, with that thick, brutal frame, leveled the catcher to jar the ball loose for a score. The Yankees were really coming through (or coming to, depending on one's expectations) and the collective whispers of New York spoke of World Series titles. The fans had broken out of their apathetic shells.

Immediately after the Hall of Fame game, the Yankees were playing Detroit, seeking their third win of the last four. Thirty-nine thousand came out for the potential sweep that Thursday night when Steve Kline started opposite Joe Coleman. But come the game's closing, it was all Lyle. With the bases loaded late, Sparky took the mound. He was a great competitor, but didn't take matters with unnecessary seriousness; he accepted wins and losses as they came. Such knowledge prompted Munson to sagaciously remind his pitcher that the bags were full — just in case he hadn't noticed. Lyle, ever defiant of logic, threw three straight balls. Thurman once again approached the hill and — with nothing else to say — reiterated that the bases were loaded and the batter had nowhere to go. Lyle looked at him sharply, with surprise dancing in his eyes. "I thought you were kidding!" he laughed, and proceeded to strike out the side.[25]

The wins were beginning to pile up. The standings of August 10 showed a dead heat.

	Wins	Losses	Winning Percentage	Games Back
Detroit	58	48	.548	—
Baltimore	57	48	.543	½
New York	55	49	.528	2

Soon the simultaneous occurrence of rookie Fred Beene's first win and Lyle's 28th save relieved the Yanks of a Munson error and pulled them to a tie at second under Baltimore. It was a miraculous recovery. Exploring their further blessings, New York dropped a whole series to Kansas

City, yet lost but a half game. They were still within striking distance at two games out.

That same day, Mayor John Lindsay officially sanctioned the renovation of Yankee Stadium. It had been only a year earlier, on July 6, that Governor Nelson Rockefeller had approved the purchase and modernization of the stadium. The announcement sounded rather elementary, but was a matter much more complicated.

Mike Burke had been establishing a favorable rapport with Lindsay, and together the two worked out a strategy for the purchase of the Yankee Stadium land and the ballpark itself. Next, they planned to condemn and modernize the stadium, as well as the neighboring highways and parking areas. Before the first two could be checked off, the properties would have to be purchased from the Knights of Columbus and Rice University, respectively. They were able to do so at a price tag of $24 million (or roughly the cost of a present-day slugger). However, the cost quickly escalated to over $100 million, municipally owned and leased to the Yankee organization.

The Yankee ballclub had been renovated itself. Come the second of September, a Yankee win in Chicago tied the team for second place with Detroit, one tantalizing game behind Baltimore. Back in New York, the brass must have seen something they liked, for Houk was re-signed to a $75,000 three-season contract. "We have made the announcement at this time," Burke commented, "to end nonsensical speculation that Ralph might not be back with the Yankees next season. We were particularly concerned about the players and Ralph's peace of mind."[26]

The Yanks responded triumphantly, managing a win in a doubleheader with Baltimore. The Orioles and Tigers were now tied for the top spot in the East, trailed in a remarkable race by New York and Boston at a half game back each. But when the Yanks defeated the Os, Baltimore dropped down to fourth place — in a single game! At only one out of first and a half game behind Detroit, the Yanks and Red Sox, eternal nemeses, were locked at the peak of the division.

In quite possibly the season's most important series, the two clashed in a battle for first place. It was perfect baseball in motion, the two participants in the most heated rivalry in all of sports squaring off for the assertion of divisional superiority. Unfortunately, the Red Sox left no doubt in the minds of speculators, sweeping New York and effectively crushing the team's morale.

Perhaps the Yanks should have employed Earl Weaver's strategy. The wily, stout Baltimore skipper admonished his club to "go out and win 23 in a row, and we [won't] have any trouble."[27]

Munson was at a very respectable .288 with 6 homers, 45 RBI, and 48 runs, but unlike 1971, that offense would outrank his defense. In a stunning reversal, Thurman tied for the league lead in errors with 15. "A lot of guys are tired," Horace Clarke explained.

Though the Yankees' performance had varied erratically throughout the season, on September 13, they were granted a scintillating opportunity, for it had been eight long years since they held sole occupancy of first place for even a day. By the hand of the Boston Red Sox, it was not meant to be; they lost 7–2 and fell a game and a half back. The situation was worsened by a defeat that pushed the Yanks to fourth place, yet merely 2½ games behind.

Some of the club's personal stories were more encouraging. Munson's batting mark hovered around .280 when on September 28 he cleared the outfield to make his seventh home run of the year, a solid personal power number. The hit could not save the Yankees, who were drowned by surges on the parts of Detroit, Baltimore, and Boston. On the night of the homer, New York stood at 79–71, with a stable .527 winning percentage, which was good for a game up on defending three-peat AL champion Baltimore. The Yankee team, which had quietly put up a great fight for the 1972 Eastern Division race — one in which a leader was never clearly distinguished — inexplicably lost all of its final five games.

For all they had accomplished, a fourth-place 79–76 record was a terrible disappointment. But the Yanks could take they solace in looking upon the Red Sox; with several games lost due to the strike, they finished a half game behind Detroit.

After the 1971 season in which Munson questioned his hunger to continue in the game, he was — by the winter of 1972 — a considerably happier man in nearly all aspects. A .280 hitter, he had sincerely enjoyed the year and had a splendid experience with his colorful teammates.

Munson never quite shook the anger accumulated from the earlier years, and one of his consequential vices was an affinity for firearms; especially pistols and his .357 magnum. During the season he had found a gun holster while scouring a magazine. Excitedly, Thurm filled out the order form. A 36-inch waist, it read, for a righthander's .357. Well, Fritz Peterson — the king of friendly annoyances — intercepted the order and erased Thurman's writing. In its place he submitted a request for a 20-inch waist (sure not to fit the 194-pound victim) and a lefty's .38 snub-nose. The parcel arrived six weeks later. Munson was ecstatic as he tore the wrapping apart. "I waited so long for it and I have to send it back!" he yelled angrily upon discovering the mistake. So he packed it up and sent it back. But Peterson got at it once again and hid the package in his locker. In the meantime, he ensured that it looked beat up and worn, as though it had been in the mail a while. They played through the scenario another time, repeating the process once more. Throughout the circuit, Thurman was baffled; he had no idea what was going on.

All along Peterson wrote the company president posing as Munson. "Thurman" said he was thrilled with the wonderful product — so thrilled that if the man was ever available when the Yankees played in California, he would save him a few tickets. Enclosing a phony number, Fritz sent it off once again.

That November, the Yankees sent off a package of their own: Jerry Kenney, John Ellis, Rusty Torres, and Charlie Spikes to Cleveland. Spikes was an outfielder of high potential, but otherwise they were giving up very little. In return, the club obtained Gerry Moses and third baseman Graig Nettles.

The latter was a power hitter and defensive wizard with a biting sense of humor. He would have a rocky relationship with the press, management, and certain teammates, but he had an outstanding 11 seasons in New York, over which he built up most of his third-baseman-record 319 American League home runs.

"Puff," as he was nicknamed, was also a stellar practical joker. In 1978, the Yankees included a solid reliever by the name of Dick Tidrow who had a habit of walking to the field from the club's hotel. The team was in Toronto one day, where the Blue Jays were in only their second season of existence, so the territory was a bit unfamiliar. Tidrow, a house of a man who was tough to refuse to those who had good eyes, asked Puff for directions to the stadium. "The ballpark is just past the needle there, that Canadian National Tower," an edifice about a mile in the distance. Tidrow thanked him and set on his way. As he would find out, Nettles *had* given the right direction; it's just that the field was an additional five miles beyond. No matter, for that was all prep time. There were still hours to go before the game began.

5

OBJECT OF NEW
YORK AFFLICTION

The more we lose, the more Steinbrenner will fly in. And the more he flies, the better the chance there will be a plane crash.
— Graig Nettles

"Why not?" Munson figured. During the months that preceded the 1973 baseball season, he gave up his clean-shaven image for good and grew a soon-to-be trademark mustache. It was hardly a novel idea, and the trend swept across the players for the first time since Dodger outfielder Frenchie Bordagaray sported one in the 1940s. Thurm was no traditionalist; others were. Detroit veteran Norm Cash would ask, not so politely, whether Munson had gotten his hair cut in a pet shop. Thurman generally shrugged off the traditional criticisms. Times, they were a-changing.

The Columbia Broadcasting System owners reluctantly conceded the failure of their venture, after nine long, failing years. CBS knew in 1972 that its investment had not been returned, and dutifully, it gave Mike Burke first shot. He immediately sought backers. Through Indians general manager Gabe Paul, who had orchestrated the Nettles deal, Burke was introduced to a 42-year-old Cleveland shipbuilder by the name of George M. Steinbrenner III.

On January 3, 1973, a syndicate headed by Burke, Steinbrenner, and numerous limited partners (including Gabe Paul) took ownership of the New York Yankees for a ridiculously low $10 million. (CBS had bought the club in 1964 for $13.2 milllion) Steinbrenner, debuting in New York, spoke in confident support of Burke, MacPhail, and Houk. "I'll stick to building ships," he assured infamously at the press conference announcing the sale, "and leave the baseball to Mike Burke and Lee MacPhail."[1]

Obviously, that didn't work out. *Cleveland Press* reporter Roy Meyers once said after working with George on a scoop, "Within two weeks we were very impressed with what a liar he was."[2]

There's no point in trying to nail Steinbrenner's character with any accuracy, but it is fair to say he was a man who sought to please everybody. A man who knew how to please everybody, no. At a Cleveland restaurant called the Theatrical, Yankee players were free to eat, drink, be merry, and sign the bill in George's name. He had no problem with that; that is the kind of guy he could be. Initially, Munson saw him as an ideal owner of similar tenacity, work ethic, and respectability as himself. In fact, he felt that if the two were not in a working unit, he and George could actually have been good friends. While that's debatable, the Boss created that impression upon his introduction to the city he had an attitude that could charm even the cynicism of New York.

On the other hand, George could be incorrigibly difficult. From his box seat in Yankee Stadium, he would flail his arms wildly in hopes of catching the managers' attention to express his various stratagems. (When that didn't work, he hooked up a phone line straight to the dugout.) Often, he ripped into players or managers, regardless of time or setting. If one of the men ever turned in a poor performance on the field, he was sure to be berated by Steinbrenner.

Such habitually neurotic tendencies all came from a sense of hyper-responsibility, almost a fear, that if the team faltered, it was up to him to fix it. This came from a life background in which he couldn't wait around for things to be done for him; it was up to his initiative to solve it. And, to give due credit, the product proved a durable success.

More or less, the Steinbrenner/Munson team was a success itself. In later years Thurman could be found in his boss's office after batting practice, feet perched on the desk as the two spoke casually. George remembered this publicly as a testament to their friendship, yet according to Thurm, it annoyed him to death; "But he never told me to knock it off."

If one were to seek the first chapter in the famed era of Yankee baseball known affectionately as the Bronx Zoo, it would have to start not with Steinbrenner, but with the twisted pact between pitchers Mike Kekich and Fritz Peterson. Worse than Ruth for cash, and Lyle for Cater, these two had traded everything: wives, children, houses, dogs.

Other Yankees knew that the pair of families had been close, but this situation was understandably disarming. Word leaked early in the camp before the two held separate press conferences a few days into it to dispel the rumors that had been circulating. The exchange created a general awkwardness within the team, for their teammates disagreed firmly with the ethics of the swap yet did not think it was their business to get involved. Personally, Thurman, who was friendly with both sides, could understand a man's attraction to another woman, but to trade children was beyond him. Though the Yankee club and its officials handled the situation rather well, the media attention brought a sense of fragility to the team that robbed the players of their focus and their game of its treasured innocence.

Small arguments cropped up between Kekich and Peterson and soon a rift developed, causing Fritz to lose his usual carefree charm. By midseason, Kekich, a valuable hard-throwing lefty, was 2–5 with a 2.38 ERA, and consequently he was traded to Cleveland. Peterson, 8–15, gave up 13 hits in eight innings of pitching at the beginning of 1974 and was given his walking papers. He too joined Cleveland, just as Kekich happened to be on his way out.

The Yanks didn't quite know it at the time, but the House that Ruth Built was being inhabited by one big dysfunctional family. As Graig Nettles put it, "Some kids dream of joining the circus, others of becoming a major league baseball player.... As a member of the New York Yankees, I have gotten to do both."[3]

Several sportswriters, before camp opened, picked the Yankees and Mets to meet in the World Series, but — as is often the case — they would prove only partially correct. The Bombers ranked at the top of the junior circuit and above all National League teams in spring training exhibition records, and were especially hungry to win a championship — of any sort — in the last year before Yankee Stadium's renovation.

Steinbrenner stayed remote that spring, though he was anxious to meet the players and get to know the personnel. He was shown around by Gabe Paul, an experienced and personable baseball man who was well liked by his players.

Gabe had not yet taken over as general manager, but it would hardly be long for that to come about — and just a bit longer before it was made official. He was a man well-suited to work for Steinbrenner, or ill suited, depending on how one looks at it. According to the masterful pen of writer Ed Linn, "Gabe has a way of remaining so unnaturally calm in the face of dissension, turmoil, and omens of doom that he has been moved to wonder himself whether there isn't a missing gene somewhere in his makeup."[4]

The team for which these men toiled took the diamond for opening day on a bright April afternoon at Fenway Park, where a powerful wind blew through the field. Ron Blomberg made history that day in his most famous role, the first designated hitter in the annals of baseball, though the position had been proposed formally as far back as a half century before and informally for nearly a century. Personally, Munson appreciated the addition, seeing it as a possible way to extend his career. Like most others, he saw it as a chance to add offense and excitement to the game, though it was not to come from Blomberg that day. With only a broken-bat single in three official at-bats, his first appearance turned out to be a walk from Luis Tiant. Often injured in 1973, Ron was riddled by inconsistency. Nevertheless, Blomberg turned in a productive season, with a .329 average in 100 games. Though his fame would be in April 7's DH debut, it was Jim Ray Hart who truly manned the role that season, though not too successfully (.251, 13 homers, 53 RBI, before being traded to San Francisco).

The Red Sox belittled New York before a packed house with a 15-run, 20-hit barrage. Asked if he were taken aback by his club's hitting, Eddie Kasko replied, "No, not a bit. Although I'll have to admit I didn't think we'd hit quite that good."[5]

In the second game, old Cape Cod League friend John Curtis was on the mound. Munson welcomed his friend by knocking a homer in the second for his first hit of the season, but in the ninth he played his starring role. Thurm was on first via a single when Gene Michael hit a beautiful double-play ball. As Doug Griffin received the putout and turned to throw to first, Munson barreled him over. The ball ended up in Boston's dugout and base runner Matty Alou scored to tie the game up. New Red Sox member Orlando "Baby Bull" Cepeda led off the bottom of the inning hoping to end the affair in regulation. "I guess I was due," he told reporters after the game. "Sparky threw me a good pitch — a low inside slider."[6] And Cepeda cranked it for a home run. The Yankees were pulled off their feet as a result.

A week later, the team was 4–6, while Thurman suffered at a dismal .219 batting average. By the end of April, however, he was on a torrid swing when, after ranking seventh in the American League at a .357 clip, he hit .556 in the next couple of games, lending a bases-loaded triple to the streak.

For the home opener in New York, Mike Burke invited various writers and artists from Lincoln Center to attend, including poet Marianne Moore who threw out the first pitch. "It's a waste of money giving those tickets to those people," Steinbrenner barked at Burke. "I don't like the people you are inviting."[7] He insisted that the tickets be sold to the general public, but Burke wouldn't budge. Prior to the game, George sought to humiliate him in front of as many friends as he could, and in this case the number happened to be about 40. In reference to Murcer, Steinbrenner shouted, "We'll see how your $100,000 ballplayer does today!"[8]

During the singing of the national anthem, George was in his box seat beside the Yankee dugout taking notes. He exhorted Houk with a message listing "1, 9, 10, 11, 12, 14, 15, 17, 19." Without even the courtesy of naming the offenders, these were the men who Steinbrenner felt were in need of a haircut. Assuredly as stunned as anybody, the Major made a melodramatic production of reading the memo. The players were startled, especially by the fact that the owner didn't even know their names. Most got trims, but either way the damage was done.

Munson a rare off-the-field shot. (National Baseball Hall of Fame Library, Cooperstown, N.Y.)

Steinbrenner was a formal man, one who did not and probably never will accept long hair and messy looks. How he put up with Munson's was most likely a matter of fear and defeat in the face of Thurman's stubborn independence. George had his bargaining tools though. One spring Lou Piniella reported with longish hair and Steinbrenner ordered Piniella to come see him. After some heated words, Lou figured he had the Boss cornered. "If our Lord Jesus Christ came back down with his long hair, you wouldn't let him play on this team?"

George rose from his chair. "Come with me." The two walked over to an adjacent hotel, through the lobby, and stopped at a swimming pool. "If you can walk across the water in that pool, you don't have to get a haircut."[9] Piniella left with no further arguments.

Steinbrenner was really making a name for himself in that home opener. After his earlier comment to Burke over Murcer, the most volatile possible situation came into play when Bobby batted with two outs in the ninth inning and the winning run on base. Sure enough, he struck out. After the game, Steinbrenner stormed into Burke's office. "There's your $100,000 ballplayer for you!"[10] he hollered. Remembered Burke, "That tore it.... I knew I couldn't work with him."[11]

"I balanced all, brought all to mind," Mike Burke quoted poet William Butler Yeats at his resignation press conference on April 29. Sitting beside

Steinbrenner in Burke's own office, he reluctantly relinquished his position, despite retaining some residual ownership.

By the end of the year, CBS-affiliated Lee MacPhail, Bob Fishel, Howard Berk, and Fred Bachman would all leave their posts one way or another. "This guy is very difficult to play for," Houk had warned of Steinbrenner in a team meeting early in the year. "But I'm not going to let him beat me. I promise you. I'm not going to quit. I'm going to stay right here until he fires me."[12]

The players, the fans, the press—they were all coming to see Steinbrenner in a fresh, new, disgusted perspective.

The Yanks and Munson picked up their play after Burke left. Though Thurm had only a couple of home runs and ten RBI, he was batting .372. Most important, his offense was helping the club. The race was again remarkably close at that point, even for such an early time in the season. New York, Baltimore, and Detroit were all only a half game under the Milwaukee Brewers by mid–May.

Munson, as was customary, remained in Canton during the spring, but in early May, he had the family come up to his rented home in Westchester County. He had never been particularly fond of this house, but it was the best he could do in the vicinity of Yankee Stadium. It seemed that as soon as the three other Munsons came, Thurman fell into a slump, before Diane and the kids returned to Canton on May 16. On the way to the airport, Diane joked that if he got two or three hits that night, the family might never come back. With a home run, a double, and a single that evening, Thurm laughed to Nettles, "Who knows, I may be getting divorced!"

Munson was back to his stroke of 1970 with homer number five a week later. Despite the fact that Thurm was fifth in the American League at .321, behind Blomberg, and three others, he batted at eighth in the order for most of '73.

To mark Thurman's 22nd birthday, George Steinbrenner gave him a couple of new pitchers. While his club fought for the top spot in the division, the Boss worked out two separate deals for the opinionated, intelligent hurler from Atlanta, Pat Dobson, and the hot-dogging Cleveland Indians flamethrower "Sudden Sam" McDowell. Altogether, the moves cost about $200,000, and almost immediately the Yankees responded. Not used to such accommodations in pennant races, the club was thrilled to see an owner who put his money where his mouth was. According to Murcer at that point, if they lost it would be their own fault. But the team was progressively moving into better shape. "This owner is giving me a lot of trouble so far with all these phone calls," Houk told Nettles, "but one thing about him, he isn't afraid to spend some money and buy some players when we need them."[13]

The team's immediate response to the trades moved them into a tie with Detroit at 29–25. New York increased that to a sole occupancy the next day at a half game up. But by the time a week passed, it was a free-for-all fight over first place with the Yankees, Tigers, and Brewers all tied for the spot. On June 21, Munson and Felipe Alou both chipped in two-run homers to defeat Mickey Lolich and regain exclusive possession of the top spot. By this time Blomberg was leading the majors with a .402 average, while Thurman launched his ninth four-bagger. Yet he still ran 82,000 votes shy of Carlton Fisk in the All-Star balloting at that point.

One of Munson's common complaints about Fisk was that he was overrated, due in part to Curt Gowdy, the famous broadcaster and great admirer of Pudge, who served as both the voice of the Red Sox and NBC. Between the two, he spread praise of the Red Sox catcher nationwide, and Thurm felt this contributed greatly to Fisk's acclaim.

To Munson as a receiver, a man who caught barely 100 games at the position as Fisk did for his first five seasons was not displaying the durability that was essential to earn the title of the best. Was Fisk the better hitter? Thurm could concede that, and in fact did. But a better catcher overall? He took issue with that.

Quite possibly, as far as the All-Stars went, the most stinging insult to Munson was the difference between local and national opinion. In New York he was the leader, the stable warrior, the reliable one; he was the best catcher in the game as far as they were concerned. Yet the national voting was unmistakably in favor of the Bostonian. Not being a charismatic personality in the public eye, Thurm was sure it all reduced to a popularity contest, one which he consistently lost.

The All-Star break came, and despite Munson's .297 batting mark which tied him with Kansas City's Ed Kirkpatrick and Boston's Reggie Smith for eighth in the American League, he was massacred by over 600,000 votes in the balloting by Carlton Fisk. Thurm didn't like being told that he was the number two catcher in the league, but he had to face that when Billy Martin chose him as a reserve. At the game in Kansas City Munson got his first chance to bat in an All-Star game, though all he had to show for it was a strikeout in a couple of ups. He handled five chances cleanly and logged an assist.

Houk knew before the break that his club, up in the division by a game and a half, needed some rest. "Just get out of here, leave the country, do what you want to do, but get out of here."[14] When they returned, rested and hungry, the Yankees took their first three games. Thurman knocked the cover off the ball in going 8–13, headlined by a triple, a double, and a stolen base.

New York closed July by opening a series at Fenway, with Baltimore breathing down their necks. As a precursor to the events of August 1, an argument erupted when Reggie Smith came to the plate in the first wielding a sawed-off baseball bat. "I had only one bat, because some I had ordered hadn't come in yet," moaned an irritated Smith. "So I borrowed a couple from Cepeda and cut them down. Munson complained that I couldn't use it."

"I don't see why not, and it was pretty petty anyway," Smith continued. "But, I changed bats that time and had the other filed down between innings so the edges would be nice and rounded like they wanted them."[15]

A crowd of 30,689 rooters crammed into Fenway Park, which ensured a volatile situation if any furor of the partisan faithful was precipitated. One had been retired before the wild chain of events took place. Munson stood at third, Felipe Alou across the diamond at first base. Gene Michael was supposed to bunt for a suicide squeeze, but he missed the offering from hurler John Curtis, and Thurm — who had already committed to home — had no alternative but to continue. "I weigh 190 pounds," he explained to the press. "I'm no Lou Brock. What good would it have done for me to get caught in a rundown?"[16]

Michael hesitated in getting out of the way, so Fisk did the moving for him. He hurled the scrappy shortstop out of the way as Munson's 5'11", 194-pound frame sprinted down the third-base line. Munson barreled Fisk over with a crushing blow, but could not jar the ball loose. The two rolled over, with Thurman holding Fisk down before being forced off. John Curtis, albeit an old friend, found no harm in the action. "I think Munson was trying to stay on top of Carlton so he couldn't see the play and stop Alou from advancing."[17]

Thurm took offense at Fisk's shove, and so he returned the gesture. "Munson didn't throw any punches," Pudge recapped. "We were just bumping chests."[18] Curtis and Carl Yastrzemski rushed in to restrain them, and the ruckus appeared to be a quick fade. Enter Michael.

"Michael came at me from the side," Fisk contended. The two wrestled on the ground and dugouts cleared. Referring to a scratch by his left eye, Fisk scoffed, "Maybe that was Michael's best shot. If it was, it wasn't very hard."[19]

Munson and Fisk were ejected by umpire Joe Brinkman, yet Michael was not, which incensed Boston further. "Michael was the one who provoked the fight in my opinion," argued Curtis. "If Brinkman didn't see that, he must have been watching the fight in the stands [a few rowdies garnered attention with some fisticuffs of their own], not the same fight I was watching...."

"I guess I'd call the fight a draw. Just another Wednesday afternoon at the fights at Fenway Park."[20]

For Munson, the issue was far from over. "So I ran over Fisk. I felt he kicked me off when I did it. He said the next day, in the papers, that the reason he kicked me off was so that he could get up and throw. Well, fine. But at the time, that explanation didn't satisfy me, so I got up and hit him."[21]

From that perspective, the incident seems to be due to a simple misunderstanding. But during the ensuing weeks, that theory dissolved. Fisk was involved in a similar melee at home plate with California's Al Gallagher; soon after, Angel teammate Bob Oliver was forcibly restrained by five other players from beating the Red Sox catcher; a little later, Fisk had a near-tussle with Hall of Famer Frank Robinson. Some say that once is an event, twice is a coincidence, and three is a pattern.

Munson owned the last word: "For me, the hassle with Fisk turned into a lot of national press. Even being notorious is better than being ignored."[22]

When dawn broke on August 2, 1973, New York was no longer the lone leader of the American League East for the first time since June 21. It had been a 41-day run. Though rain interrupted the game in Boston, the club was drowned eventually, 10–0. Utilizing Gaylord Perry's "stratagems" (in other words, spitballs), which defeated Baltimore, the Yankees stayed tied atop the circuit. Munson got a hit, as did Fisk, but the latter's was a home run. "That's the best kind of revenge there is," Fisk told reporters victoriously after the game. "I've got to admit that I was sorta pleased when Michael struck out twice, but the best thing was that we came right out and beat [them] on the field."[23]

New York went into a spiral. A split doubleheader against Texas sent them a game down on the Tigers and a half game shy of the Orioles. That quickly deteriorated to two and a half and a tie for third with the Red Sox. At the time, Munson ranked as the tenth best hitter in the league, but he was more concerned with his team's regression. During that time, the writers bore down on the Yankees, calling them gutless and generally demeaning the team. Thurman defended his club, which did not endear him to the press. Despite that loss, it was at this time that some people feel Munson began to assert himself as leader of the New York Yankees.

Munson's role as leader was a quiet one, a calming influence based on the loyalty of his teammates. Fellow players had too much respect to voice negative words against him. Even the fans were loyal and appreciative, which was uncommon for a New York crowd. Thurm didn't always have a high opinion of fans; he rarely posed for photographs, and was known to spit tobacco on the shoes of some who sought them. Despite the memory of Mike Garcia, he thought autographs were meaningless (how quickly he forgot) and resented the exploitation of people pawning signatures. As far as Thurm Munson was concerned, a handshake and a hello were just fine, thank you.

Some spectators' behavior disarmed Thurman. Often as he'd stand on deck, someone would run up to the screen and yell whatever he could to get Munson's attention, as though he had something important to say. Most players ignored them, but the voices were easily heard all over Yankee Stadium. While Munson was distracted by this, he still considered the Yankee fans to be the best and most knowledgeable patrons in baseball, and they treated him generally well.

The press, on the other hand, did not treat Munson well. In addition to the Michael/Clarke criticisms of earlier years and his defense of the heart of the Yankees, the media rift was exacerbated by his angry or sarcastic responses. Sarcasm was Thurman's sense of humor, but the writers didn't quite get it. They began identifying him as a cold and grumpy man. In fact, as the grumpy image evolved, he took on the role. Steinbrenner saw it as being "overprotective," but according to Lou Piniella and Catfish Hunter it was a defense mechanism, a buffer against his insecurities and awkwardness around strangers, a fear of getting close, all as a result of his childhood. In Thurm's opinion, the grinding two dozen scribes present every day mostly did poor work. Certain ones he liked, especially those from other cities, such as Los Angeles, Boston, and Chicago. He would depend on a few for stats and box scores to size up opponents, then discuss the findings with teammates. But often he was asked "stupid" questions by the media, and repeatedly so. To these writers and for these questions Munson was sarcastic, or didn't even answer them, although that was the exception, not the rule.

The press fought back by publicizing the gruff image and — in Thurman's opinion — by omitting favorable quotes of his and instead emphasizing the negative. After seeing many players try to get in the press's good graces and fail, Munson became disgusted. He did not understand why public opinion was driven not by a player's skill and achievements on the field, but rather by his charisma when dealing with the press. So Thurm became uncooperative, almost delighted with his intimidation of the media. Diane believed it was a cover. "It almost seemed like if Thurman didn't like you, he wouldn't bother cracking on you," she told Armen Keteyian. "Some people might see that as sarcasm, or maybe even hurtful.... He hid a lot behind that."[24]

What Thurman truly wanted above all was not headlines; it was respect. By the daily beating of his body, Munson felt he had warranted that from everybody, but his treatment of the writers foiled any realistic hope of achieving it. He was an enigma to them, intermittently approachable and terrifying.

Teammate Fred Stanley offered a remembrance of this years later. "Thurman had this way of walking up and down the clubhouse when he wanted some press attention," the utility infielder claimed:

> If he didn't want it, he could hide. But when he walked, he knew one of the writers would be brave enough to stop him and ask him a question. He was waiting for them one day after hitting a game-winning home run. But they never came to him. They had all stopped at Reggie [Jackson]'s locker, and he discussed the latest rise and fall in the stock market or something.[25]

According to Stanley, that really set Munson off.

The ironic piece of the puzzle is that Munson was actually a talkative man, often highly energized and pleasant. But Thurm did little to show this side to the media, out of either fear or indifference. He liked to "needle his teammates and insult reporters"[26] and was "a rather well-known grouch," Marty Appel remembered in description of the press's opinion of Munson. He was "noncommunicative with most of the media and thus, seldom quoted, seldom heard by fans."[27] Nonetheless, the masses in attendance at Yankee Stadium did not seem to be dissuaded from loving number 15. In a baseball city where one play can turn a hero into a hissed-at and loudly jeered degenerate, the fans appreciated Thurman throughout, seeing him as the unappreciated underdog. And he was, whether champion or MVP, forever an underdog.

During August, Munson's rank in the batting order was lower than his position in the American League batting race, seventh and fifth, respectively. Meanwhile, the Yankees' drop in the pecking order happened more easily than a Little Leaguer mishandling a fly ball. A terribly long skid coincided with Baltimore's 14-game winning streak, and by the time New York wrapped up a 9–18 August the team's deficit had plunged to 10½ games. Houk took the blame. All through September, he was booed unmercifully for it. The Major was no longer so optimistic and bright; he was frustrated, disappointed, and restricted by Steinbrenner.

Opening the month of September, the fact that Munson was batting .309 must have triggered a different perspective for Houk, for Thurm was batting cleanup during a match against Detroit on the third. Munson had been noted for the rare ability to bat absolutely anywhere in the lineup, especially the 2–5 slots, and still produce. That day in the four spot, he made an exhibit of that specialty, when he came to bat in the sixth with two outs and blasted a solo shot to bring the Yanks within a run. With two out in the eighth Munson cleared the yard once more for his second of the day, numbers 19 and 20. The total was a remarkable upgrade for Thurman, who was said to have never failed in improving at least one facet of his game during every new season. Though he didn't slug another homer that year, this ranked as a department high for his career.

The Yankees plummeted to .500 by the middle of the month. September became more and more frustrating as it dragged on. In Fenway Park, Munson reached on a single with one out, and moved to second via Murcer's base on balls. Jim Ray Hart stroked a line drive to left field in which the relay was cut off, and the fielder, eyeing Munson as he shied away from the bag at third, threw and gunned him down.

Four days later, the Baltimore Orioles clinched the American League East. Thurman could not believe he had seen the deterioration that he had, but personally he shone with his 20 homers, 72 RBI, and .303 average. Though that digit hardly stands out, his clip was high enough for third in the junior circuit, only behind stars Rod Carew and Willie Horton, and tied with Baltimore's Tommy Davis. To prove how close the pack was, Munson dropped to sixth after one day.

Sparky Lyle skipped New York's last game on September 30, 1973, and while that was of minimal consequence to anyone concerned, the aftermath of the game was much more harrowing.

Late in the last-ever game at the old Yankee Stadium, Ralph Houk walked out to make a pitching change. He was booed callously, all the way out and then given the same treatment on the way back. He faced signs that read "Fire Houk" and "Houk Must Go." Rejected, scorned, helpless, the man called the Major looked at that moment more like a beaten soldier.

By the time the final score of a Detroit 8–5 victory was recorded, word had spread around the team that there was yet more to be done that day. "Stay around until the end of the game," they were told. "Ralph is going to make an announcement."[28] At the game's conclusion, fans tore to the field, ripping apart whatever they could. Symbolically, the Yankees were being torn apart simultaneously. Inside the clubhouse, with tears in his eyes as the players sat quietly on stools by their lockers, Houk reluctantly conceded his position. "I got to tell you guys something," he addressed them. "I've had enough. I'm quitting."[29]

Houk explained to the press:

Sometimes when you have been with somebody as long as I've been here, when you don't accomplish what you are after, you get the feeling it is better off for the Yankees, who have done so much for me and my family, to resign....

The owner and general manager have done everything they can do to give us a winner, and we didn't do it. I think everybody will welcome a change. It might put some spice into it.[30]

Off the record, Houk was much more candid. "I have to quit before I hit the guy," he told Nettles in reference to Steinbrenner. "I don't want to leave the game of baseball by punching an owner. But if he keeps on bothering me like he does, I'll end up hitting him."[31]

Nettles was furious over Houk's departure, a man Puff had waited anxiously to play for. Munson was also deeply disappointed by the loss. He felt that although ownership might not have pushed Houk to exit, little had been done to dissuade him from leaving. Throughout the experiences of the past year, Munson had found an insulting coldness in the brass's dealings. He had watched in disgust that August as Johnny Callison, a skilled major league veteran, was released days before the end of a road swing. Now out of a job, the club saw to it that his allowance of meal money was subtracted from his travel check home.

Shortly after the final game of 1973, Houk took over as manager of the Detroit club and MacPhail was promoted to president of the American League. In just one year, CBS had become but a memory.

On October 1, 1973, ceremonies were held at Yankee Stadium in which first base was given to Mrs. Lou Gehrig and home plate to Mrs. Babe Ruth, memorabilia that the fans remarkably had not absconded with the day before. The demolition commenced a month and a day later, on November 2, and would actually end up finished five weeks ahead of schedule.

By December 7, the 32nd anniversary of Pearl Harbor, it looked as though a bomb had rocked the stadium. Behind the scenes, the Yankees were conducting deals to fix up their ballclub. In a trade with the Kansas City Royals, Lindy McDaniel, a great man who was even better out of the bullpen, was exchanged for a mediocre pitcher by the name of Ken Wright and a fiery Spanish outfielder four seasons removed from being named Rookie of the Year, Lou Piniella.

Piniella — Sweet Lou to teammates — became a close friend of Munson's and a valuable man for the Yankees. Even when Yankee feuds grew to the height of controversy, Lou often managed to remain friends with all sides. He spoke the common language of hitting often, and was extremely critical of his fine offensive prowess.

On the other hand, Munson's prowess, offensively and defensively, had allowed little room for criticism. After leading the league with 15 errors in 1972, the figure dropped to 12 in '73, which proved sufficient to capture his first Gold Glove. A .301 batting mark, 20 homers, 74 runs driven in, and 80 runs were to his credit, not to mention a hefty 147 games—142 of which were spent behind the plate.

As mighty a leader as Munson had become, he could not right the Yankee ship. They had been reduced to a pathetic fourth place, 17 games out. At 80–82, they even fell shy of .500. Munson wasn't the man to straighten them out; they needed another shepherd. But could the Yankees find one?

6

EASTERN CIRCUIT RACE

Baseball gives you every chance to be great. Then it puts every pressure on you to prove you haven't got what it takes to be great.
— Joe Garagiola

According to Dick Williams, he had been contacted through a middleman about joining the Yankees in mid- to late- September. Williams had been unusually successful in his tenure as manager of the back-to-back (and eventually-to-back) world champion Oakland As, but had reached his breaking point in dealing with owner Charlie Finley. When he was informed through the middleman that Ralph Houk was "getting ready to be thrown out the door," according to Williams (which adds a twist to Houk's "resignation"), Dick jumped at the opportunity.[1] But Finley stepped in to complicate the transaction because Williams was still under contract to the As. Finley demanded compensation, but the Yanks said his requests were too large. The deadlock had to be broken, and the buck stopped in Boston.

In 1935, Joe Cronin had been a young star shortstop for the Washington Senators. He enjoyed great success as a player-manager in the capital, highlighted by a World Series berth in 1933. But the Red Sox pursued him intently, and in order to execute a deal for him they would have to compensate Washington with $250,000. With that and other deals as precedents, what better judge to preside over the Williams case but American League president Joe Cronin, in his final ruling before stepping down from the post to make room for Lee MacPhail.

On December 20, Cronin ruled in agreement with the law of his transfer nearly four decades ago; in order for the Yankees to obtain the services of Dick Williams, the club would have to supply Charlie Finley and his Athletics with satisfactory compensation. New York chose not to do so.

In one cruel piece of irony, Cronin also judged on the departure of Ralph Houk, who was still under contract to the Yankees at the time of his resignation. Though this and the Williams case seemed to have no concrete difference's, Cronin ruled that Houk's departure was legal and valid.

With Williams out of bounds, the Yankees hired Bill Virdon. He had been signed in 1950 by Tom Greenwade, the talented scout who discovered Mickey Mantle, to play for the New York Yankees club. Virdon was a quiet man, narrow-minded, almost cold, but at least he knew his baseball well. After a solid major league career that included a Rookie of the Year award, Virdon moved on to a progressive managerial career. By 1972 he had led the Pittsburgh club he had recently played for to the Eastern Division championship, and the subsequent September the team was still a steady runner-up. Yet, "what have you done for me lately?" the Bucs asked and kicked him out in favor of Danny Murtaugh.

Munson had kept abreast of the wild Yankee occurrences through newspaper accounts. On January 4, the news came to him that Bill Virdon had been hired to manage the New Yorkers. Thurm was taken aback. He had expected Dick Williams to be employed and was encouraged by this. Thurm wasn't so sure about Virdon, who was reputedly all business, rules, and regulations. Plus he was a National League man.

On February 3, Munson was paid his due with a substantial increase in salary to $75,000. It was higher than any of the past Yankee catchers, though he conceded "in no way was I ready to stand beside Bill Dickey, Yogi Berra, or Elston Howard." Compared to his salary of 1970 — merely four years removed — this was a 400% increase. Gratefully, he noted to Lou Piniella at one point that spring, "George is a very generous man. He'll do anything for you if he likes you. He also pays well. I think there isn't a guy on this club who doesn't think he is getting a fair salary, maybe even better than he would be getting any place else."[2]

Munson was resting at his locker on February 28 next to Murcer, Nettles, and Blomberg, when Piniella strolled in with his newly issued number 14. "Welcome, Lou," Thurman promptly greeted, "glad to have you."

Nettles wasted no time in ribbing the new guy. "Leave him alone," he piped up in speaking of Piniella. "He has to squeeze that bad body into a uniform."

"Ahh, shucks," drawled Blomberg, "he doesn't have a bad body. Now, Thurman has a bad body."[3] Munson plucked a nearby bat and whacked Blomberg with it. This was Piniella's pleasant first impression of the Yankee contingent.

Obviously, Munson wasn't unfit, though he did boast a notoriously reckless diet. On the road he often succumbed to his affinity for pizza and cheeseburgers. In the baseball world, to his chuckling chagrin, his teammates couldn't care less about the distinction between overindulgent and fat. They kidded him endlessly. Many times Munson would find pictures of fat people pinned up in his locker, and upon the discovery, he would laugh as hard as they did.

Hours after Piniella arrived, Bill Virdon held a meeting to tell the players his objectives. "I just want you to hustle," he announced, "every minute you are out on that field. You'll find that I'm an easy guy to get along with if you do that. If you don't do that, we'll have a lot of problems."[4]

Oh, if it were only that simple. As much as Munson hustled, his problems were just beginning.

In Columbia, South Carolina, on April 2, the New York Yankees were wrapping up what had been a grueling spring training. Virdon had run them to exhaustion, excessively pitting his men against their once-revered, now-despised pitching machine. With only three exhibition games remaining on the docket, the Yanks had detoured to Columbia to accommodate former star second baseman Bobby Richardson, who was then manager at the University of South Carolina. A sizable crowd turned out to watch them square off against the New York Mets.

Early in the game, a 24-year-old Met came to the plate, a .199 lifetime lefty who had bounced around the organization for a couple of years before this game: Dave Schneck. Thurman apparently committed the cardinal sin of leaving his bare right hand exposed as opposed to tucking it behind his back, as had been popularized a decade earlier by Cubs backstop Randy Hundley. Schneck took a hard cut and on his backswing connected with the unguarded webbing between Thurm's thumb and forefinger. Munson collapsed to the dirt on his knees immediately, in deep pain. The recovery was quick too. In a few moments he was back on his feet.

What Thurman didn't know was that he'd actually suffered a threatening injury. It was eventually diagnosed as a serious inflammation of the medial nerve and would later in the season develop into tendonitis. Undaunted, he gritted out another four innings until a Jon Matlack pitch jammed him so badly that he could not even grip the bat. After the game, trainer Gene Monahan checked it out and had an x-ray performed which showed nothing anomalous—no broken bones, nothing more serious than a bruise. Although that did not turn out to be so, Thurman was not feeling the injury much at first.

It didn't take long for Munson's thumb to become useless. Simple tasks grew impossible, and baseball was difficult, to say the least. Though he toughed out the remainder of spring training, Thurm was forced to compromise his technique. Whereas he normally fired with a three-quarters motion, he was now reduced to either a sidearm or underarm throw, which changed the normal flight of the ball and in the end would bring about bursitis in his right shoulder. Thurman could barely make the distance to second base, word spread through the league. The fear that had long kept runners idle subsided quickly.

Munson's injury wasn't the only problem the Mets were giving their crosstown rivals. Due to the Yankee Stadium revampment, the Bombers were forced to put on their show elsewhere, and the only logical solution was the Mets' Shea Stadium. Ultimately, the move was a nightmare; it felt like a two-year road trip. Their counterparts at the ballpark were shabby in their hospitality. Granted, the Yanks were the guest's, but they were refused any cut of the concessions or parking, had to downsize their ground crew in favor of Shea's men, and the Met's fans would come out just for the sake of booing the Yankees. Conditions at the park were difficult: heat, the distraction of planes constantly flying overhead, and a bullpen with Plexiglas so scratched and worn that the relievers could scarcely see through it.

The Mets were also dealing with a well-founded fear that New York City would not end up funding the renovation and the Yankees would be stuck in Shea for good. They were so afraid of this that a clause was written into their contract that if the stadium project were not completed by the 1976 season as expected, the Yanks would be obligated to take over Jersey City's Roosevelt Field, which was hardly a major league complex.

Munson had no problems with moving to Shea, at least on the surface. He wrote in his book of Yankee Stadium, "There were days I wanted to blow the place up."[5] He had difficulty with Shea's lengths, which was largely due to the hand injury. "I think I could have hit more home runs if it had been stronger," he said to the media, though he was emphatic that the pain would not serve as an excuse. "I wasn't getting that extra ten feet that can mean the difference between a homer and a drive to the wall."[6]

In the opening day game, the Yankees' first appearance at "home," Stottlemyre closed down the Indians and old buddy Gaylord Perry 6–1. Tacking on three more wins straight, it was an unusually fine start for the Yankees. They were in first place.

Munson's early season was less satisfying. To his discouragement, the hand had actually worsened in this time, instead of having improved as expected. As April closed he took a slide from Carlos May right in the thumb, and this was enough to sideline him. Rick Dempsey replaced him in the meantime, which was a plus because he had been frustrated over a lack of playing time. When Thurman returned, though, a play similar to May's put him out of commission for another week. It was not a good way to start the season.

A surprising event rocked the Yankees on April 15 when Steinbrenner was indicted by the federal government for making illegal campaign contributions to President Richard Nixon's successful reelection campaign of 1972 under the auspices of the American Shipbuilding Company. George — who progressively bought out several of his limited partners throughout the year — would claim that he did this under pressure, but it was not enough to wash his hands clean. His confession would not come until August 23.

Mel Stottlemyre pitched the New York Yankees to victory at Shea over Texas's young Rangers. It was his fourth triumph, and the club was winning as well, only a half game out; yet April 26 came to be known among the players as the Friday Night Massacre.

Fritz Peterson, Steve Kline, Tom Buskey, and Fred Beene went to Cleveland. Dick Tidrow, Cecil Upshaw, and Chris Chambliss moved Bronxward. New York had rid itself of half of its pitching staff (four of eight) and been reimbursed with only two. The Yankee players were stunned, and they were angry. Four good friends, some with families (Fritz with his former teammate's family), were now gone. Besides, the team was now full of old Cleveland men. Nettles, Piniella, Sam McDowell, Gerry Moses, Walt Williams, Fred Stanley, and then these three — all through the dealings of Cleveland businessman George Steinbrenner and former Cleveland GM Gabe Paul. It was as though they were being crafted into the hapless Indians in order to imitate failure.

The announcement was made in the clubhouse after the game. Gabe burst in with a smile chiseled on his face, according to Munson, "as though the friendships of the four men he'd traded didn't mean anything to us."[7] Obviously, Gabe was just happy to make the move for some fine ballplayers: Tidrow, a 6'4", 230-pound power reliever, Upshaw, an effective pen man in his own right; and Chambliss, the 1971 American League Rookie of the Year. But in reaction to the initial shock, as reporters begged for comment, the Yankees aired it out. They hadn't had much time to evaluate the situation, so much of the open criticism was pure anger — and a good sum came from Munson. As so often, they needed someone to blame, and in this case it was Gabe. After all, Virdon was not consulted and had nothing to do with the deal; he probably would not have let it go through had he been asked.

Summarily, the Friday Night Massacre was anything but. All the pitchers traded to Cleveland developed sore arms and were hardly any help.

Upshaw for the Yankees was slated to replace Beene as middle reliever, but he hurt his finger and was unable to fulfill the role. Tidrow on the other hand was a cornerstone of the club's impending success; he alone was worth the trade.

The Yanks had not counted on getting Chambliss. Chris was an intelligent, sensitive, soft-spoken son of a navy chaplain who immensely impressed Munson with his character and superior sportsmanship. He generally did not complain to umpires, lose his temper, or badmouth anyone. Chambliss had not wanted to leave Cleveland, where his wife, Audrey, authored a regular newspaper column. He was happy there, comfortable, and had little desire to enter the rapid-pulse world of the Yankees. But at least he had been shifted to a winner.

After 33 games, an 18–15 record to their credit, the Yankees were holding firm in first place. One of the prime reasons for this was Mel Stottlemyre, who started a night game at Shea that June. He threw a few innings to the Angels before suddenly gripping his shoulder while on the mound. Munson, Virdon, and Monahan converged on Stott. He was hurting, but wanted to finish the inning, suspecting it was just a twinge. It was no twinge, but a torn rotator cuff, the worst three words a pitcher can hear. After going on the disabled list, he would return for a short relief stint in August, then audition the subsequent spring as a member of the roster. The Yanks told him he had as much time as he needed to get back on track, and so he set his regimen accordingly. Due to his stunted progress, with the end of spring training would come a pink slip.

The Yankees rolled through early July with an explosive offensive barrage, yet the club's statistics were alarmingly anemic: second to last in the league's team batting average (.253) and at the bottom in several other categories. Munson, manning the sixth spot in the batting order and in team production, was hitting only .247, with 32 runs scored. His power numbers were strangely erratic — nine homers and only 27 ribbies. He addressed this inconsistency to the press:

> I definitely would have had the better numbers if it wasn't for the hand. I'm not trying to make excuses, but I really couldn't grip the bat properly and my whole defensive game was hurting. It's disappointing to me because I felt I could have helped the club a lot more. Maybe if I didn't hurt the hand we would have come out on top.[8]

Defensively, the Schneck injury was still plaguing him, but Thurman kept plugging away every day except for those early stints on the disabled list.

The Yanks seemed to be rolling when they edged the Royals 2–1 to pull out of the cellar. Oddly, though, Virdon chose to give the order a little change of pace. Munson, after going 11–26 (.423) with nine RBI over the previous six games, was reduced to eighth. His subsequent performance gave credence to the drop, for he fell hitless. The team regrouped back in the West where a five-run fifth was highlighted by Munson's double and six Yankee singles. Whereas before, Virdon dropped Thurm two places after a two-hit game, before this one he moved Thurm up four places to cleanup, following an eighth spot 0–fer. Munson answered the call with a couple of hits. Perhaps Virdon was a reverse psychologist.

Virdon didn't have the same successful effect on the team, however, as New York occupied the East cellar with a 44–45 record. The .494 winning percentage did not go over well in the highly competitive six-team pack where only 4½ games separated last place and first. In an odd move, opposing clubs challenged the Yankees with 43 left handers in 83 contests. This was a trend that continued for the rest of the decade — teams would pull southpaws out of the minors *specifically* to throw against the New York Yankees.

Munson was again rejected in the American League All-Star catcher voting.

Carlton Fisk	1,626,874
Thurman Munson	1,243,779
Bill Freehan	946,625

However, Fisk was hurt in a collision against Cleveland on June 28, injuring his left knee severely. He was released from Boston's Hahnemann Hospital on July 7 following reconstructive surgery and — doubtful to play for the rest of 1974 — was scratched from the midsummer classic. Though the feat was thus cheapened, Munson would start an All-Star game for the first time. At the event in Pittsburgh on July 23, he caught a myriad of greats, from Gaylord Perry and Luis Tiant to Rollie Fingers and Catfish Hunter. All four gave up runs en route to a 7–2 NL triumph. Thurman doubled, scored a run, and committed an error, but his most memorable thrill was the ebb and flow of receiving Hunter.

June and July were shaky months for the Yankees. Having kept within 8½ games the whole season, a strong August in which they took 18 of 28 placed them in the heart of the pennant race, right at the top. But in September, it was do or die.

After a crucial pair of wins in Boston and a dramatic split doubleheader in Baltimore, the Yankees were still breathing. The credit was being given to Virdon for New York's winning streak, though in reality the players were simply producing well. And Munson was the star. Despite a .261 average over the whole year, he straightened out in his last 49 at-bats with a .408 clip on 20 hits. He had expected better from himself with the more luxurious power alleys of Shea. But if at any time Thurman needed to lead with his bat, it was down the stretch, and that's precisely when he did it.

The Yankees entered Detroit cruising at two games up (a hearty lead in the East for 1974). They swiped two out of three from Detroit before preparing to take on Baltimore, Cleveland, and Boston. Unfortunately, the Yankee patrons were irresponsibly apathetic. Only once during the ten-game stretch did attendance peak 40,000, while it dipped under 25,000 four times. Overall, this constituted a 40% letdown from normal figures. The decrease was largely attributed to Shea, where the environment was uncomfortably foreign to Yankee rooters.

As the New York crowds lacked vigor, their team reacted in kind. Facing a threatening trio of starting pitchers in Jim Palmer, Mike Cuellar, and Dave McNally, the Yanks were discarded 4–0, 10–4, and 7–0. Though they were out of first by only a half game, many discounted their chances after that series, even with 12 games left to play. Steinbrenner was one of those nay-sayers. Before the Indians came to town, he sent in a tape for Virdon to play to the team, a nasty one that Munson disregarded as belittling and "high schoolish." Most of the team took similar offense, but—whatever the inspiration—the Yanks swept Cleveland in four meetings to give them first place once again at one game up in the division. The Tribe was a simple and bumbling challenge, an already beaten contingent before they even came into town. The Boston Red Sox would not succumb so easily.

The Yankees were energized and intense entering the Red Sox series, their last regular season set at Shea. The Sox triumphed with a double-header sweep to put the Yankees at a half game deficit under Baltimore, which was devastatingly strong in response. The Orioles went on a torrid streak down the stretch: 27 wins in their last 33 chances, 15 of them one-run games. The Yanks knew there was barely a margin for error. Their final game at Shea, closing out the series, was a milestone—but not for the team.

The right field wall in Yankee Stadium had measured 296 feet from home plate, whereas Shea's was 338. Bobby Murcer, a steady power hitter, shot many 330-footers to right that year, yet they fell for long outs, and he was dubbed "Warning-Track Murcer." Finally, in that last game of the series, he hit his one and only homer at Shea of 1974. Doc Medich picked up the win, his 19th of the season, to defeat Bill Lee. Unfortunately for the Yankees, Baltimore won as well, and New York was embarking on a road trip at a half game back with five left on the schedule.

Stormy, wet weather killed Cleveland that Friday. George Steinbrenner and his club were in town, and the Boss wanted to impress those of his old stomping grounds. That wouldn't be the day, though, for the game was postponed and rescheduled for Saturday. Defending against the Orioles' win on their off-day, New York was hopeful that the Tribe's performance would be as poor as the previous week's. Only about 8,000 were on hand to witness a 9–3 and 9–7 twin killing by the Yankees. Rudy May took the mound Sunday to face old friend/new foe Fritz Peterson. It was expected to be a superb pitcher's duel, but Peterson's faltering earned him an early dismissal, and the Bombers went on to trounce Cleveland by a 10–0 score.

The club took a 36-hour rest before flying to Milwaukee to close out the season. Though the Orioles' magic number was down to two, Ralph Houk's optimism proved right even a year later. New York was hungry for the division title, but the club's sentiment was that even if it didn't get it, at least it had proved the experts wrong.

Only 4,000 showed for the game that night, and frankly it was getting on the team's nerves to be in the thick of the pennant race and not draw a decent crowd so many times. Doc Medich sought his 20th win amidst the knowledge that if his team lost this one, that was the season. A tenth-inning George Scott single broke a 2–2 tie to win the game for Milwaukee. Now the Yankees had to be content with proving the world wrong. Baltimore secured the division the next day by two before dropping the American League Championship series to Oakland in four games.

Prior to the final game in Milwaukee, Steinbrenner threw a party for the team. His generosity was overshadowed by a comment of his to the team. "I know Baltimore won last night. Ralph Houk let them win. Ralph pitched a bunch of young kids so Baltimore would win."[9] Strike one. Most of the players loved Houk, who in throwing his young Detroit Tigers was no different from all other teams out of contention who try to get experience for their youths when the wins and losses become relatively inconsequential. George continued, "Tomorrow is one of the biggest games of the year." Heads turned. "You go out and show 'em that you can win tomorrow, and that way you'll get your minds off losing the pennant."[10] The players were insulted. Not only had it been an incredible year of unforeseen success, but they had worked awfully hard to get there. Yet the Boss— their boss— was deeming the season a forgettable failure. Inspired or not, they defeated Milwaukee 2–1.

There were various minor victories for the 1974 Yankees. Beside's the fact that the team went 89–73, Lyle was 9–3 with 15 saves and a 1.66 ERA. Not bad at all. Piniella made a stellar transition; not only did he lead the team in hitting, but shortly after arriving, Sweet Lou was translating for Celerino "Cellie" Sanchez in his contract negotiations.

Munson was productive as well, especially with his power numbers of homers and 60 runs batted in. But the .261 average was atypically low. This was certainly in part due to the hand injury. Of course, that affected his defense even more. His 22 errors ranked as the second worst of his career and even the worst in the American League. But Thurm did lead the league with 75 assists, plus he caught 144 games (after missing nearly two weeks at the beginning of the season). Later, Thurman would regret not having taken more time off.

Munson's fellow players respected his season enough to vote him a Gold Glove, based primarily on his incomparable ability to call the game of a pitcher. Some fans and press did not understand that, not having experienced the value of such a task.

Wrote Munson, "With the season over, all I wanted to do was go home and rest. I had no desire to lift a bat, or even a golf club. I had played in pain, and didn't like it."[11]

In October the Yankees were looking for a quality starter and a righthanded power man. On the 22nd, in the early hours of the morning, Bobby Murcer was awakened in his Oklahoma home by the ring of his telephone. It was Gabe Paul. Murcer had been traded straight up to San Francisco for Bobby Bonds. "The trade came," he remembered sourly, "just after I had told Gabe I could finally accept right field if I knew I would be a Yankee the rest of my career. He said there was no way the Yankees could trade me. Three days later, I was gone."[12]

Bonds, the father of baseball's best left fielder, Barry Bonds, was also the godfather of the 30–30 season. He wasn't the first—that honor goes to St. Louis Brown Ken Williams—but he was one of the first and the best. He was also one of the league's elite players, though 1974 was a weak season for him. His arrival at the Yankees, however, initially overshadowed Bonds's potential. Murcer had long been of great assistance to Steinbrenner, occasionally speaking on George's behalf to teammates in contract struggles. Munson was much affected by losing one of his best friends; it really stung him that the promise to Murcer was broken. He felt less secure himself after seeing that, and angry as well. The truth is, one of his closest buddies had just been sent away; he would have been angry no matter the circumstances. But the fact that Bobby was lied to fueled his furor. Steinbrenner blamed Gabe—nicknamed by now "Monty Hall" for all of his trading—for the miscue. According to George he had no say in the trade.

After being fined $15,000 by the federal government three months earlier, George M. Steinbrenner III was suspended for two years by Commissioner Bowie Kuhn on November 27, 1974.

During the 1974 World Series between Los Angeles and Oakland, Jim "Catfish" Hunter announced that he would become a free agent. Few people took him seriously.

Before the season, Hunter had entered contract negotiations with team owner Charlie Finley, amidst an amazing run of five consecutive 20-win campaigns. They worked out a two-year deal, for which Finley acted as his own attorney. One of the pact's stipulations designated half of the pitcher's salary to be issued to an insurance company, to be named by Hunter, for the purpose of purchasing an annuity. It was to be paid in installments, issued every payday during the season. In the spring, Cat named the insurance company, but still Finley neglected to contribute any cash to the fund. Toward the close of the regular season, union head Marvin Miller sent a written notice to the Oakland club notifying it of the default, to be rectified within ten days. A clause in the uniform player's contract stated that if the club failed to do so, the player had the option of terminating his contract.

In early October, accompanied by league president Lee MacPhail, Finley sought to pay all the money at that time. Acting on his attorney's advice, Catfish refused, since accepting Finley's terms would have incurred unwanted tax complications. So, legally, Jim Hunter became baseball's first true free agent.

Hunter was now truly the hunted. Twenty clubs jumped into the fray — 20 of 24. Surely never before nor since have so many people traveled to Ahoskie, North Carolina, as numerous organization men came to speak with Catfish and his lawyers. Try as they might, no two would be as instrumental as Clyde Kluttz and Thurman Munson.

"I remember when the Yankees had a chance to get Catfish," Diane later recounted to Armen Keteyian:

> Thurman was really pushing. I remember he called information —
> and I'm not trying to make fun of the size of the town — but I know
> when he called and said I'm looking for a Jim Hunter, the operator
> said "Oh yeah, Catfish" and gave him the number immediately.
> They didn't even have an unlisted number. That's what down-to-
> earth people they are. Thurman got a real kick out of that.[13]

Clyde Kluttz was the man who had originally signed Hunter for the then–Kansas City Athletics in 1964, sticking with him even after Cat accidentally shot off a toe on his right foot. By '74, Kluttz was in charge of the

Yankees' scouting operation. Gabe's high stakes negotiation helped as well, but to Hunter, Kluttz — a man he truly liked and trusted — was the clincher, though he acknowledged that Munson's promotion of the club was effective as well.

On New Year's Eve 1974, Catfish Hunter — with his cheap, drugstore pen — signed on to play for three years with the New York Yankees. There are several different price tags attributed to the signing: $3.5 million, $2.85 million, $3 million. Whatever it was, it involved a bonus, life insurance, and lawyer's fees and was a mighty impressive figure. Munson, who as Marvin Miller wrote in his autobiography, *A Whole Different Ball Game*, "later became a member and staunch supporter of the Players Association," saw such figures as reasonable.[14] He believed that since minimal amounts of personnel across the country were qualified to play major league baseball, such high salaries were justified. He cited the money raked in by management from television, radio, tickets, parking, concession commissions, and merchandise as proof that high payrolls could be maintained. But Thurm was careful to acknowledge that the beneficiaries of this system needed to be cautious and invest it in something, for in life after baseball that player would likely not be making that kind of money.

Shortly after Hunter signed, Diane and Thurman held a party for the team. It was a real blessing for the club when they acquired Cat's services, something that made them almost instantly believe in their chances for 1975. Intoxicated with joy, among other things, the celebration grew rowdy at the Munson home, led by Sparky Lyle. Sparky had a penchant for mischief. Once, Bill Virdon had a chair bought for himself by the Yankee front office, a director's chair. Lyle knew that when Virdon held a meeting he would unfailingly stand before Rudy May's locker, so after he chopped the furniture up with a hacksaw, there the weapon went. "I got a birthday present today," Virdon announced to the team. "And I really liked it. It was a chair with my name on it. Which somebody cut in half. And I have a pretty good idea who did," as he looked directly at Lyle.[15]

Just then, Virdon turned around and caught a glimpse of the hacksaw. May looked up and saw it. "It wasn't me," he protested, springing to his feet. "It wasn't me. I know who did it, but I can't tell you."[16] Virdon got another chair but didn't feel like putting it together. Such was the case at the Munsons' home after that party. The place was an eyesore, and Diane — pregnant at the time — couldn't put it back together. Jim and Helen Hunter, newly anointed millionaires and celebrities, were the only ones who offered to help.

As good of a person as Catfish was, he was an even better baseball player. The eight-time All-Star tossed a perfect game in 1968, plus tacked on three hits and four RBI in the same nine innings. He was one of only four men to win 200 games before his 31st birthday, along with immortals Cy Young, Walter Johnson, and Christy Mathewson. Cat, calm and cool with the press, at his Hall of Fame induction speech of 1987 opined that playing under both Charlie Finley and George Steinbrenner was reason enough for his election.

The light $5,000 raise Munson received for 1975 can be looked at two ways: number one, he simply did not have that great of a season in '74, or number two, the Yankees blew all their money on Catfish Hunter. Thurm was still reeling from the Schneck incident of the year before and kept in close contact with trainer Gene Monahan so he would know what to stay away from, what not to worry about, etc. He felt a strange tingling in his hand throughout the winter and wondered if it would require surgery. He saw a neurologist, who conducted some tests but found no reason for an operation. Thurman was leery, though. He certainly did not want to play a whole career in such pain.

Bill Virdon, on the other hand, was feeling great. He was much more relaxed that spring training, uncharacteristically confident. In fact, the whole team was cocky in light of the addition of Bonds and Hunter. Double workout sessions for practice were set up, in the morning and afternoon, which allowed for more personal focus.

Munson returned that March to Puerto Rico, where the Yanks engaged in a couple of games on the 17th and 18th in San Juan. The short series was carried out to benefit Roberto Clemente's Sports City, an organization which supported young Puerto Rican athletes. Clemente, Thurm's old winter ball amigo, had spearheaded a fatal mission to deliver goods to Nicaraguan disaster victims on New Year's Eve 1972. The plane, overloaded with supplies, crashed at sea and killed everyone on board. Thurm was floored by the loss of this friend, who he enjoyed and respected, and with whom he shared numerous similarities.

The trip was a small bright spot in a bleak spring. New York was only 14–17 in spring training, but did not invest much concern in a series of spring exhibitions.

Doc Medich was handed the opening day assignment in Cleveland, thereby saving Hunter for the home opener that Friday. Medich, a 19-game winner in 1974, was losing his interest in baseball. It had started on September 5, 1972 when he, the starting pitcher, walked as part of a top-of-the-first rally in which the order batted around against the Orioles. As he pitched the bottom of the inning, Doc couldn't set down a single batter. The next day was his first class at the University of Pittsburgh, where he worked diligently toward a medical degree. The only place *that* ever got him in baseball was prior to a game in Baltimore when he performed a heart massage on an injured fan to save his life.

Fifty-seven thousand showed up to see the perennially dismal Cleveland Indians; it was no ordinary day. On opening day 1975, Frank Robinson was making his debut as the first black manager in major league history. The weather was ugly, but Rachel Robinson, wife of Jackie Robinson, and Commissioner Bowie Kuhn were on hand. Robbie inserted himself as designated hitter, and in the bottom of the first he majestically cleared the fence for a home run. It was quite possibly the most eloquent punctuation among 585 other clouts. He paused at home, gave a wave of his helmet, and the fans and news cameras stormed the field. It was a classic Hollywood scene. Though the Yankees lost 5–3, Munson was consoled by the fact that he was involved in that piece of history.

The Yankee stance on race, historically, is one of the more visible demerits on the franchise's record. On September 20, 1969, Mike Burke addressed this issue with a reporter: "[African Americans] felt unwanted at Yankee Stadium because no one ever attempted to convince them differently. Even to this day there's a residue of that attitude."[17] On the team, black players generally sat together and white players the same. Both sides would rib each other relentlessly — not before the cameras, just jostling between teammates. It would go on until one side grossly outdid the other. Munson got in on it, too. Hardly one for political issues and ways, he would often call Bobby Bonds "boy" openly, and reciprocally Bonds referred to Thurman as "honkey," and they would go about arguing playfully in this manner.

A more playful trio had developed elsewhere on the ballclub. Munson, Hunter, and Piniella spent the first month of the season together, and in doing so drew close. The three roomed at the Sheraton Centre Hotel on Seventh Avenue in New York, and often went to that street's Stage Deli. They usually indulged in dinner and some drinks, nothing really excessive — except perhaps their standard 2 A.M. check-in time. Munson and Hunter hit it off immediately. Early in the year, Thurm took to calling Catfish "Blowfish." "Your cheeks puff out when you pitch," he explained. Some writers misinterpreted this as mean-spirited, but Hunter understood its innocence. To return the favor, whenever the team was on the bus and Cat saw a heavy pedestrian, he rolled down the window and called, "Hey, Thurman, we'll be right back to get you!"

One night, after Munson, Hunter, and Piniella took in a few rounds of golf, the three stopped by a swanky Italian restaurant, still clad in golfing outfits. They were preparing to order when a man walked in, and the whole room stopped. With the employers breathless, he tugged at his gloves, nodded once, and moved toward a reserved table. It seemed like a scene out of *The Godfather*. The entire room remained motionless until, almost simultaneously, they all got up to go kiss the man on his cheek — well, all but three dumb jocks. Hunter turned to Munson and assured him firmly, "Thurman, this is the last time we eat in this place."

Cat's first game in pinstripes began as a letdown, and didn't stray much from its course. Reporters clogged the tiny Shea Stadium clubhouse beforehand. The lights, cameras, and writers fractured Munson's nerves so that he was decidedly uncooperative in response to their pleadings. On such a momentous day, it's not a good idea to project an image of grouchiness, but that's what the media saw, and that session only served to perpetuate the trouble between him and them. Most of the games Hunter pitched that year sold out, but, surprisingly, only 26,000 showed up at Shea for the home opener to see him shoulder the loss, 5–3. Steinbrenner attended as a fan, sitting beside the dugout. He was careful not to break any rules, careful to act in compliance with Kuhn's ruling in hopes of getting off suspension early.

Five to three was becoming a consistent Yankee score when on April 15 they took the losing side again against Boston in Cat's second start. His next game was a loss to Mickey Lolich and the Tigers, which dropped the club to 2–7. This was followed by a no-decision loss to the Red Sox. As a casualty of Hunter's early ineptitude and Bonds's slow start, New York hit the cellar.

Hunter finally improved his perspective after a talk with Piniella. That showed on April 27 when Milwaukee challenged the Yanks at Shea Stadium. At one point the batter knocked a foul ball just back of the dugout, but it landed in the seats. Munson chased to no fruition, stopping just short of a gorgeous woman in the front row. Thurm found his way to home plate and — after calling time — trudged to the mound. "Cat," he said, "see if you can throw another pop-up right there again."[18]

The light moment lifted Hunter, and he cruised to a 10–1 win, his first as a Yankee. It was a real turning point for Cat and a catalyst for the team. The win picked them up from last place and raised their collective spirit and hope.

Hunter wasn't the only catalyst. By Bonds's bat, glove, and base running, he carried the team after heating up in May. He had initially endured a sluggish start due in part to his placement at the cleanup spot where his 137 strikeouts were deeply harmful. So he was shifted to leadoff where the Ks would not sting so badly and responded immediately. The club was full of confidence in him and many figured Bobby as an early favorite for Most Valuable Player. However, in Chicago on June 7 he misjudged a flyball over his head and struck the fence in right. Slamming down hard, his knees were hurt badly in the first serious injury of his career. Though Bonds was not sidelined long, it was a heavy blow to the team's batting, and even when he returned he wasn't himself.

Bonds wasn't alone in the class of the disabled. Elliot Maddox also hurt his knee and would not regain his earlier form; Nettles injured his leg; Roy White, his foot. Munson was the only everyday, consistent, productive player on the club, which was no small feat. Throughout May, he hovered around the .350 mark, a phenomenal high for him. In fact, from the 4th until the 25th of that month, Thurman led the circuit in batting. Apparently, his positivity was all-encompassing. On top of feeling well psychologically, he genuinely believed the Yanks would win the pennant, and in June the team was playing as though it could. Eight consecutive wins opened the month, and consequently on June 24 they took over first place, only to drop down to second several days later. They would never see that spot again in 1975.

Munson, on the other hand, was finally seeing the light of day in his fight for justice when Carlton Fisk was sidelined long enough with a broken arm for the voters to elect Thurman to the All-Star game. He got a hit in the Milwaukee contest, but it wasn't until late that month at Shea that he displayed the instinctual talent that made him great.

The Yanks were facing Boston when out from the bullpen stepped a 160-pound cagey southpaw out of the Louisiana bayous, Ron Guidry. Munson and Virdon waited on the mound as Gid approached, calm, cool, cocky as usual. "Don't get nervous," Thurman warned. "Just throw strikes." It was a strange time to ask for his pitcher's repertoire, but that's what he did. Slider and fastball, Guidry replied. "OK," said Munson, "one's a fastball and two's a slider." Gid had thrown 62 innings and struck out 76 at Triple-A Syracuse, and three dominating innings and three strikeouts later, he had yet to see a second finger.

Munson's inclination to not play by the book worked against him. That July, after he knocked an RBI single off Minnesota, the Twins manager emerged with a protest for home plate umpire Art Franz to check the bat. Franz took out a tape measure and found that the pine tar exceeded the legal length of 18 inches. Thurm was called out, the runners were retrieved, and he just lost it. As Munson fumed, Franz insisted, "Hey, this is the rule. The rule stands." (Though Franz was indisputably correct, the same offense was committed a fortnight later, but that umpire simply ordered Thurm to wipe it off.)

Thurman had no vendetta against umpires; he actually got along with them generally well. He argued on many of the calls that inevitably become

Munson stands beside a pair of umpires before a game at Yankee Stadium. (Courtesy Louis Requena)

an issue as a catcher, but was rather proud of the leaguewide arbiters, especially the new school that was ushered in toward the end of his career. Impressed with their vigor and hustle, he felt the crews were a much-improved lot compared to what had recently existed.

But Munson was not done dabbling in misbehavior. At one point that year, Mike Torrez of the Orioles clipped Thurm with a few inside pitches, and he charged the mound. Unfortunately, these were only glimmerings of a darker side, a residue of the past.

According to Catfish Hunter, he and Munson were headed to Shea early one Sunday morning in 1975. While cruising at 60 down Broadway, a jaywalker attempted to cut in front of them. Thurman, who was driving the car, didn't like it, and immediately chased the man down a sidewalk with the vehicle. "I'll get him!" he hollered madly. "I'll get him!" Scattering pedestrians as he rode, Thurman eventually cornered the man at a wall.

"Gun!" Hunter yelled, as the man reached into his suitcase. "He's got a gun!"[19] Thurm slammed into reverse, and laughed merrily the rest of the way.

The car he used was a beautiful, sleek vehicle, with less than 100 miles on it. One time Munson walked out of Shea after a home game, with Hunter. Looking over at the windshield, he found it shattered, and Thurm was incensed. He jerked open the trunk, pulled out a .357 magnum, and fired several shots at a neighboring fence. "Thurman!" Cat screamed in disbelief. "There's people over there!"[20] Reluctantly, Thurm put the gun away. Reckless driving at the expense of some fans then cooled him down.

"People whom he cared about saw an entirely different side of Thurman," Diane disclosed in 1987. "He was the most two-sided personality I've ever known. He was the finest father I've ever seen. He spent time with the children before it became fashionable. He wanted to have a close-knit family, that was his number one priority, because he didn't have a good family life."[21]

On July 29 Michael Munson was born. "A little squatty," his father noted fondly, recognizing a distinct resemblance. Unfortunately, Mike suffered from hyperactivity. "When Thurman is around," Diane said four years later:

> you wouldn't know he is the same child. Usually, Michael gets up ten or eleven times a night and calls for me. But when Thurman is home, he says 'Michael, I don't want you getting up at night and calling Mommy.
>
> And he sleeps until morning. And then when he wakes up, he calls Thurman. When I see that, I know we need Thurman around. This little boy needs his dad.[22]

Back on the field, the Yankees were in need of a little sanity, for there was mutiny on the club. Down by 11 to Boston and virtually out of contention, they had just lost a four-game series to the Red Sox. The pressure was falling on Virdon. The losses were taking their toll on Steinbrenner's nerves, and — with Gabe Paul out of town for a few days — it was George's opinion that counted, suspended or not. The players were not happy either. Virdon's mistakes were largely responsible for the numerous losses incurred under his watch in 1975. The players tried to put a stop to it in Texas when Sparky Lyle organized a team meeting in his hotel room. From White to Tidrow to Piniella, they were all there. The men didn't particularly enjoy doing this; they liked Virdon personally. They didn't want to go behind his back, but it was their only opportunity.

The team's most outstanding conflict with Virdon was that he seemed not to manage much, for he was used to the power of Clemente, Al Oliver, and Willie Stargell taking him over the edge for wins in Pittsburgh. Many games were two-run losses due to a lack of strategy. Much was gotten off the collective Yankee chest at that meeting; ultimately, the players just wanted to institute a style of "little ball." Together they agreed that if there was a bunt situation that came up and the sign was not given, bunt anyway.

The first night the Yankees implemented this system, they were beaten, but soon after that they put together a small string in the win column. Virdon easily caught on after a few games—and smiled.

On August 1, Hunter and the Yankees defeated Cleveland's Indians 5–4, with Fred Stanley making a marvelous catch to close it out. Back at the clubhouse, reporters were everywhere, centered on Virdon. They wanted to know if he'd been fired. Bill was an honest man, and he was being honest when he told the press that he had no official word to that point on his status. He also didn't know where Gabe Paul was. The reporters soon left, and then the phone rang. It was Gabe. He asked Virdon to cross the street after dressing to meet in the Yankee offices. And there he was fired.

"How could a guy be Manager of the Year," Yankee old-timer Hank Bauer wondered, "and supposedly get so bad over the winter?"[23]

In the middle of July, Gabe Paul was visiting Minnesota Twins owner Bob Short at the latter's office. While the two conversed, Texas owner Brad Corbett paid a call. He had just fired his manager, Billy Martin. "That's the end of Billy Martin," Gabe said confidently, according to Short. "He's been fired by the Twins, Tigers, and Rangers, and no one else will hire him now."

"You gotta be kidding," Short replied. "There will always be someone in this game to hire a manager like Martin." The disagreement grew into a $500 bet. "He'll be hired within ten days," continued Short, who then probed deeper by supplementing this with an additional wager on where Martin would end up.

"Tell me," Gabe urged him.

"The Yankees."

"You're crazy," Paul laughed, appalled. "I know Steinbrenner better than you do, and George would *never* hire him."

So Short upped the ante. "Five hundred to five thousand that Martin will be the new Yankee manager."[24]

Gabe later denied the bet ever existed, and it quite possibly didn't. However, if it did, he was getting royally hustled. What Paul didn't know was that Steinbrenner had all the while been using Short to help acquire Martin.

Later that day, George told Gabe, "That man is a fiery manager. Let's get him."

"I think you'll be making a mistake, George." Gabe was dead set against it, warning Steinbrenner, "We'll have to be able to control him."[25] Some believed his objection was due to a fear that Martin would second-guess his moves and attempt to manipulate the farm system. Gabe, a sound baseball veteran who often saved the Yankees with his advice, was only foreseeing the problems that actually did end up turning the New York Yankees into the notorious Bronx Zoo.

George *was* concerned about Martin's character, but not dissuaded. "I want him," he persisted. "Let's get him."

Martin initially told Steinbrenner that he'd like to take the job, but the price was not right. George countered by playing on Billy's known desire to lead the Yankees. "This is where I always wanted to be," Martin once said of New York. Steinbrenner was well aware of this. "If you don't take the offer now," he prodded, "you will never get it again. C'mon, Billy, be the manager.... Here's your big chance to manage the Yankees, something you've wanted to do."[26]

Martin remained noncommittal. But on the next day he signed an eerily prophetic — if not simply calculated — contract. One part called for Martin to "personally conduct yourself at all times so as to represent the best of the New York Yankees and to adhere to all club policies." The pact further forbade criticism of management and contained a section requiring that he remain available to management for consultation on certain unspecified matters, all nonsensical to Martin. The last sentence decreed that if he did not follow those three stipulations to the satisfaction of the powers that be (aka George Steinbrenner) he could be immediately fired without compensation. Martin had left himself vulnerable to complete censorship based solely on Steinbrenner's judgment.

Billy Martin was born Alfred Manuel Pesano on May 16, 1928, in Berkeley, California. Legally, he was named Alfred Manuel Martin, Jr., after his father, who his mother, Jenny, disgustedly regarded as a "bum." One day, as little Alfred lay in his crib, his Grandma Nonna picked him up and admiringly repeated "Bellisimo" or "Bellino" — no one's quite sure — which developed into the permanent name of Billy. If someone dared to call him Alfred, that itching reminder of his despised father, Billy would drop him quickly. A scrappy, rough, bombastic, 170-pounder of only 5'10", he was an integral cog in the 1950s dynasty of the New York Yankees under the tutelage of "The Little Perfessor," Casey Stengel. As their second baseman, Martin captured the 1953 World Series MVP and was named an All-Star thrice in the decade before being exiled for his involvement in 1957's famed Copa Cabana incident.

A masterful tactician, Martin was a natural for a managerial position. As the skipper for six teams over 16 seasons, he won the Manager of the Year award four times. But Billy's hair-trigger temper kept him from solidifying any permanence on the teams he managed. Perhaps it was all a strategy: "Every time I'm fired, I get a better job," he said. There was no better job for Billy Martin than manager of the Yankees. He was perfectly suited to lead New York to victory.

Billy Martin played "little ball" as the team wanted, part of a long stream of strategies and tendencies that endeared him to his players. He had a certain chemistry with them that shook the best out of their bodies. When he made a move, Martin explained his motivation to the team while pacing the dugout. He treated them like men. No curfews were imposed; all they had to do was ask to stay out late, for he remembered what being one of the guys was like. He respected them. He drank with them. He fought with them.

Martin was not a stranger to the team members. He had managed shortstop Jim Mason in Texas and Elliot Maddox in Detroit and Texas. Both were strained relationships, but Billy swore that there would be a clean slate in New York. Nettles had also played under him at Triple-A Denver in 1968. The whole team was, of course, familiar with Martin, mostly by reputation. That was Munson's source.

But they came together easily. Billy respected Thurm greatly and saw him as a fine competitor. Munson often teased him and tried to get on Billy's nerves, encouraging him to display his famous temper, and Thurman laughed. He loved it. Some players felt Munson, Piniella, and others received preferential treatment from the manager, that he'd be patient with a regular, but not so with a backup. On one stance, however, he was not so endearing to Munson; Martin believed that bringing children into the clubhouse proved a lack of intensity, and was set firmly against it. Thurm must have not liked it, but Steinbrenner was of the same school of thought as Billy on this, so he presumably figured it was just a scuff in the brass.

The radio proclaimed on August 2, 1975, that Billy Martin was not only in New York but would hold a press conference at noon. The announcement was made, and then he was publicly presented at the Old-Timers game festivities. In a nervous daze, Billy was introduced last of all the old ballplayers. He received a loud ovation, cheapened by the fact that it happened at Shea instead of Yankee Stadium. Loyal Virdon fans had their boos. The return of Martin must have brought about a change of fortune, for the Yanks were actually on the winning end of a 5–3 score against Cleveland. It was pure chaos that day, and lots of press; Munson was thoroughly annoyed.

On Martin's second day, the riotous affair had calmed to quiet discussion, which he chose to have with each player separately. Munson took the opportunity to clear the air. He told Billy that *he* would call his own game, for Thurman knew the hitters, had good experience with the pitchers, and — bluntly — that he was simply more qualified to do so than Martin. He asked for a few days to prove this, and was so obliged, much to the Yankees' success.

Many things were beginning to swing in New York's favor. Starting with Martin's arrival in the Big Apple, the Yankees won six of their next eight. In one of those first games, Munson established a degree of respect between him and his manager. Rudy May was faltering on the mound and Thurm went out to meet with him. Out of the corner of his eye, he caught a glimpse of Martin. Without hesitation, he ordered him to turn back and leave him alone to work. Billy Martin, the incorrigible, pugnacious, tough guy Billy Martin, changed direction and headed back to the dugout.

Despite Martin's initial success, New York basically remained in third place for the rest of 1975. Toward the end of the season, at 75–71, they were battling the Indians for that slot. At three games up on the Tribe, they faced Cleveland with a strong determination not to end up slighted. Catfish Hunter, on two days' rest, was sent out in sub-40° weather to secure these hopes. Cat put in seven gutsy innings and fought to a 6–2 win at home, his 22nd of the year. After the game Martin encouraged his club to grab first place, even though it was 11 games out — with about a dozen left to be played.

In the last week of the season, Bobby Bonds — already listed in the lineup — told Billy that he wasn't playing because his leg hurt. Martin was compliant: "Well, okay, you're not going to play." Based on this, he recommended — and then insisted — that Bonds be traded at the year's conclusion. Billy was proud of this move, but if he had done his homework he would have seen the stupidity of it. Bonds had been remarkable that season, stunning to his teammates with gallantry in overcoming his injury. And since this incident was the only explanation Martin gave of the deal, it is fair to assume that he was making a decision possibly detrimental to the team without even consulting the facts.

New York ranked in third place when the season closed, 12 games below Boston. That wasn't bad considering all the injuries and transitions overcome. On the positive side, Bonds captured a Gold Glove and Hunter was superb. As a relief to the relievers, he threw 328 innings and 30 complete games. As far as the latter statistic, Cat was the last to reach 30, with the highest number in about a half century prior. With a 23–14 record, he was only the third to win 20 games for five straight seasons, paralleled only by Walter Johnson and Lefty Grove.

Munson's season was quite possibly the best of his career. His .318 batting mark — a personal high — ranked in the top five for the junior circuit. In an anxiously awaited adaptation to Shea, he drove a dozen home runs and 102 RBI, plus 83 runs, and 190 hits. Out of 157 games, Thurman hit safely in an impressive 117, while 56 contained two or more. But the most notable testament to Munson's talent was that, despite leading the league with the most errors (23), he earned a third consecutive Gold Glove award. Yet something was missing.

Seventy-five million fans watched the seventh game of the 1975 World Series. Munson was undoubtedly one of them. Carlton Fisk, after batting .417 in the ALCS, kept the Boston Red Sox alive with his historic game 6 clout, waved fair at the pole. "I'm little," Thurman once conceded to the press. "I'm pudgy. I don't look good doing things. Those big tall guys look super. But nobody plays harder than me."[27]

7

THE EXPERIENCE WOKE UP

People consider me a gamer. That's the best thing they could say about me.

— Pete Rose

He was a gamer.

— Jay Johnstone on Thurman Munson

The Yanks now focused their attention on turning their disheveled contingent into a champion. Gabe Paul, the chief orchestrator, was most determined to set their record straight in light of his contempt for the previous season. "There have been ups and downs in my baseball life," he lamented to reporters, "but this year has been very frustrating for us. We all expected better. The whole country expected better."[1] And so on December 11, 1975, after biding his time at the winter meetings, three key deals were executed within the space of a few hours.

First, Pat Dobson was sent to Cleveland in return for Oscar Gamble, a steady right fielder and all-around performer, who came to the Yankees sporting the largest afro in all of sports. Naturally, Steinbrenner ordered him to cut it.

A deal with the Angels followed, and a stunning one at that. Bobby Bonds was off to California in exchange for Ed Figueroa, an emotional, driven pitcher who had started off 1975 as a minor leaguer, then collected 16 victories in the big leagues. The second part of the package was Mickey Rivers. Often cantankerous but consistently valuable, Rivers's centerfield play had a profound effect on the 1976 unit. To Bonds the trade was unexpected — many thought he would wear pinstripes for several years. It cost them power, it cost them some strong righthanded hitting, but apparently that's what Billy Martin deemed necessary to prove a point. Fortunately, the deal was a grand success.

Next, to Pittsburgh went Doc Medich, and New York reaped a finer harvest: Dock Ellis, Ken Brett, and a 21-year-old unknown, Willie Randolph. Ellis, though famously recalcitrant, was a quality pitcher skilled enough to start for the National League in the 1971 All-Star game. His 17 wins that year were as important as his presence, for when he was comfortable the team seemed comfortable. For Dock, a man who, despite his hard outer shell, sometimes sported hair curlers about the dugout, that came easily. Brett was a decent moundsman in his own right, but he did not fit in with the Yankees.

Those two were helpful, yet the Yankee objective was Randolph. Having played only a few weeks in Pittsburgh the previous season, the second baseman was virtually unknown. Due to his quiet nature, he was almost completely void of controversy. In some ways that proved harmful, for Willie often felt underappreciated or unaccepted. He played hurt, but few seemed to notice. Randolph was motivated in his play by the knowledge that the club had gone through with the trade primarily for him. Inspired by the confidence that had been invested in him, Randolph beat out Sandy Alomar — just off a great '75 season — for the starting job at second while capturing the James P. Dawson Award in spring training.

Thurman Munson took his standard reserved approach to the trades, but — internally — must have realized their risk. Three of the players traded for — Gamble, Ellis, and Rivers – had troublesome reputations. Paul was undaunted. "I believe there is no substitute for talent," he said. "It's the manager job to handle talent. I'd rather have a louse who hits .300 than a nice guy who hits .200."[2] (Likewise, Martin was fond of boasting that he'd play Hitler, Stalin, and Mussolini as long as they had the talent.)

Munson and the brass didn't argue much that winter. Player salaries had shot up to a median of $52,000 with a minimum rate of $19,000, and he wanted a cut of the wealth. Negotiations began in December with Paul, but nothing was resolved. Free agency was imminent with the Andy Messersmith case (in which he boldly sought to abolish the old reserve clause) pending. Munson coveted a three-year deal to provide security in a location where he was happy. Though he rejected the free agency money sure to come if Messersmith won his case, the numbers it would take for him to stay were hardly minimal: $120,000 for 1976, $130,000 for '77, $140,000 in '78. In early March, he expressed interest in staying a Yankee, but if unsatisfied, "I'll play out my option and be a free agent," he told George Steinbrenner, who was reinstated by Commissioner Kuhn nine months early for good behavior.[3] Thurm didn't really want to leave the club, but Gabe and Steinbrenner were not paying heed to the Messersmith case, which they felt would undoubtedly fall through. "You're going to be surprised with the Messersmith case," George vowed. "It's not going to be decided the way the players want."[4]

Spring training began without Munson's signature, so in reaction his salary was cut the maximum of 20 percent. One day at Fort Lauderdale, he lingered in the outfield where Steinbrenner soon approached. "Hi, Thurman," he greeted unassumingly.

"'Hi'?" Munson bit back. "You're talking to me like a friend — you're no friend of mine. You cut my salary twenty percent a year after I'd gotten only a $5,000 raise."[5]

Neither side was moving an inch as spring training rolled along. At one point he told Steinbrenner flat out, "Fine, trade me to Cleveland." Then the ruling in the Messersmith case came in favor of free agency. Munson now knew that he would be better off financially if he didn't give in, and George knew that, too. He was called to the owner's hotel, where the silver-haired fox was sullenly resigned. "You want the $120,000, $130,000, $140,000 for three years? Okay, you got it."[6]

"Well, wait a minute, George," Munson replied comfortably. Here's where the greatest side of Thurman came out, that uncanny, innocent, childish smugness. It was the point where he reclined easily with a satisfied grin, as if to shout "I got ya.'" "That was then and this is now," he reminded Steinbrenner.

When Steinbrenner heard this, the 20 percent reduction was reinserted into Munson's contract in order to set a positive mood for negotiations. A couple of weeks later, on March 24, the two tied up all loose ends. Steinbrenner gave him the three-year deal described earlier and told Munson that as long as he was with the Yankee franchise, he would be the highest-paid man on the club — words that Thurman would not soon forget. Nor would he forget Steinbrenner's promise that Thurm would have the right to renegotiate his pact if the team won the American League pennant. Also that year, George promised Billy Martin that if they won the pennant, he would give him a tugboat. The terms of both his and Munson's deals became conveniently unclear to Steinbrenner by the time their contents became relevant.

With the new salary, Munson reached the zenith of $100,000 that only five other Yankees had previously received: Joe DiMaggio, Mickey Mantle, Bobby Murcer, Bobby Bonds, and Catfish Hunter. Thurm was of a strong belief that a player's stipend was to be in accordance with his statistics, and that the recipient should repay his employer with the designated season's accomplishments. By participating in 152 games in

1976 — among other acclaimed efforts which will soon be discussed — he certainly proved that he meant what he said.

Baseball started off on the wrong foot in spring training. The owners, fearing a strike, locked the players out before camp began. Fans, players, everyone detested the situation, but it bore the fruit hoped for when a basic agreement was reached in which chronic troublesome issues were ironed out. Informal workouts had been held in the meantime by the athletes, leaving no doubt that they were ready to hit the field.

Prior to the season, Munson and all the players received a letter from Martin. In it he stated his objectives for the 1976 campaign and warned of a difficult spring training, stricter discipline, tight dress code, and clubhouse regulations. Billy further informed them that mediocrity was out, that now they would exhibit pride, desire, and the will to win. "I have never been with a loser," he wrote, "and I'm not going to start now."[7]

Martin's actions spoke as loudly as his words. The training camp was rigorous, for he was taking no chances on producing a failure. He procured two separate fields for more activity, and then set the program into motion. Relays, rundowns, pickoffs, supervised bunting, pitchers covering first base. As far as the batting routine, on the hitter's first pitch, he practiced the hit-and-run stroke to right field. On the next pitch, he made a hit to send the runner from second to third. Following was a sacrifice fly, a suicide squeeze, and a pitchout so the battery could practice that maneuver. The batsman then took to the base paths to serve time there.

Overall, this routine stressed the fundamentals while working the player thoroughly in every area, and with the little time it took, it conserved energy for the season. Despite the intelligence of such workouts, Steinbrenner often came to the field to question it. It was an early chapter in the pair's trouble, preceding a spring shouting match in which Martin ordered his boss out of the clubhouse.

The tranquil bull of a legend, Lou Gehrig, was born on June 19, 1903, or rather, Heinrich Ludwig Gehrig was. The son of German immigrants grew up powering thunderous clouts about the dusty New York sandlots, perfecting the science of baseball. Starring at his college, he became "Columbia Lou" until an infamous first baseman by the name of Wally Pipp wanted to take a day off in 1925 for a bothersome headache and hence Gehrig became "The Pride of the Yankees." The man's legend is well documented: 2,130 consecutive games, 493 home runs, .340 batting average for his 17-year career. Roger Peckinpaugh and Babe Ruth had both been Yankee captains. But it wasn't until Gehrig took the station that it became such a matter of pride. Upon his death in 1941, his manager, Joe McCarthy, decreed that no man should ever again assume the title of captain for the New York Yankees. Until George Steinbrenner said, *"Fuhgedaboudit!"*

There were only a couple of weeks left in spring training 1976, when Pete Sheehy shuffled over to Thurman Munson's locker. Thurm had been sorting through fan mail and discussing a fishing contest with Graig Nettles when the clubhouse man interrupted to inform him that he was wanted in Martin's office. Munson dressed and headed toward the end of the locker room. "You wanted to see me, Billy?" he said, stepping in.

"Oh, yeah, Thurman, come in. Listen, George thinks it would be a good idea if we had a captain on the club — you know, sort of an official team leader. And we agreed that you're the best choice for the job, so I'm appointing you captain. We'll make an official announcement to the press in a few days, but I wanted to let you know myself now."[8]

According to Thurman, he paused for but a moment. "Okay with me," he shrugged. "Thanks!"

Munson was no baseball historian, and hardly a traditionalist. What he did know came primarily from being a member of the historic Yankees, which was often ruined by the corporation it had become. Sadly, that could have been the drive for Steinbrenner naming him captain, for Thurman believed it was done to bring respectability, prestige, and some of that traditional charm to his club. Only the sixth Yankee ever to be so honored, he initially did not grasp the whole concept. He wasn't alone.

When the captaincy was announced, Marty Appel, public relations director for the Yankees, spoke up. "When Gehrig died, Joe McCarthy said no one else would ever be captain of the Yankees."

"If Joe McCarthy had known Thurman Munson," shot back Steinbrenner, "he would have approved."[9]

Not long before the players went north to open in Milwaukee, Munson was catching in a game when a foul ball broke his finger. Out of fear that a release of the full details would hinder them in fairly acquiring an adequate alternate, the club merely announced it as a sprain. The writers could not be fooled, though, and they quickly figured it out. In the meantime, Rick Dempsey was put on full catching duty for the rest of spring training. Nevertheless, Thurm told Martin that he'd be catching on opening day. Billy did not stand in his way, whether he believed it or not.

The team came out of spring training with a 10–7 record, but it looked less like the Yankees and more like an Olympic club thrown together with borrowed hands from all across the nation. Here's the lineup: catcher Thurm Munson (Yankee organization); first base, Chris Chambliss (acquired from Cleveland); second base, Willie Randolph (Pittsburgh); third base, Graig Nettles (Cleveland); shortstop, Jim Mason (Texas);

outfield, Oscar Gamble (Cleveland); Mickey Rivers (California); Lou Piniella (Kansas City); pitchers, Catfish Hunter (Oakland); Dock Ellis (Pittsburgh); Ed Figueroa (California); relievers, Sparky Lyle (Boston); Dick Tidrow (Cleveland); and Ken Brett (Pittsburgh).

Despite the unfamiliarity, the club was surprisingly cohesive. "We have fun together," Munson wrote in his book. "We like each other. In the past there were factions, cliques, a division on the team. But this ball club is fun. This ball club is together."[10] According to some, though, there was a definite clique, composed of Munson, Hunter, Rivers, Piniella, Nettles, Randolph, Carlos May (who came from Chicago a month and a half into the season), Gamble, and Fred Stanley. They stuck together, on planes and buses or social outings.

United, the Yankee contingent took the field on a chilly day in Milwaukee for their season opener. Martin initiated the season with a meeting that day. He was a capable leader of the club, and while not completely well regarded all the time by his players, there was one quality that made the players simply want to win *for* Billy: he stuck up for them, he'd risk his job for them.

Early that season, the Boss prepared a tape-recorded pep talk that Martin was to subsequently play to the team. Billy refused to do so, leaving the motivation up to himself. "You know," he started the meeting:

> we're going to win this thing this year. You're all good enough to win. The only way you won't win is if you don't listen to me and do what I tell you. Anybody who doesn't want to do it my way can leave now, but I'm guaranteeing you right now, if you do what I tell you, you'll win this thing — easy.
>
> Anyone who doesn't think so can leave now, no hard feelings. I might be rough, but I'm going to treat you like men until you act different. I'm not a guy checking curfew, just be ready when the bell rings.[11]

Munson actually ended up not being able to answer the bell that day because of his finger, so Dempsey caught in his place. But he did DH, though he was rather ineffective as a result of his difficulty gripping the bat. This was due to either his finger or the chill hanging over Milwaukee that day. Hunter lost the opening assignment 5–0 on a mound that he claimed to be inadequate. Martin filed a protest over the mound. But not all fights were so clearly aimed.

"It was opening day [and] I can remember Lou Piniella and Rick Dempsey fighting with each other," Ellis wrote. "I wouldn't even go in there. Who knows what they were fighting about.

"On that team guys were always arguing. 'You should have caught that ball.' 'You shouldn't have called that pitch.' But they talked baseball all the time."[12]

While it's unfair to assume that Munson was exempt from such banter, it's a matter of record that he generally accepted responsibility for what he did on the field. Lou Piniella told of a situation with then–Yankee pitcher Larry Gura. In a close game, the young hurler hung a curve that left the park for a loss. Afterwards, even with teammates around, Thurman told Gura, "I should have called a fastball. We had the guy set up, that was my fault. I never should have called a breaking pitch in that spot. He was looking for it."[13] Fortunately, not all pitches that he called ended up proving harmful.

Back in Milwaukee, the two teams played again the next day in a battle that came down to the bottom of the ninth, 9–7 Yankees. Dave Pagan was on the mound, characteristically erratic and edgy. With the bases loaded, he gave up a grand slam to Don Money. The game should have been over. But Chris Chambliss had been granted a time out just before the pitch, which only he and the first-base umpire realized. Chambliss was hysterical and Billy the same. Eventually, they coerced the arbiter into admitting it, thus the money shot was null and void. Ken Brett came on to quietly record the save.

Ellis personally theorized that his manager won at least five games that season by sheer intimidation of the umpires. "Billy believed in intimidation. And that's what he wanted the team to do, intimidate the other team. Billy wanted to be in charge."[14]

On the plane ride from Milwaukee, where the third game proved victorious as well, Martin turned to Bill Kane, sitting nearby. "I got these guys now," he said triumphantly. "They'll do whatever I tell them.... We'll win this easy. You watch. We'll win it *easy*. They will do everything I tell them."[15]

On their fourth game in Baltimore, New York took hold of first place with a win. As Munson DHed that day, he grew concerned about whether he'd be able to catch the opening game at the House that George Rebuilt within the week. The team at least was heading there on the right track. After taking all three in the Orioles series, it seemed first place would not be as elusive as previously experienced.

Steinbrenner was being pummeled by the press over anything they could get their hands on: his suspension, Gamble's haircut, Munson's contract, Watergate, and especially Yankee Stadium, the expense of which he had to defend, even though it was the CBS syndicate's original project.

On April 14, the Yankees got their first chance to see the new Yankee

Stadium on the occasion of a workout. The house was beautiful and the players loved it. Where they had endured a minuscule, uncomfortable locker room at Shea, the refinished one awaiting them was relaxing, and spacious, with new lockers and a new training room. The park itself had been rid of obstructing poles, as well as most of the famous white facade, and — in a move virtually unknown to most — the upper deck was raised, making fair balls traveling out of the stadium an extinct sight.

While left field was extended 11 feet to 312, it was to Munson's advantage that the wall was decreased gradually as it converged into center field, an area whose boundaries had dropped from the deathly 461 feet to 417, with Death Valley reduced to 430.

On April 18, 1923, Yankee Stadium, erected across the Harlem River from the Bombers' old rented house at the Polo Grounds, was introduced after a mere 284 days of construction. Babe Ruth hit the first home run there, pitcher "Sailor Bob" Shawkey the second, and the latter defeated the Red Sox 3–1. Three days shy of 53 years later, Shawkey, age 85, threw out the first pitch at the field's renovated version. He was watched by Mickey Mantle, Frank Gifford, Joe Louis, Whitey Ford, Mrs. Babe Ruth, Mrs. Lou Gehrig, and Joe DiMaggio. DiMag, the "Yankee Clipper," was nearly impossible to keep away from the stadium, participating in 36 consecutive Old-Timers Days, a run that ended in 1988 when he was sidelined by hospitalization.

Munson didn't need any hospitals that day. His finger was feeling fine, and he caught the game. But Steinbrenner was more concerned with Thurm's hat. When "The Star-Spangled Banner" played, he lined up before the song without putting it on. George called Martin in the dugout and ordered him to fine the incorrigible. Needless to say, Billy was disgusted.

Rudy May — nicknamed "The Dude" — started versus the Minnesota Twins. In the first inning, Dan Ford touched May for a smash into the left field bullpen. Munson corrected that quickly, following with the first New York home run in the new Yankee Stadium to basically the same spot as Ford's. No clouts would reach that area for the entire remainder of 1976. Dick Tidrow came on to finish up the win, 11–4.

Yankee Stadium was a refreshing success. Fans relieved not to see their club calling Shea home turned out in droves, more than 2 million, to outdraw the Mets for the first time in 12 years. All over baseball, there was a mass resurgence of interest, which especially surprises in light of the lockout. Numerous attendance records were broken, and network television revenues shot up. It was theorized that the prime generator for all this was simply the success of the New York Yankees. Since the days of Ruth, the club has consistently been the most passionately loved and most passionately hated, depending on which side of the fence a fan stood. Yet a period of Yankee superiority transcends all barriers to extract and promote the love of baseball. When the Yankees excel, so does baseball.

After winning 15 of their first 20, the Yanks appeared insurmountable. Hunter was not starting off well, though, at 1–3 in his first four decisions, and his right shoulder was bothering him, the result of throwing 627 innings between 1975 and '76.

He and Munson were very close that year. While Diane and the children stayed home in Canton for the early part of the schedule, Thurman became an honorary member of the Hunter household. There was a drive of only half an hour between the stadium and Cat's house in Norwood, New Jersey, where Thurm and Diane were building their house. Nettles was just across the street from Catfish, and the three would often drive together to games, Munson dominating the conversation with his discussions of real estate. After games, he came back and slept on the Hunters' living room couch. Upon awakening, he would make some phone calls— mostly concerning business—and go back to dreaming, all without leaving his "bed."

Also at that time, Thurman developed a friendship with Cat's son, Todd Hunter, who grew to be like a nephew to him. Often Munson would joke, "He's gonna look like me, Cat. Short and fat. He's gonna be a catcher just like me."[16] In order to protect that investment, he gave Todd an autographed catcher's mitt, with which the two played catch constantly: in the clubhouse, on the field, or in the Hunter backyard. Besides his own children, Thurm had a great time with those of others.

Called a "player's player," Munson was more notably a people's person. He could be generous with his time, such as at an event in Morristown, Pennsylvania, at which he spoke to 250 Little Leaguers, then stayed around and signed autographs for two solid hours.

By mid–May, New York was clearly the most formidable of the Eastern Division. And to the circuit's distress, the team chose to upgrade. First, Ken Brett and outfielder Rich Coggins were traded to the Chicago American Leaguers for Carlos May, a big bat and great personality. While contributing three home runs and 40 RBI, he shared designated hitter duty with Piniella, who when in that slot was replaced by Roy White in the outfield. Second, Larry Gura was shipped to the Kansas City Royals for backup catcher Fran Healy, a well-liked, amiable teammate.

Billy was more than happy to get Gura off his hands. The pitcher's complaint was that he was promised a starting role that never materialized. Martin complained that Gura allowed too many base runners and was unreliable, though the young man thought himself a star moundsman.

Billy allowed no illusion concerning that status. "As far as the coaches are concerned," he told Gura, "you happen to be a low man on the totem pole."[17]

The true reason for the trade was an incident in the spring when Billy saw Gura and Coggins dressed to play tennis, a sport he looked down upon in macho arrogance. They were practicing for exercise, but, acting in unnecessary spontaneity, he dismissed that as ridiculous. After all this blew over, the Yankees were ready for some on-field fighting.

Boston came to town after Baltimore for a well-hyped series of the coming and defending champs for the 1976 season, though New York held a dramatic six-game lead over its challenger. In a night game on May 20, the Yanks were up 1-0 with two retired in the sixth. Nettles waded off of first and Lou Piniella loomed at second when Otto Velez lined a single over the second baseman's head to Dwight Evans in right field. Evans fielded it and fired, a true throw straight on the mark, and Carlton Fisk applied a hard tag. Said the catcher afterwards, "The throw came in, I went down and tagged him and all of a sudden his knees were at my head. He was screaming, kicking, and trying to hurt me so I buried the ball in his face."[18] Piniella claimed he was tagged by a mitt and a fist. The two were fighting in seconds, prompting both benches to clear. Munson was right in the thick of it, along with Nettles, Darrell Johnson, and Mickey Rivers.

Nettles had run in toward the plate to assess the damage when starting pitcher Bill Lee, originally there to back up the play, started giving him lip while embroiled in the fracas. "I ran in to pull him off," Puff said.[19] He did more than that. Nettles, a powerful man by any estimation, picked Lee up and threw him down. The impact injured Lee's shoulder, tearing cartilage that rendered him inactive until July 12. Realizing his arm was dead, he screamed at Graig, who, misunderstanding the situation, responded by giving Lee a shiner. Even a fan came out to beat on the boisterous hurler. He wasn't the only one injured: Piniella bruised some ligaments and tendons, and Carl Yastrzemski hurt his knee.

The game resumed as a tie after seven. Then Fisk walked and Martin brought in Tippy Martinez to face fellow lefty Yaz. The fans were still rowdy and flung beer cans angrily onto the field, forcing third-base coach Don Zimmer to don a batting helmet. (Mickey Rivers would be forced to do the same in Boston that summer.) The pitch to Yaz left as a towering home run, which he stopped to watch momentarily.

In the ninth inning, Guidry was on the mound with Fisk again at first. Like deja vu, Yastrzemski crushed a fastball into the seats. The Red Sox ended up winning 8–2, yet they lost more than they gained. Jim Rice, Fred Lynn, and their only lefty pitcher, Bill Lee, were all injured.

Martin reveled in the shutting of Lee's mouth. "Lee always said the Yankees would be a good team to get in a fight with ... that we hit with our purses. Did he get hit with a purse tonight?"[20]

Honestly, Munson was really sick of Fisk. Nineteen seventy-six was another year in which the Boston catcher won the All-Star vote and garnered constant media attention. Though Munson denied harboring any bitterness toward Fisk, he was fond of ranking himself ahead of Fisk as a backstop, going so far as to state boldly that if he and Fisk were to play for the same club, the latter would have to find a different position.

Often the phrase is uttered that it is not bragging if one can back it up, and Munson backed up his soundbite. It was at this early point of the year, in May, that he reached .300, never to come down again that season; he also had 54 games of two or more hits, 17 game winners, and defense that was at its peak. Unbreakably confident, he withstood the rotation changes and handled the staff deftly. With a strong offense in addition to a stellar defense, Munson was a player with valuable influence on a dominant team. And as the season wore on, he felt exceedingly proud of being designated the Yankee captain. Writers and others spoke often of his captaincy, to his initial obliviousness. But progressively, Thurm grew to understand his role, his place in history, and the life and gripping legacy of Lou Gehrig. He embraced the link with the "Iron Horse." Munson insisted it had no effect on his play, and probably didn't, but he'd say most anything to downplay it. He did not want a superficial title to take away from his ever-neglected talent. Something had to give. It wasn't going to be his pride.

For all the talk and testosterone being thrown around on May 20, the Yankees and Sox had a few games to play. In the dozen wild innings of their next game, Kerry Dineen, freshly plucked from Syracuse, contributed the winning hit in the 12th. On Saturday, Hunter was untouchable: three hits, no runs. Fifty-three thousand came out for the finale in gleeful knowledge of the Bombers' comfortable lead on the Orioles. Well into June, they were disposing of the league handily.

Martin was feeling confident in his club, hovering around a baker's dozen edge on the competition. Then: "This trade just won you a pennant," Steinbrenner boomed to Martin that 15th of June. "You now have the best team on paper, and now you're just a push-button manager."

"Who'd we get?"

"We got Ken Holtzman."

"Who'd we give up?"

"Tippy Martinez, Scott McGregor, Rudy May, Dave Pagan, and Rick Dempsey."[21]

This account, given by Martin in his autobiography, *Number One,* is

a clear exaggeration; George Steinbrenner is a businessman, not a school-
boy. The deal with Baltimore was actually those five for Holtzman, Grant
Jackson, Doyle Alexander, Ellie Hendricks, and minor leaguer Jimmy Freeman. According to Martin, the deal was driven by George's 13-year-old
son. As an example of Martin's lapses in memory, Hank Steinbrenner was
17 at the time that Holtzman impressed him. Holtzie was 30 years old, 6'2"
and 190 pounds, out of Lincolnshire, Illinois. In his previous five years in
the American League, he had averaged an indomitable 18 wins per, with
a total of 91. To his credit were a pair of no-hitters and four World Series,
yet he spent only ten weeks in Baltimore before the trade. Upon witness-
ing one of Ken's good showings, Hank prodded his father to obtain Holtzman. He was given not only a substantial five-year pact, but also a no-trade
clause. His contract would have made him the highest-paid Yankee, so
George — true to his word —called Munson into his office and raised him
back to the top in salary. Thurman was pleasantly surprised.

Alexander was a quality moundsman who, a decade later, was enticing enough to be dealt from Atlanta to Detroit for a promising young
fireballer, John Smoltz. For New York, Alexander threw well and even came
close to a few no-hitters. Munson, who was never a victim nor a recipient of such a game, anxiously awaited the opportunity. Grant Jackson was
the best acquisition. While Lyle was the ace out of the bullpen for the first
half, 7–8 with 23 saves on the year, it was Tidrow and Jackson who took
over after the All-Star break. Jackson was also a grand personality, and the
club was disappointed to see him opt for free agency after the season. Hendricks became a misused second-string receiver, and Freeman failed to
materialize.

For the Orioles, it was quite likely their best move since St. Louis to
Baltimore. On the negative side, Pagan's following year and a half were
spent in Seattle and Pittsburgh before his last major league appearance in
1977. All the rest were positive. In McGregor's next nine years— all with
the Birds— he won ten or more nine times, 138 total. All of his 13 years
were pitched there. Dempsey, given the chance, became an All-Star, while
May went 18–4 the next season before closing out his career with four
campaigns back on the Yankees. Martinez was a perennial quality reliever
who lasted ten and a half years in Baltimore. He took with him a fond
vision that he expressed years later of his rookie season when Munson
would take him out to dinner and not let the kid pay a red cent. "I'll always
remember him saying, 'When you're making a lot of money, then you can
take the rookies out to dinner,' he recalled in 1979."[22]

"Who's Thurman Munson?" enigmatic Detroit pitcher Mark Fidrych
asked facetiously before a Monday night baseball game on June 28.[23] The

rookie's insult irritated Munson, especially after he had spent July offering his body as a sacrifice for the team's quest. That month he suffered a staph infection in his right hand after getting spiked, then injured his right knee when he collided with Spikes, Cleveland's Charlie Spikes. He refused to take time off, and for one stretch in July rapped out ten hits for ten RBI in 13 at-bats.

Whatever disrespect Munson received from the youngsters, a prevailing wisdom secured him selection to a starting role at the All-Star game, set for Philadelphia in celebration of America's Bicentennial. President Gerald Ford was not only in attendance, he was also in the locker room to shake the players' hands. When he got to Munson, Ford was surprised that the tough, solid catcher wasn't nearly as tall nor as imposing as he had envisioned. Thurman on the other hand found the experience larger than life; he was thrilled to meet a president even if he had little use for politics. Right before a photograph was taken of the three together, Ford threw out the first pitch to Munson and Johnny Bench. Thurman proudly kept that photo for years.

Bench's team, the Cincinnati Reds, was well represented that July 13, with five starters out of nine. Reds batters hit one of the National League's two homers, drove in four out of seven runs, scored four out of seven tallies, and collected seven of the ten hits. Before 63,974 fans at Veterans Stadium, the third largest All-Star attendance to that point, the senior circuit once again was victorious, 7–1, with Fidrych the loser. Munson had a hit and a passed ball, but he knew that those games weren't the ones that counted.

At the break the Yankees were 20 games over .500, for a lead of 10½ on the Orioles. There was much talk of an easy stretch run. Deep into July, they were 14½ up, and overconfidence was setting in. Ellis was on the mound on the 27th facing Baltimore. Dock was having an outstanding season; he wound up 17–8 with a 3.19 ERA and won the Comeback Player of the Year Award. He was also giving Steinbrenner gray hairs with his enticing comments to the press. Ellis wasn't in a pleasant mood; in the game against the Orioles, he hit Reggie Jackson with a fastball in the face. Accidental or not, the incident was twisted in its familiarity, for Martin had been ordering him thrown at for years in hopes of intimidation. Fortunately, Jackson recovered well from severe facial bruises. The Orioles retaliated in the ninth when Palmer beaned Rivers. That really agitated Billy as he spoke to the media after the game. "That was about the weakest knockdown I ever saw in my life. It belongs in the Hall of Shame. Knowing Jim, I'm sure he was directed to hit Rivers. He's not that type of guy. I'll deck Earl [Weaver] at home plate the next time one of our guys is deliberately thrown at."[24]

To add to those frustrations, the Yankees dropped six of seven in early

Munson stands in the line of revered New York Yankee catchers at the 1976 Old-Timers Day game. Lined up chronologically, Bill Dickey is at the far left, followed by Yogi Berra, Elston Howard, and Munson. (National Baseball Hall of Fame Library, Cooperstown, N.Y.)

August. At the beginning, they were beaten in four straight, and a few weeks later lost three in a row to California. Steinbrenner asked Martin if he could come into the clubhouse for a pep talk, to which Billy consented. "You guys don't want it bad enough," George informed his players. "You're not giving a hundred percent. You guys are Yankees, and you have to play like Yankees."[25] The speech continued awhile as Billy stood ashamedly in the corner with his head down in humiliation. His team was nine games up in the division.

Around that time, Steinbrenner invited Dick Williams, the former Oakland manager, now out of work again, to sit with him the owner's box next to the Yankee dugout. It's not likely that there was any shady business going on there, but that's how Martin saw it. It played to his paranoid insecurity, the fear that he was going to be replaced. This was the true beginning of the rift between Martin and the Boss.

Steinbrenner was not Billy's only sparring partner. At the Old-Timers Day game he got into an argument on the mound with Doyle Alexander over whether the pitcher should come out. Earlier in that afternoon, the rare opportunity came for a photograph of Dickey, Berra, Howard, and Munson, the historic lineage of Yankee catchers. Thurm played it down and at first opted not to pose. He came around. The 16 × 20 photo later hung in the Munson den.

Hunter got his 200th win that month. He managed to go 17–15 for the year, making for 40 wins between 1975 and '76. But his season was riddled with injury and inconsistency. After the game, Munson approached him. "Maybe you're a better pitcher when you pitch once a week," he joked.[26]

New York had its fair share of ups and downs that season. And when the Yankees faltered, the Orioles threatened. Earl Weaver, at ten games down, spat, "I'm not predicting that we're going to catch them. I wouldn't want Billy Martin to get excited."[27] In their next meeting, Jackson homered and doubled to bring his club within 8½, yet when August closed, the lead was increased by three games over that.

September began with a four-game series in Baltimore, the last Oriole's chance if they were to somehow capture the East. The Yankees won the first game 3–1 and in a doubleheader the next day the Os took advantage of a bad hop double, walk, flyball, and sac fly to take a 1–0 edge. The Yanks then scored two runs in the sixth, but Lee May balanced that with a run-scoring single. Munson's single then drove in Rivers, and Nettles homered in the ninth to seal a 4–2 victory. The series ended up split, with New York up by 10½.

After a two-game sweep of Boston, the magic number was down to three as champagne chilled on ice for the Yanks' three-game home set. Palmer went against Ellis in the first game of a twin bill. According to Palmer, "Dock told one of our players last night that he wanted to beat me in the game that clinched it for them. Maybe that's his way of psyching himself up. It's all right, but he still has to beat me."[28]

Ellis was having a tough game by the time Palmer took the mound for the ninth with a two-run lead. Randolph opened the inning with a single, only to be retired when Roy White hit into a fielder's glove. Puff was up next, a bat that Palmer did not like to face. "Why Nettles?" he said. "Why did he have to come up in the ninth?"[29] So Weaver trotted to the mound in contemplation of bringing in Tippy Martinez. He told Palmer that the worst possibility was a game-tieing home run. "That wouldn't make me happy," he responded, and later added, "You have mixed emotions about walking him and bringing in Tippy. But you can't do that, so that left my mind."[30] Palmer remained to get Nettles on a right field fly out, then closed the game with one to left from Chambliss. This gave the Baltimore ace his 22nd win, as both he and Ellis threw complete games.

The Yanks lost round two behind Palmer's closest contender for the

Cy Young, Figueroa, by the score of 5–2. They were defeated again the next day. "Mathematically, we still could win it," Palmer stated, "but realistically, with the club they have and the way they've played all year, we can't do it. We're just postponing the inevitable…. I know we're not going to catch them; that's even silly to think about at this point. But it's fun to beat them."[31]

Still, any combination of Yankee wins and Oriole losses adding up to three clinched the division. New York dropped the first game of a doubleheader in Detroit with Grant Jackson pitching. They came back to take the night game 8–0, while Wayne Garland won his 19th to keep Baltimore close.

By September 25, the magic number was down to one. New York scored ten, the Tigers six, and Boston's Luis Tiant shut out the Os 1–0; the Yankees were division champions, crashing the playoff pool for the first time since 1964. When they found out at a Detroit restaurant of Baltimore's defeat, a celebration was launched, something that hadn't been enjoyed in the six long years since the 1970 second-place party. Munson and White were the only two still around to remember that, and so to them it meant the most. The champagne soared across the room, soaking everybody. Steinbrenner got drenched. Gabe — savoring his first win since his days as traveling secretary for the Cincinnati Reds of 1939–40 — was soaked as well.

From then on, the games were just a tune-up for the AL West champion Kansas City Royals.

Kansas City was a solid team in 1976 whose strength was offense. Third baseman George Brett led the junior circuit in hits, triples, total bases, and batting average (the first of three decades in which he topped the latter category); Amos Otis led in doubles; Hal McRae was first in on-base percentage, second in doubles and batting average. On the other hand, the individual pitchers failed to crack the top three in a single category, though collectively their 3.21 earned run average was second only to the New York Yankees (3.19).

The Yanks went into the American League Championship series with an intense outlook. "We still haven't done anything yet," Martin warned his men.[32] It was a new season in which nothing previous counted. So they came a few days early to practice on the Royals Stadium field (currently known as Kauffman Stadium). The dimensions measured 330 in both left and right, and 410 in center, not too much different from Yankee Stadium. The New York club knew the astroturf would be a disadvantage, and the early workout was a clever attempt to negotiate the quirks of the surface.

Larry Gura was named as the starting pitcher for Kansas City. Gura had thrown only 61 innings and had gone 4–0 with a 2.29 ERA. A former All-American, he was adamant about conditioning and had excellent fielding skills. However, Gura had a penchant for getting himself into tough situations. And of course, he and Martin couldn't stand each other, a sentiment the two verbalized openly in the newspapers. The Yanks personally held nothing against Gura, who was scheduled to face Hunter. But the tension was certainly there. Further intensifying the series was the presence of old Royals fan favorites Lou Piniella and Fran Healy.

The game was on a Saturday afternoon, October 9, considerably late to start the playoffs. Gura was hungry for the win to shut up Martin and his barking which persisted throughout the contest, to either cause the pitcher to lose concentration or try too hard. It worked. The game opened with an uncharacteristic George Brett error at third. Brett had also been making angry comments through the papers, particularly because of the trading of his brother, Ken, earlier that season. Later in the inning, he erred again. Yet that wasn't nearly as discouraging as what happened in the bottom half when star Amos Otis sustained a leg injury running to first and was lost for the series. Hunter, controlled and masterful in the clutch as ever, allowed only five hits and led his club to a 4–1 victory.

Munson made two errors the next day, to his dejection. (They would be the only postseason errors he ever made.) His two hits were hardly enough as Kansas City beat New York and Figueroa, 7–3. Figgy had twice that year missed an opportunity to become the first Puerto Rican player to win 20 games and was stuck instead at 19. The series shifted to New York, where the Yankees had won 45 at home as compared to 52 away — but there were no guarantees.

The series went back to the Bronx, where 20 World Series championship banners had been hoisted up the stadium poles. Chris Chambliss had 17 home runs in '76 along with 96 RBI and a .293 average. And he continued to produce in the postseason, slugging a homer and driving in three that third game. Munson had two hits as part of an early streak in the series. Dock Ellis opposed Andy Hassler, a southpaw who had been traded from the Angels at midseason and was only 5–12 by the schedule's end. Manager Whitey Herzog thought that his pitcher could handle the all-important game. Hassler's performance was decent, but the contest ended on a 5–3 score, with Lyle in to ice the Yankee win.

New York was anxious to wrap up the best-of-five series in four games, in light of the taxing effort it had taken to set down Baltimore for the division championship. Munson got caught up in that — allowing it to penetrate his impeccable focus — and had to keep refreshing his memory that the Royals still had 27 outs left to spare. Game 4 was a rematch of the opener, Hunter and Gura. This time the game would not be as pretty. Hunter was yanked in the third and Gura in the fourth. In for Kansas City was, first, reliever Doug Bird, off of whom a run was scored. Then Steve Mingori gave one up to the Bombers. Despite Nettles's slugging of two home runs and Thurm again collecting a couple of hits, the Royals won 7–4 to force a fifth game in New York.

The whole club was eager to play, for it was truly anyone's game. Each player knew that his own singular action could spell a win or defeat. As Munson drove to the stadium, the prospects were tantalizing to his mind, prodding him to perform well. As Thurm rode in his car he went over how Dennis Leonard pitched him in game trying to separate and capitalize on every detail. The vision grew as he pulled up to Yankee Stadium on October 14, 1976. All that had to be done was to win one simple game.

Holtzman was available, but Martin chose to pitch Figueroa. "If I had Holtzman, I sure would use him," Herzog told the writers.[33] One can only imagine how Steinbrenner fumed.

The game opened up in Kansas City's favor when first baseman John Mayberry homered off Figgy to put his team up 2–0. The Yankee half started off with a triple by Mickey Rivers and a Roy White RBI single. Chambliss—a reputedly dangerous clutch player even though it was his first appearance in the playoffs—eventually brought White home. 2–2 deadlock.

By the third, the Yankees were taking advantage of Leonard's replacement, Paul Splittorf, for a pair of runs. Now it was 4–3 and the Yankees, whose confidence had hit a pivotal turn when they tied the game in the first, were now feeling well. Martin was rambunctious the whole game: yelling, screaming, ranting, raving. It was his enthusiasm throughout that kept his players at a sustained pace. Two runs off Andy Hassler in the sixth put them at a comfortable lead of 6–3. Figueroa was cruising, but in the eighth he allowed two men on base, and Martin came to the mound for a discussion with the battery. Figueroa, Munson, and Martin all agreed to call for Grant Jackson to take on the young, cocky batting king, George Brett. Figgy was allotted a grand ovation as he exited, consistent with the high decibel level the fans had provided all night. But they soon became numb when Brett homered to right. The most theatrical home run to that point in the year, it was a deep and crushing bomb that easily could have made history had there been a simple conclusion to the game. The Yankees were in a spiral, completely demoralized. They had to pick up their heads and travel back to square one. 6–6.

A 23-year-old fireballer named Mark Littell worked the bottom of the eighth for the Royals. A former minor league Pitcher of the Year, the

6'3", 210-pound reliever was the ace of Kansas City's bullpen. He had given up only one home run all season, and Munson wouldn't be the second, for he was the third man retired. Dick Tidrow, who had ten saves and four wins, shut down the Royals with the clock reaching the eleventh hour.

Chambliss stepped to the plate to lead off the ninth inning. He was not the man that the Kansas City Royals wanted to see. He hit .524 for the series, collected a record ten hits and seven driven in. Unfortunately, as he eased into the box, the crowd began littering the field with paper bags, scorecards, sandwiches, fruit, and rubber balls. The cleanup crew came on but the shower didn't stop. "Fans who insist on throwing things on the field," public address announcer Bob Sheppard warned, "will be removed from the stadium and subject to arrest."[34] But this was New York; they kept on throwing. Nettles turned to Carlos May during the delay of 15 minutes. "Get ready to pick up all the gloves off the dugout. When someone hits a home run this inning, all the fans are going to come streaming in."[35]

Sandy Alomar, who had come in earlier to pinch-run for May, waited on deck, while Nettles stood by the bat rack, due up third in the inning. Right before him was Munson, crouching on the top step of the dugout clad in full catcher's gear and praying for a run. Chambliss had no plans to let Alomar or Nettles take their strokes. "I wanted to swing at that first pitch," he later recalled. "I thought the fuss on the field might have cost Littell some concentration. No matter how long the delay was, I was just going to jump on that first one."[36] On the opening swing, he took a deep cut and pulled the ball to right. It was a steep drive that seemed to hang forever. No one was quite sure whether it would hook fair or foul. When the ball landed in the lower right-field stands, there was no doubt he'd shot a home run.

Chambliss hit the air in elation. Munson launched off the dugout step, a couple of feet high. The body that had been so ravaged throughout the season was suddenly indestructible in its airborne, slanted position. No injury, no distractions, no reminder of reality could snap him out of that moment's dream state as he clutched the climax that had taken an entire life of dedication to reach. As Munson bounded from the ground to the air and back to the ground, Chambliss attempted to circle the base paths. But as he neared second he was taken down by a fan. He pushed away the man, grabbed for his helmet, and pressed on. By the time he made second base countless fans and policemen had swarmed him. The idea of completing his run was abandoned when he instead headed straight for the clubhouse, doling out shoulder blocks and whatever evasive maneuvers it took to get out alive.

An emotional scene unfolded in the packed clubhouse. The Yankees were amid crowds of families, reporters, hot lights, even the mayor of New York, Abe Beame. Wrote Munson in his autobiography:

> We were like Little Leaguers in the clubhouse. We had no idea what was going on outside, but we could be sure the place was in a state of destruction. Inside, bright television lights glared, strange faces appeared everywhere, and we looked for every teammate we could find to embrace with big bear hugs. Somehow Cary Grant appeared before me — Steinbrenner had brought him down. I could swear there were fans in the clubhouse, but I really didn't care. I wasn't in charge of security. I was in charge of enjoying one of the happiest moments of my life.
>
> Sure, I was still a young man — 29 years old and a veteran of only seven big league seasons. But I'd wanted to play baseball for as long as I can remember, and when you want to be a baseball player, this is what it's all about. Winning the pennant![37]

Martin sat on a trunk in the middle of the clubhouse, remembering his mentor. "I wish Casey was here to see it," he said, speaking of Hall of Famer Stengel, who had died the year before. "This was his pennant."[38]

"Those guys who didn't think we could do it, who picked against us, who said we'd never win one — where are they now...? I won it. The Yankees are back where they belong, on top."[39]

The Yanks stayed in the clubhouse for nearly three hours, dousing one another incessantly with champagne. The party was then transplanted to the Hasbrouck Heights Sheraton in New Jersey and proceeded several hours more. The buses including one to accommodate the wives, left for Cincinnati early (considering the players' state), at 10 A.M. The joy of the night before encouraged Martin to invite numerous others onto the buses — Stadium police, bat boys, batting practice pitchers. The guests were so surprised that they didn't bother to bring along baggage.

On the bus, Munson mulled over the fact that he had finally made it to the World Series. He wanted to savor the simple thrill of being there, for he might never return. In contrast, the general emotion of the team was frustration over a snag in obtaining tickets for their families, which became more complicated than expected. Thurman endured an endless stream of phone calls at home for them, too.

Snow and rain prevented a workout the Yankees had scheduled in preparation for the next day's opener. Still, they pulled on their uniforms, spoke with the abundant media, took a few snapshots, and played catch.

New York was in for a challenge against the heavily favored Reds. The Big Red Machine of 1976 is generally considered one of the greater clubs in baseball history. Pete Rose, Johnny Bench, George Foster, Rawly East-wick (who led the majors with 26 saves and won the Fireman of the Year award in his sophomore season), Don Gullett, Tony Perez, Dave Concep-cion, and back-to-back National League Most Valuable Player Joe Mor-gan powered the juggernaut. Cincinnati dominated the 1970s, finishing below second only in 1971, averaging 95 wins a season, and showcasing six MVP awards. This did not look like an even playing field.

The Bombers took an old army bus to the ballpark on October 16. Munson was impressed by the monstrous Riverfront facility and the crush-ing amount of reporters that crowded the cage. The Yanks weren't really prepared for the series, nor for the distraction of all the attention, whereas Cincinnati had several off-days to get their emotions straight. The Reds, who had been on the World Series stage three times already that decade, were on their home field that night, and they had developed an advanta-geous tolerance of the Ohio weather that gripped the air. For the opening game, it was so cold that portable heaters were brought in to warm the benches.

Martin thought he'd catch Cincinnati off guard by starting Doyle Alexander, which stunned most people. Opposing him was a Kentuckian lefthander who was said by one writer to "throw nothing but wall-to-wall heat."[40] Don Gullett had gone 61–26 over the previous four seasons as the ace of a top-rate ballclub. He was a tough man to open up against, on the road, in the pivotal game 1.

The city of Cincinnati was baseball-insane that year. This was the site of the Red Stockings, the sport's first all-professional contingent; in 1869 the club, headed by owner Aaron B. Champion and led by English man-ager and "centre fielder" Harry Wright, toured the nation on an unmatched winning streak that propelled the American national pastime into an insti-tution. At that juncture, Cincinnati was the baseball capital of the world; 109 years later, the residents had no intention of relinquishing that dis-tinction. Needless to say, tickets were not easy to come by. As game time approached, the players still didn't have tickets for their friends and fam-ilies, but Steinbrenner did. He ensured that his people got in, yet the play-ers' families did not, which the team took to indicate that it was less important to the organization than the Boss's business buddies. Amidst their screaming, the men finally got their stubs, made suddenly available by the uproar, five minutes before the national anthem. That was their mindset before game 1 of the '76 World Series against the Big Red Machine.

Gullett took his warmup throws in front of a rowdy crowd before Mickey Rivers struck out to open up the fall classic. White grounded out, and Munson — batting in the three slot after a .435 American League

Championship series—could not surmount Gullett's heater. He struck out to make it a 1–2–3 inning. The Reds had a specific plan to deal with his bat, according to manager Sparky Anderson. Apparently, they would let Thurman slap singles to right all he wanted, just so long as he didn't utilize his power.

Munson must have been excited by his performance, for he was especially gregarious in this World Series. As the Reds batters filed to the plate, he talked to them all. According to them, Thurm was the only Yankee having a good time. With two out in the first, one of those observers, Joe Morgan, stepped to the box. "Little Joe" stood 5'7" and 150 pounds, yet he was possibly the most towering presence on the field. In that year he had extended a string of five All-Star games, four Gold Gloves, and two MVPs. He hit 27 home runs, a career high, and drove in 111 (only the fifth second basemen to crack 100 in a season); he also registered a .576 slugging percentage, .320 batting average, .516 on-base percentage, and 60 steals. He did damage. Flapping his back elbow like the tick of a clock, Morgan uncoiled a swing that launched a solo homer to give Cinci the early lead of 1–0.

Lou Piniella was the first designated hitter in World Series history, and he started in style. On the first pitch of the second inning, he slammed a double to left. Advancing on Chambliss's groundball, Piniella scored on a Nettles sacrifice fly to tie the game. Unfortunately for the Yankees, Pete Rose also sacrificed to put the Reds up 2–1. The lead increased to 3–1 after six, 5–1 after seven. At one point, Roy White reached on an error, Munson singled to right, and Piniella then lined one over second base. It looked as though the Yankees were ready to break through, but Morgan managed to track down and stab the ball.

Gullett hurt his ankle in the eighth and had to come out. This would be his last appearance in a Reds game, and coincidentally the same was true for Alexander. Both left via free agency, this their final performances for their respective teams. Pedro Borbon relieved and stopped the Yankees stone cold. New York had lost its first try.

Munson was truly enjoying himself and enjoying the Queen City. On Sunday, with game 2 to come that night, Thurm and Diane spent the afternoon talking with fellow players and their wives. His internal concerns were intense. The whole team knew how important the second game was, for if the Yankees won, the momentum would be swinging in their favor, tied 1–1 going back to the Bronx. Falling to 2–0 to the Reds was to take a walk blindfolded through quicksand.

Hunter started against Fred Norman. Cat was the ideal man for the job, calm and composed, someone who despised being taken out of a game.

And it was his fourth World Series. In the second inning, he uncharacteristically surrendered three runs on four hits. The shoulder might have been hurting still, but he ended up improving as the game wore on. Munson, in his second at-bat, stung a ball to Pete Rose at third and just beat the throw. Nettles later scored him on a single, and three frames later Thurman's RBI grounder put the game at a deadlock, 3–3. There it stayed into the ninth inning.

The Reds started off the bottom of the ninth with a Dave Concepcion flyout. Pete Rose then came up and harmlessly flied to Roy White in left field. Hearts pulsated quickly. Just one out and time for another miracle. Ken Griffey was induced into a groundball to shortstop Stanley, who threw it past first and into the Cincinnati dugout. A simultaneous flatline swept across the Yankees as Griffey advanced to second on the overthrow. Handling the next batter, Morgan, was fundamental. He was intentionally walked. Tony Perez, who Morgan had been passed to get to, ripped a single to left that won the game, 4–3. Going back to Yankee Stadium, the home team was down two games to none.

Afterwards, Billy was a wreck. He refused to cooperate with the writers or go to a press conference which both managers, Martin and Cincinnati's George "Sparky" Anderson, were expected to attend at a downtown hotel. When the former failed to show, Munson was called on to represent the organization. He was rather uneasy about the assumption that he wouldn't mind taking on such a responsibility, not to mention enduring the repetitive inquiries that are the hallmark of a World Series.

The return to Yankee Stadium, an October hallmark in itself, was designated a night game by Bowie Kuhn in order to attract the late night viewership. As a result — with it being autumn in New York — the weather was frigid. Dock Ellis was to oppose Pat Zachry, who had tied with San Diego's Butch Metzger for the National League Rookie of the Year honors in 1976.

Three runs came off Ellis in the second, causing his early exit after but four innings. With the score 4–0 in the seventh, shortstop Jim Mason batted for the Yankees in his last appearance with the club. With nobody on, he slapped a home run in what was his first and last World Series at-bat; Mason, the light-hitting shortstop, was the only ballplayer ever to do that. Unfortunately, circumstance has no sentiment: the Reds scored two more in the eighth and won 6–2. If New York fell once more, the season would be over.

The clubhouse was deathly silent. The euphoria was gone. No longer were the Yankees content just to be there. They wanted to win, but that possibility was slipping out of grasp. And if they were going to lose, a sweep was the ultimate humiliation.

October 21 was armageddon as far as the New York Yankees were concerned. Ed Figueroa, pitching the night game, received early support courtesy of a Munson run. It was the first time they had held a lead all series. Bench raised his team up in the fourth by blasting a shot so deep into left field that it landed in a spot virtually virgin to righthanded hits. Another run was scored for the Reds to draw within one and Bench again struck a homer — to the same crevice of left field to give them the lead. Martin got into an argument with the umpire, earning an early departure from the game — yes, the fourth game of a World Series he was about to lose that night. He picked up a ball in disgust and launched it across the field.

Martin's relationship with the men in blue had never been pretty. He was famous for kicking clouds of dirt onto umpires and for a quote made after one particular blow-up with an umpire, in which he likened the rule book to the funny pages and asserted that the only way one could be put to use is if he ran out of toilet paper while deer hunting. Apparently, that didn't earn him many brownie points with the umpires.

But it was the game that mattered, not Martin. Last inning, bottom of the ninth; the Yankees were shot down, 1–2–3. On the field Cincinnati celebrated, but to the New York players the world was muted, silent, slow motion, and unfeeling. All that remained were lost possibilities, and the cry of "Wait 'til next year!"

After the last game of the series, as described in chapter 1, Munson had his run-in with Sparky Anderson. Anderson saw the incident as an unfortunate blemish blown up by the media. What he didn't recognize, or somehow was not aware of after 15 years, was that Munson was insulted by what he had heard with his own ears. Forget the press; Thurm was right there. Sparky announced that he sent a letter of apology within a few days to the stadium intended for Munson. Thurm never received it.

Munson helplessly anticipated the voting for the American League MVP. "Geez, I'd really like to win that award," he told Martin.[41] Many believed that teammate Mickey Rivers deserved it, with numbers of .312, 95 runs, and 43 stolen bases. In Billy's opinion, Rivers became sluggish as the season wore down, a common and debatable criticism of the fleet center fielder. On the other hand, as the schedule concluded, Munson was told as he traveled through the league that his play merited the accolade.

He did not lead in any categories; the closest he came was in runs batted in, four short of Baltimore's Lee May. What impressed the voters was a steady stream of productive numbers in varying facets of the game. Thurman batted .302, the same as his other award-winning campaign of 1970. While playing in 152 games, he belted 17 yard jobs, collected 105 RBI and

27 doubles, scored 79 runs, and rapped out 186 hits, fourth in the league — not to mention a speedy 14 swipes.

Most important, his crafty handling of the pitching staff was invaluable. Despite the fact that, except Lyle in saves and Hunter in innings, the individual hurlers did not make the top five in any major statistical division, they did spur the Yankees on to 97 victories. And if the thought occurs that the wins were due to the bullpen's proficiency, consider the undermanned size of it: three or four men all year. Guidry was in mop-up work after a spat with Martin; Brett was traded early; Lyle and Tidrow were the only ones down there throwing a whole lot. With new faces like Brett, Gid, Figueroa, Holtzman, Jackson, and Alexander, there was a considerable amount of transition to be worked through. These men, faced with the high-pressure pennant crunch, turned to Munson. Consequently, all had quality seasons, save the first two, but of course Brett didn't figure much and Gid was up and down. As Figueroa put it: "When I came from California, he made me a pitcher. He taught me how to pitch to the batter."[42] Taking that into consideration — coupled with his fine offensive standing — Thurm Munson was one of the most valuable players of the era.

Munson didn't know what to expect from the 23 voting writers. He knew they did not like him, and they were aware that the sentiment was reciprocal. Nervously, he phoned the Yankee offices throughout the day of the announcement, and eventually decided to set up an address at six o'clock that evening in order to coincide with morning paper deadlines. The call ended up coming in around three o'clock. Out of 23 ballots cast, Munson was named first on 18. By garnering 75 percent, he was the American League's Most Valuable Player, and he was a compelling definition of the term. A few votes ranked him at second or third, but 87 points separated him and George Brett, while Rivers placed third, then Hal McRae, and Chris Chambliss. Said Munson in reflection of the 1975 and '76 season's, "The only reason I got more recognition in 1976 was because we were winners."[43]

A small press conference was thrown together, and though it accommodated the morning papers, the announcement came at an awkward time for afternoon papers and especially television stations. "I'm proud I won," Munson stated to the few reporters. "I know it wasn't politics. I won this on my ability."[44] He also inserted a small mention of his contract, which made Steinbrenner squirm uneasily. After a series of Q&A with the reporters, Diane was asked to step up and pose with Thurman for a few snapshots.

A lot was made of Munson's being named captain and MVP in the same season, but he supposedly did not think much of it; Thurm was just

Munson in his throwing stance behind the plate at Yankee Stadium. (National Baseball Hall of Fame Library, Cooperstown, N.Y.)

proud. And thrilled. The ecstasy lingered a few days, while he ranked the honor alongside the All-American selection of 1968. But not above.

Out of the embers of failure come the sparks of hope.

The World Series sweep convinced Steinbrenner that his club was in dire need of progress. So he and Gabe carefully examined the possibilities of 1977's free agent draft. First on the docket, Don Gullett was signed and added to an impressive staff already consisting of Hunter, Figueroa, and Ellis. A flashy press conference was held in which Munson was invited to appear as the Yankee ambassador, welcoming to the fold the former farmboy Gullet, decked out in a comfortable hunting vest. Thurm had a sure feeling that this wouldn't be the last of such festivities, for the Yankees were still allotted one more free agent to ink.

Bobby Grich left the Baltimore Orioles as a powerful All-Star second baseman and owner of four straight Gold Gloves. New York wanted him badly, despite the emergence of Willie Randolph. However, when it became increasingly clear that Grich was headed for the California Angels, the Yankees turned their attention elsewhere.

In 1973, Steinbrenner was taking in an Oakland ballgame that featured the impressively powerful performance of right fielder Reggie Jackson. Midway through, he turned to a nearby friend, Peter Callahan. "Pete," he said, "I got to tell you, I'm going to get Jackson, and I'm going to get Billy Martin."[45] After obtaining the latter 16 months earlier, he finally saw the opportunity to bring that union to fruition.

Jackson had led in slugging in 1976, won the '73 AL MVP, led the league twice in home runs, and boasted six All-Star performances on his resume. He negotiated with nearly every major league club after becoming a free agent, including the Yankees on November 4. Gabe was adamant about Grich, but when Steinbrenner consulted Munson, the push for Jackson went into full swing. "Go get the big man," Thurman implored the Boss. "He's the only guy in baseball who can carry a club for a month. And [who cares] what you hear. He hustles every minute on the field."[46]

It was the eve of Thanksgiving when the talk came to action. Steinbrenner had wined and dined and hunted his player as only he could, before clinching the deal with an offer of $60,000 to purchase a brand-new Rolls Royce. "I will not let you down," Reggie inscribed on a hotel restaurant napkin. "Reginald M. Jackson."[47] Offered a five-year contract worth $2.96 million, Reggie hardly hesitated to pull the trigger. Little did he know, the barrel was aimed at his own head.

8

THORN IN THE PRIDE

Reggie's really a good guy, deep down he is. I really like him. I always did. He'd give you the shirt off his back. Of course, he'd call a press conference to announce it.

— Catfish Hunter

Munson flew in from Ohio on November 26, 1976, for a press conference at the Americana Hotel in New York City. Willie Randolph, Ed Figueroa, and Roy White joined him there. To the side of them stood a young man flanked by his father, brother, and girlfriend, clad in a gray flannel suit, complete with gold buttons, and a vest. The gold watch and championship rings he wore were countered by a midnight blue New York Yankee's cap, and the smile underneath stretched from ear to ear.

Gabe Paul rose and stepped to the microphone. He cleared his throat, then positioned a pair of reading glasses upon the bridge of his nose. "The New York Yankees are pleased to announce that we have come to terms with free agent Reggie Jackson."[1]

Jackson soon was granted the microphone. "The reason why I am a Yankee is because George Steinbrenner outhustled everybody," he informed the assembled press:

> George Steinbrenner dealt with me as a man and a person.... For me get applause from the crowd or slaps on the back or have George Steinbrenner say to me that he felt he wanted me to play here and always wanted me here, that's something I never had. I never felt wanted like that....[2]

Fielding questions as fluently as Nomar Garciaparra would a grounder, Jackson called every writer by his first name, and those he did not recognize were asked their name and affiliation before receiving an answer. That took a while, too; the place was packed.

Reginald Martinez Jackson's skills on a baseball diamond were undeniable. He had stolen well over 150 bases by the time he signed with the Yanks. On top of being an excellent clutch player, his power and prowess created 563 career home runs and drove his clubs to 11 postseason berths in his 21 seasons. On the other hand, he struck out a record 2,597 times, once made five errors in a single game, and was the ultimate driving factor in christening the Bronx Zoo.

To his benefit, Jackson held a magnetic effect on the writers. He could often be found huddled with reporters, holding official or unofficial press conferences. He could insulted teammates regularly, but was thoroughly surprised when they took offense. His fellow players generally did not retaliate, so as not to practice that against which they preached. Consequently, most shied away from him or did not try to work out their differences. Teammates would usually find out Reggie's opinions in the sports section instead of straight from the source as would have been preferred, and this created a tense, noncommunicative atmosphere. Even the writers found that at times.

Once, after a game in Oakland, Jackson was on the radio claiming the New York writers were uninformed, that they didn't know what they were talking about. Turns out he didn't know who he was talking *to*—the writers were listening in the clubhouse. When he came there following the interview, the reporters were angry. "You guys heard that?" he laughed, caught off guard. "If I knew you were listening, I wouldn't have said it."[3]

Writer Murray Chass was not seduced by Jackson's "quotability." "Reggie is obsessed with money," he wrote in the *New York Times.* "Amateur psychologists view him as a tremendously insecure person who feels that money gives him instant status and importance far beyond his standing as a baseball player."[4]

Defensively, Jackson had the speed to be potent but had difficulty catching the ball, and unfortunately he didn't do much to improve it by neglecting to shag flies in practice. But there were some times when he saved the game with a grab. Ron Guidry was once on the mound when a lefty sliced a ball to Reggie in right field. Initially, he lost it somehow, then recovered, sprinted over, and dove for the catch. It looked great. The players all knew it was an easy play that appeared difficult and dutifully took the opportunity to rib him about it afterwards. Munson started off by joking about Reggie's inferiority on defense, and wouldn't let him live it down. Jackson rebutted by bringing up the catch, to which Munson just laughed in response. Reg turned to Guidry, a supporter of his, at the front of the bus to ask about it. "Honestly, Reggie," Gid said, innocent as could be, " I didn't see the play. I had my glove over my face the entire time."[5]

A lot of the on-field hype Jackson precipitated was completely avoidable, but he liked what was expected, because, as he said, "When I get up in a pressure situation, I swell up with relaxness [sic]. It's like everyone is saying 'Reggie's up. Everything's going to be OK.' He was also attributed the quote, "I go to pieces in turmoil, but I thrive on pressure."[6] While he denied saying it (and probably didn't), the sentiment was nevertheless accurate. That was the Bronx Zoo—dissolving in turmoil, thriving on pressure.

Back in the press conference, Steinbrenner continued:

> I have brought not only a colorful personality who can pull in paying fans, but a player who produces under pressure.
>   Thurman played a major role in our decision to go after Reggie. Gabe Paul wanted to go after Bobby Grich instead. But I was always a Jackson man and Munson encouraged me.[7]

Thurm explained this upon his chance at the mic. "I felt we needed a left-handed power-hitter," he reasoned, "and an outfielder who could throw. Jackson fits the bill. I'm thinking of the team."[8]

The signing was not all positive for Munson. When his 1977 contract came around, he trusted that Steinbrenner would remain a man of his word by keeping his salary the most lucrative on the payroll. He knew that wasn't going to happen as soon as the two discussed the first issue on the table. George now claimed that the previous year's offer was that Thurm would be able to restructure his contract if the team won the World Series, not just the pennant. As if that weren't frustrating enough, Thurm felt there was another promise being broken. When it came to salary, Munson knew that Jackson outranked him, but had no way to prove the exact amount Reggie earned, and in fact never really did. He called Players Association head Marvin Miller to inquire about Jackson's and Gullett's contracts. "Funny thing," Miller told him, "those are the only two that haven't been filed in the league office."[9] Miller had signed one, but told the Yankee lawyer that it would not qualify as the final contract, and another would have to be drawn up.

Munson wisely spoke up. At a banquet in Syracuse that winter, he stated that he would want a trade if he were unable to depend on Steinbrenner's word. He was hoping that the Boss would receive bad press over this—which he despised—and consequently rectify the matter. Unfortunately, the story did not catch and Steinbrenner presumably never got word of it. Later that week, Thurman spoke in Canada to reiterate his comments. This time the wire services took notice and spread it through the papers.

The night it came out, Thurm was playing a game of cards with his buddies back in Canton. At one in the morning — two eastern — the phone rang. Steinbrenner. George wanted him to fly to New York to sign a press release denying the quotes. Happy to have caught his attention, Munson hopped a plane eastward and found out Jackson's exact pay (according to Steinbrenner). Unmentioned was the fact that, though Reggie was below his teammate in actual salary, he was raking in thousands in deferred payments. In accordance with Jackson's base figures, the proper contractual

Thurman Munson on one of his scruffier days, in pinstripes at Yankee Stadium. (National Baseball Hall of Fame Library, Cooperstown, N.Y.)

adjustments were made. As Thurman held his pen poised above the paper, he looked Steinbrenner directly in the eye. "Am I the highest salaried player on this club?" he asked.[10] George said yes. Though suspicious, he signed the contract with gratitude despite his reservations.

For months, Munson attempted to find out Reggie's true salary, for he was a man that demanded honesty. He wasn't sneaky about it; he simply asked. Thurman's lawyer sought Jackson's, but to no avail. One day, driving to the stadium with Catfish, Thurm lamented, "I don't think he's ever told me the truth. I like him as a player, but I can't stand the fact he lied to me. He won't tell me the truth. I know, because I've caught him in a lie two or three times."[11]

It bothered Thurm that he had trusted both Jackson and Steinbrenner, and yet been deceived. Insecure, shy, doubtful, he didn't commit faith to people easily. As the insecurity pressed, his emotion turned to humiliation. Throughout, Munson shook his head wearily, thinking of George, "He lied to me. He made a fool of me."[12]

"I'm going to show him who's boss around here," Martin spoke of Jackson in January. "One of George's boys isn't going to come in and run the show," he said, using his favorite derogatory term for one of Steinbrenner's pursued free agents.[13] He was just setting the tone.

In Hawaii, during the winter of 1977, Reggie was preparing to participate in an ABC program called "The Superstars." There he met Lyle and Nettles, both of whom allegedly ignored him. Despite the fact that the two were famously close with the likes of Randolph, Ellis, May, Gamble, and Rivers, and despite the fact that Jackson himself had already alienated the club with his mouth at this point, he labeled the two as racists.

It's safe to say Reggie Jackson didn't feel welcome.

Reporting late and overweight, Jackson's first day was a zoo. Munson fought his way to his locker through the mass of media. "Can you believe this?!" he said to Lou Piniella, with a deeply disturbed countenance. "You'd think we had just won the World Series or something." Piniella later mulled it over with Thurman. "We're not in baseball anymore," Lou mused, "we're in show business. Baseball is just a sideline here."[14] Those two and Nettles were particularly disgusted. Thurman was torn up internally but disguised it with the image of grumpiness. As insecure as he was, he had come off his greatest season — MVP, captain, pennant winner — and on that day, who cared? As Fred Stanley once told the writers, "See, the thing that people forget when Reggie joined the club was that Thurman was the captain. He was Mr. Yankee. He also wanted attention. He probably wanted it as badly as Reggie did. He just didn't know how to go about it."[15]

Reggie did. Early in the spring, he held a press conference. He carried a shining black baseball bat to the microphone. "You see this? This is the Dues Collector. This now helps the Yankees intimidate every other team in baseball. That's what I do just by walking into this clubhouse. Nobody will embarrass the Yankees in the World Series as long as I am carrying the Dues Collector."[16]

The truth is, Munson would have respected Jackson if he had not been so genetically immodest. Brandishing the Dues Collector, Reggie told the writers at a later point:

> I'm the big fish and now I'm in the big pond. I've got a big job to do, but I've got the big bat to do it with.
> All I read is that I'm supposed to create controversy. I don't look for it. It follows me around. I can live with it. I've learned how to handle it.[17]

On the third day, Martin called Jackson into his office. "You just feel at home here and do your thing," Billy said. "If you do your job nobody will bother you."[18] Noting that Munson had been disturbed by Reggie's audible assertion that he was the star and leader of the team, Martin expressed hope that the two big "fishes" would get along.

Ken Holtzman, a former Oakland teammate of Jackson, warned the team, "You definitely won't believe this guy. You wait, pretty soon Reggie says how he's the leader and how he's the key to the team."[19] And, sure enough, later in the season Reggie called Munson a bad captain, to which Thurm replied, "I thought Reggie was the captain." Steinbrenner shut out Munson's doubt. "When I want Reggie to be the captain, I'll name him captain. You're the captain. Now be the captain."[20]

According to Reggie, he later regretted not having phoned Thurman early to say, "You're the captain and I know that. I'm just glad to be here. Glad to be playing for you."[21] That would have cleared up a lot.

Jackson developed a sore arm while throwing early in the spring. His camp was a poor one with characteristically high strikeouts, and he was booed nearly everywhere he went. "Reggie is a Bozo" signs were strewn across several parks, to the subject's stunned dejection. One thing Jackson often did in the face of rejection or turmoil concerning his offensive personality was to cite racism.

Reggie's claims of racism were so erratic that they often blurred the prejudice that undoubtedly existed. "Racism is a constant undercurrent," the *Boston Globe* wrote of his views, "and sometimes Jackson may be seeing an issue that isn't there. At other times, it too obviously is."[22]

His first exposure with the Yankees was an incident in March when the group of Munson, Martin, Nettles, Tidrow, and Lyle made jokes about Jewish teammate Ken Holtzman as he ran laps in the outfield. Reggie scorned it as immature and noted how foreign it was to his days in Oakland. Of course — if one may toe the line of justification without betraying the truth — the difference was that the As were a tense, bitter group in his time, while the Yankees (at least before Reggie entered the picture) were a club that had no problems with ribbings and insults. Face to face they most likely would have said and did say these things to Holtzie just the same (like the Munson/Bonds jesting described earlier). There was a common respect and fondness for this pitcher who, after all, they had overwhelmingly elected as player representative.

Some racial jokes crossed the boundaries quite clearly, such as a game in which Martin was approached by Nettles. "Skip, that's the first time I've ever seen that," he said, quizzically.

"What's that, Graig?"

"A player," Puff replied, pokerfaced, "with his home address on his back."

"What do you mean?" Billy asked. Nettles looked out toward a large African American by the name of Wayne Cage.

"Look at their first baseman."[23] Initially, Martin didn't get it, but soon he laughed so hard that he left stumbling out of the dugout.

After Jackson spoke out on racial issues, Roy White, exposed to a uniquely transitive decade in New York, commented to him, "It's about time somebody said something like that around here."[24] Other black players on the team seemed to disagree. During the 1977 season, about ten of the players were at a hotel bar in Detroit, one being Jackson, who, without warning, burst into tears over a glass of beer. "If I were white, I'd own the world," he lamented.

Chambliss was not moved. He turned to Jackson disgustedly. "Reggie, you know what you'd be if you were white? Just another white boy. Be glad you're black and getting all the publicity you do, getting away with all you do."[25]

Wrote Dock Ellis, who was also an outspoken political activist, "I spent eight years with the Pittsburgh Pirates and in all those years on the Pirates, not one of those teams had the camaraderie that the Yankee's had in one year.... We would diss each other. They didn't care."

The bottom line is that Jackson didn't seem to know what he thought racism was. In his autobiography, *Reggie*, he cited the word "articulate" as a manufactured white label for intelligent black people, "something of a racist cliché" (p. 21). Yet 11 chapters later, he refers to himself as "black, articulate, and a pretty successful businessman" (p. 163). He encountered some terrible bouts with racism in his life, most notably being passed over by the Mets in the 1967 draft because, according to his college coach, "They're concerned that you have a white girlfriend."[26] Overall, it would be just to stand on the front lines with Jackson in every fight had he not caused confusion with his use of racism as a personal escape clause. Ultimately, what Reggie Jackson did by his complaints was to demean the many genuine claims of bigotry.

New York was an exciting team for the campaign of 1977, seeming to perform best when the big crowds were out or something was on the line. On April 7, they kicked off the season before one of those big crowds. Reggie Jackson banged his cleats with the Dues Collector and shouted, "Showtime!"

Cat was starting that day, hoping to follow through on a fine spring training. The fans were in a rowdy state, already employing the thunderous chants of "REG-gie, REG-gie." Meanwhile, the club defeated Milwaukee 3–0 behind Hunter and Lyle. However, amidst the excitement, Catfish took a liner off his instep. He had to go on the disabled list for a month, and the doctors soon discovered a sore arm, a urinary disorder, and what was thought to be a hernia. All this was damaging to his pitching, throwing off his mechanics and hips. It would not be much of a season for Hunter, who, by his frequent trips to the DL, ended up 9–9 with a 4.72 ERA.

New York lost their next two games and the first six of eight. As the month progressed bleakly, it was apparent that the pitchers were largely responsible, but not for faults all their own. Hunter, Gullett, and Figueroa all suffered arm problems early. Holtzie had been relegated to the bullpen, where he was ineffective. Ellis started with a win, a loss, and a no-decision. A lingering contract haggle diminished his already dismal devotion to the game. Relations with Steinbrenner, crude in its original form, were increasingly strained. In early April, George entered the clubhouse and was enraged to find Dock wearing an earring. His frustration pleased Ellis, so much so that he offered to wear it on the mound if it upset Steinbrenner further. "The only reason I don't do it is 'cause I don't want to rock your little boat," Ellis barked.

"If you do, you wouldn't rock the boat a second time."

Ellis was fuming. "OK, get ready to trade me! This is war!"[27]

Earlier, Ellis had come to the defense of Martin against Steinbrenner. "We don't need [George] riding in here like the Lone Ranger. Steinbrenner had better stay off Billy Martin's back, because the players are in Billy's corner."[28]

"If anyone says I've been on Billy Martin's butt," George argued, "he's a liar. I've had no conversations with Billy Martin about the ballclub since spring training."[29] Of course, it was common knowledge that he had in fact been meeting with Martin daily to discuss the club.

Steinbrenner must have circulated word quickly that Ellis was not wanted. A couple of days after the earring dispute, Charlie Finley responded. George wanted to trade Ellis and Rivers — another Yankee in the doghouse — to Finley's As for Mike Torrez, a solid pitcher with a large frame who was to become a free agent at the end of 1977, and star center fielder Bill North. Gabe insisted George forget about his personal contempt for Rivers because it was a bad trade. The Boss relented and was next approached by Finley seeking Ellis, Guidry, Mickey Klutts, and a fresh infielder — just for Torrez. Steinbrenner actually wanted to do it, but Gabe again dissuaded him. Other proposals were Ellis and Marty Perez — a versatile 32-year-old infielder — or Lyle and Ellis, for Torrez. Once more, George had to be talked out of it by Gabe and, this time, Martin. At this point, Gabe was still in the hospital recovering from a cerebral spasm, and of course Finley stepped in to visit. Finally, both sides gave in and dealt Torrez for Ellis straight up on April 27.

Torrez, who won 15 or more games every year between 1974 and 1979 for five separate clubs, was a 6'5" righty out of Kansas. On April 29, he was scheduled to make his initial Yankee start, but had to skip it when his wife fell sick. Steinbrenner wanted to fine him $500, though he told the papers that Billy was the one who demanded the punishment. With injuries plaguing the staff, Martin turned to Guidry.

On the day Guidry replaced Torrez, Martin told him, "All I want you to do is give me five innings."[30] In the first inning, he gave up two hits and retired two. Seattle first baseman Danny Meyer, a lefty, racked up a two-ball, two-strike count. Gid hung a slider and Meyer crushed it foul by an inch or two. Guidry stepped off the mound in relief, drew a deep breath, and rung Meyer up with a nasty slider. Gid called him the most important batter of his life. It was a major turning point in his career. Fortunately, Munson then struck a two-run homer, as he did in all three games of the sweep. Over eight and a third innings, Gator shut out the Mariners 3–0.

Late in the month, Billy was receiving complaints about the batting order, so he used an old strategy from his Denver days—let a player organize it. "The way you pick 'em," Martin told Reggie Jackson, "that's the way it's going to be."[31] The lineup ran as Randolph leading off, Munson second, then Jackson, Nettles, Rivers, White, May, Chambliss, and Bucky Dent. Chambliss racked up more RBI from the eight spot during that period than any player, Dent hit a grand slam to beat California on the second, and Thurm had a four-hit, home run game. On the strength of six straight wins, the club took over first place on May 7.

Early that month in Milwaukee, Jackson was standing in the outfield during batting practice when Munson sidled up. One on one — no media — they were a natural link. As balls flew across the diamond, the two exchanged an easy conversation about the team. They agreed that the unit was yet to come together, and that they should take the responsibility to change that. In reference to some grumblings Thurman had made in the paper about Reggie's Rolls Royce, he laughed, "I sure wish George would buy me a car."[32] Reggie appreciated the effort of Munson, for he knew that it was tough for Thurman to come around like that. It had all been in front of the club, who looked up to Thurm for influence in many ways, and were now ready to ease into acceptance of Jackson. Of course, the press caught it and gave the colloquy a good measure of publicity.

In that series, Jackson told the media of his sore arm, for which Martin benched him for a game. Reggie opined that this was nothing but a power trip. Billy also made Munson ride the pine, but for more sympathetic than offensive reasons. As Billy said, "His legs have been bothering him for a whole week."[33] With only Fran Healy to back him up, Billy ordered the front office to call up Elrod Hendricks, an experienced quality catcher in Syracuse. Instead they promoted Del Alston, who was hitting .338 primarily in the outfield as compared to Hendricks's .105. The Yanks were in Seattle on the 12th when Billy told the papers, "I don't want an outfielder. I need a catcher."[34] They lost that night to the Mariners, an abysmal expansion team, amidst the lack of a lefthander off the bench like Hendricks. "I've been asking for Elrod for a week and a half," Martin sounded off to the press. "But George and Gabe think I'm kidding. Why are we going with 24 players? It cost us tonight's game, as far as I'm concerned."[35] The papers were more than obliged to make this a headline.

Billy flew the next day to New York and spoke on the phone with Gabe Paul for a couple of hours. Strangely, Gabe ended by asking him to drive out a half an hour to the George Washington Bridge. Billy said no, figuring what was the sense in driving an hour total to discuss something they could do over the phone?

That night Munson allowed three stolen bases, though his arm had returned to a three-quarters motion for the first time since 1973, before exiting with leg cramps. "I can't visualize a major league team without three catchers," Martin commented publicly in reaction.[36] He was fined the following day for criticism and failure to meet with Gabe, who said:

> Frankly, if we have to depend on a player batting .105 at Syracuse to enable us to beat an expansion team, we are indeed in bad trouble.
>
> Certain comments directed at Mr. Steinbrenner ... by Billy Martin, concerning ... the twenty-fifth player, are totally inaccurate and unfounded.
>
> Martin was asked to report to my office on May tenth prior to leaving Seattle, and at such time the determination of the twenty-fifth player was to be made. He agreed to be there. However, Billy failed to show up for the meeting with me. If we had had that conversation as scheduled, the twenty-fifth player would have been added and the matter would have been settled then and there.[37]

In a home game against Baltimore that week, Lee May collided with Munson and knocked him out of the game. The score was tied going into the later innings, with Randolph, Rivers, and Healy due up, a runner at second, and one out on record. Orioles manager Earl Weaver was sure to get to Healy — a .224 hitter that year — because Billy couldn't put anyone else in to catch for him. Hendricks came up two days later.

According to Reggie Jackson, he was approached in spring training by a dark-haired, innocent-looking sportswriter named Robert Ward. He wanted to author an article for *Sport* magazine, a "warm" welcome-to-the-Big-Apple deal. "I'm not out to get you," Ward assured him. "The story will be in a positive light."[38] Jackson declined, in his book citing feelings that *Sport* had treated him unfairly in the past. Yet in 1973 the magazine gave him a sports car as the star of the World Series, when teammate Bert Campaneris (.290, three RBI, three stolen bases, an 11th-inning game winner, and seventh-inning two-run homer as the impetus to Oakland's championship) was felt to have clearly deserved the award, but was forsaken for his low visibility.

"I'm very tentative about doing anything for *Sport*," Jackson explained to Ward. "I'm afraid they're looking for something from me that would make a splash and do me harm. I just don't want to get involved."[39] Ward persisted for days— before workouts, after workouts— and said he wanted no trouble. Finally, one day at the Banana Boat Bar in Fort Lauderdale, Reggie relented. He offered Ward a seat, though a page later in his book said Ward asked if he could sit down. Rhapsodizing nearly a decade later of a time with a beer at hand in casual conversation, Jackson felt certain of the way the conference took place.

The two were supposed to be having an easy exchange about baseball, the team, and Jackson. He didn't think Ward was doing a story; he was just speaking off the record. No notes were said to have been taken as they first spoke of Nettles and Lyle and the Hawaii reception. Jackson kidded about Munson's grumpiness and gruff nature, then expressed an enthusiasm for playing with such a fiery competitor, with whom he was yet to have problems. "Well, everywhere I've been, I've been lucky enough to be the center of influence on the club offensively. I'm the kind of guy, the kind of power hitter, who fits the last piece of some puzzles. I can be the kind of guy who can put a team over the top."[40] Reggie didn't think much of the comment, just that he was describing his ability to fortify a club. At this juncture, he raised a glass to compare his addition to the production of a complex drink. Munson, Randolph, Chambliss, Nettles, Lyle, Rivers, Hunter, they were all part of the substance. "Maybe I'm the kind of personality that can jump into a drink like that and stir things up and get it all going."[41] The two wrapped up having established no clear topic of conversation.

Teasers were leaked to the press throughout the ensuing months, and both sides knew the story would be big. On May 23, Robert Ward's article, "Reggie Jackson in No-Man's Land," hit the newsstands. Late that afternoon, word had spread quickly, for it seemed all the players were huddled in small groups, reading *Sport* and glaring at Jackson. No one spoke with him. As he sat at his locker, Munson crossed by with the magazine peeking out of the pocket of his uniform pants.

Martin didn't want to read the article, but called Reggie in to his office to address the ambiguous dilemma. Jackson seemed to be upset it was ever published and said he didn't intend to have the interview come off so strong. After they finished, Billy spoke with Munson and came away with the overwhelming impression that he wasn't going to forgive Reggie this offense.

In the clubhouse, Fran Healy — noted to be the only Yankee consistently on Reggie's side — stood at his locker. Assistant trainer Herm Schneider came over to tell him, "Thurman's in the doctor's room. He'd like to talk to you."[42] The doctor's room, connected to that of the trainer, held Munson, gripped by the *Sport* issue as Healy walked in. "You know, this team ... it all flows from me," the article read. "I've got to keep it all going. I'm the straw that stirs the drink. It all comes back to me. Maybe I should say me and Munson ... but really he doesn't enter into it."[43]

Ironically, later in the article, Martin was asked if there would be any leadership conflict on the team. "Not a chance," he said, confused. "We already have a team leader. Thurman Munson."[44] Jackson continued his quote by saying Thurm was being so "insecure about the whole thing. I've overheard him talking about me.... I'll hear him telling some other writer that he wants it to be known that he's the captain of the team, that he knows what's best. Stuff like that. And when anybody knocks me, he laughs real loud so I can hear."[45]

At this point, Ward asked why Reggie didn't simply talk out his problems with Munson Jackson replied:

> No, he's not ready for it yet. He doesn't even know he feels that way.... He'd try to cover up, but he ought to know he can't cover up anything from me. Man, there's no way. I can read these guys. No, I'll wait, and eventually he'll be whipped. There will come that moment when he really knows I won, and he'll wait to hear everything's all right, and then I'll go to him and we will get it right.[46]

Ward couldn't believe his ears. "Do you want this printed?"
"Print it," Jackson answered, and expounded further:

> The way the Yankees were humiliated by the Reds, you think that doesn't bother Billy Martin? He's no fool. He's smart. Very smart. And he's a winner. Munson's tough, too. He is a winner, but there is just nobody who can do for a club what I can do. There is nobody

who can put meat in the seats the way I can. That's just the way it is. Munson thinks he can be the straw that stirs the drink, but he can only stir it bad.[47]

It's so apparent, why can't Munson and Chambliss and all the rest of them understand the sheer simplicity ... the cold logic?

Don't you see, that there is just no way I can play second fiddle to *anybody*. Hah! That's just not in the cards...! There ain't no way![48]

Ward asked again. "Are you *sure* you want me to print this?"[49]

"Yes, print it. I *want* to see that in print. I want to *read* it."

Munson looked up at Healy. "Did you read this?" Fran answered no, and he never actually would. So Thurm read it for him. As he stopped to draw a breath, Healy offered a suggestion: "Maybe he was quoted out of context."

"Quoted of context for three pages?!"[50] Healy couldn't help but laugh. He then returned to his locker, leery of considering this anything but a blip in the Bronx story line.

Still in the trainer's room, Ron Blomberg — out for the entire 1977 season after only two at-bats in '76 — came in to check on Munson. "I just go out everyday and play," Thurm stated bleakly. "I helped the Yankee's win the pennant. I was MVP. What's so bad about that?"[51]

The game that day was against Boston, their first match with New York of the season, and before a nationwide television audience. The team was all together at the batting cage when Reggie approached. At the sight of him, the whole unit disassembled. Once the game started, Jackson doubled and scored with what turned out to be a vital run by the end of six, with the score 2–1 Red Sox. Reggie again came up, versus Bill Lee, and rocked a fastball into the right field stands to tie the game. Giving his customary admiration, he stood to watch the ball momentarily after the crack of the bat. He came back to the dugout in front of 30,000 onlookers to find the team waiting en masse with hands extended. In his head flashed the hypocrisy of ignoring him, rebuking him, dissolving groups at the sight of him, and then putting forth their palms in a blanket of congratulations. Perhaps they were putting it in the past, and perhaps by that Jackson would be conceding defeat. Sharply, he turned away — no handshakes, no acknowledgment — and went into the other side of the dugout. The players found it to be bush, as the old baseball term goes.

Munson remembered his old friend Alex Johnson, who did not shake hands after homers; that was okay because that was his style and consistently had been. A reporter asked Jackson that night why he had neglected to shake their hands. "My hand hurt," he answered.[52] Thurm was not laughing. A "liar," he spat out emphatically, was Jackson.

Reggie went out to dinner that evening with Lou Piniella, neutral as usual, and agent Matt Merola at a restaurant called Harper's. Jackson suggested he apologize to Munson, but Healy didn't think much of his idea. By the next day, Mickey Rivers and Carlos May had moved their lockers away from him, while Chambliss was offering nothing but silence. In the locker room, Jackson approached Munson to provide an explanation. Thurm simply walked away without a word.

The Yankees were beginning to fall apart, not exclusively from the internal turmoil, and Steinbrenner did not like it. He spoke with Munson and told him he better be friendly to Jackson or else *Billy* would be in jeopardy. Thurm was startled to be handed such a weight of responsibility. Regardless, he asked Healy to put together a dinner for him and Jackson. The meal failed to solve anything but allowed the two to get much off their chests and clear up certain issues. If anything, Thurman was ashamed that a flaw between them had now been aired nationally. He did not go easy on his teammate and, in fact, was harsh on Jackson in his autobiography. Was Thurm jealous? "Tell me one thing you have that I'd want," he demanded of Reggie at dinner, looking him straight in the eye. "I have three beautiful children and a lovely wife. I have a happy home life. What do you have? You have nothing." Jackson didn't answer.[53]

By the middle of June, Boston had taken first place primarily on account of a ten-game, 33-homer run. The Yankees' downfall was a 10–15 record versus lefthanders, despite a 25–11 mark against righties. As in earlier years, rival clubs promoted southpaws from the minor leagues just to face the Bombers. To combat this trend, on June 15 they acquired from the Astros righty slugger Cliff Johnson, who Munson nicknamed "Heathcliff" after the cartoon character. Dave Bergman, Randy Niemann, and Mike Fischlin all went to Houston, a trade that Steinbrenner tried foolishly to reverse for a full year, even though it was a good one. Johnson was a powerful man of a 6'6" frame and tremendous clubhouse presence.

Johnson and his new club were in Boston for a three-game set on June 17 in which Cat — back from the disabled list — took the mound. Rick Burleson led off the bottom of the first by driving a ball deep and gone over the outfield wall for a home run. Up next was Fred Lynn. Home run. Finally, two outs were recorded. Carlton Fisk dug in. Homer. George Scott followed. Again. Six were hit in the game off Hunter, yet Billy was still employing the theory of little ball. Bucky Dent had been pinch-hit for many times in the year, then Fred Stanley would substitute for him in late innings at shortstop. The lack of confidence was beginning to diminish his game. So, early in the Boston thrashing, Martin had him squeeze bunt when Bucky wanted to swing away, which hurt him. The game was a lost cause.

On Saturday, June 18, Martin sat with Dent in the dugout in the waning hours before game time. He explained the move to his player and, during the conversation, turned to Jackson, who sat alongside on the bench. "It was the right move at the time," Billy confirmed, "wasn't it, Reggie?"[54]

"Skip, if you're asking me for my honest opinion, I wouldn't have had him bunt," Reggie claimed to have said:

> It's only June. It was early in the game when you had him do it. Something like that might affect Bucky's confidence later in the year when you'll probably have him hitting away in that situation. You're going to need him then. It's too early in the pennant race for that kind of stuff. So, anyway, no, I wouldn't have bunted him.[55]

When some writer's approach the subject of Reggie Jackson, some of his stories are met with inordinate cynicism. In most cases it's difficult to discern what's true and what's myth or exaggeration. But for Reggie Jackson to go on record as having responded in that witness-stand manner is one of the reasons why credit is not given to his accounts and his word is often met with skepticism. His account might have been truthful, but in Reggie's words, one must "understand … the cold logic."[56]

"I disagree with you," Martin supposedly snapped at him. "I do things my way."[57] That's Jackson's explanation for what was about to come.

By this time Reggie was sick of New York. Not just the team, but the city, the atmosphere. Allegedly, he had a verbal agreement to dissolve his contract at any time if he were unhappy, but Steinbrenner did not honor it. He was booed everywhere and angry not to be batting cleanup. He batted third, fifth, or sixth, but not fourth. His teammates still ignored him, even Cat and Holtzie, Reggie's old brethren. However, as the month progressed, Jackson and Munson began to say hello and even converse. Reggie seemed awkward about it. Wrote Munson:

> I think he felt very uncomfortable and self-conscious about our relationship. I think when I confronted him with the reality of life — that baseball may be a great ego trip, but there's a lot more to this world than baseball — he found himself unable to deal with it. For the sake of the team, we did no more interviews on each other. But we didn't become the best of friends either.[58]

The Saturday match at Boston, a nationally televised game, was an important and heralded one. The Sox came up with five home runs, and yet were only winning by a 7–4 score in the sixth. With a man on first, the powerful Jim Rice was up. That year he hit .320 and led the league in slugging (.593) and homers (39). With the latter statistic, he became part of a Red Sox team that for only the second time in history—besides the '56 Reds—consisted of five players who hit 25 or more home runs: Rice, Carlton Fisk, George Scott, Butch Hobson, and Carl Yastrzemski. In betrayal of his power, Rice took a crushing cut but only blooped a Texas Leaguer to Jackson in right. According to Reggie, he froze initially, hoping to gauge the ball. Soon he saw the small magnitude of the blow and thought Randolph might grab it. When he saw that wasn't happening, he slowed up— with no real chance to catch the ball—in order to keep it from passing. By almost every other account, he "loafed." Rice capitalized and hustled into second, beating the throw. Martin felt he had been allotted too many hops on such a weak hit.

Billy took to the mound to yank Torrez for Lyle. "I'm going to get [Reggie] for not hustling," he is supposed to have said.[59] Jackson retreated to right and began talking to Healy, who was serving as bullpen catcher. "You better turn around," Healy said. Reg thought he was kidding and asked why. "Because I think Billy wants you." Paul Blair was headed to right field; he was often a late-inning replacement but usually albeit between innings, not in the middle of one.

It didn't click for Reggie at first. As Blair drew closer, Jackson asked, "You here for me?" Nod. He asked what was happening.

"You've got to ask Billy that," Blair answered.[60]

As Reggie passed by Nettles at third, he slipped Puff a warning glance. He proceeded to the dugout and—in a move that many considered to be antagonistic—took off his glasses and placed them on his glove. Billy had been waiting at the top of the steps, an NBC camera covering the entire scene. Veins pulsed through the skin of his neck as he barked, "What do you think you're doing out there?!"[61]

"You showed me up," Reggie yelled back. "You showed me up. How could you do this to me on television?"[62]

"You want to show me up by loafing on me," Billy responded. "Fine. Then I'm going to show you up. Anyone who doesn't hustle doesn't play for me."[63]

"You're not a man," Reggie rebutted. "Don't you dare ever show me up again."[64] He hollered and called Martin a racist. The two inched closer. "Nothing I could ever do would please you. You never wanted me on this team in the first place. You don't want me now. Why don't you just admit it?"[65] Yogi Berra and Jimmy Wynn were standing by to ward off chaos.

With Billy shouting threats, Jackson lost it. "Who do you think you're talking to, old man?"[66]

"What?! Who's an old man? Who are you calling an old man?" According to Martin, something was mentioned about his mother, and so he lunged for Jackson. Elston Howard tried to stop him, but Billy threw him out of the way. Berra managed to contain Martin, though, while Wynn held Reggie from behind.

"You're an old man," Jackson yelled. "You're 49 years old and you weigh 160. I'm thirty and weigh 210. Let me tell you something: You aren't going to do [anything]. What you are is plain crazy."[67] The argument had been presented to Billy many times before, but as the larger man customarily fell crippled to the ground, it was apparent that larger stature could not suppress the force of Martin's right arm.

By this time, one of Billy's assistants, Ray Negron, had finally covered up the NBC camera with a towel. Martin, now held by Lyle, was still screaming at Reggie as the latter wisely bypassed his teammates and walked through the tunnel into the clubhouse. Ready for a fight, he tore his uniform shirt off, waiting for Billy. "He's wanted this fight all season," he told Fran Healy, who had by now come down from the bullpen: "Even before the season, from the day I signed the contract. It's time I gave [him] his chance.... I did not loaf on that ball." He paced anxiously as Healy tried to talk him out of it. "I'm going to stand right here by his office and wait for him." He figured if Billy wanted the fight, it was put up or shut up. But eventually Reggie just gave up and walked away.

That night, Jackson called Phil Pepe of the Daily News, Steve Jacobson of *Newsday*, and the *Times's* Paul Montgomery to explain his version of the incident:

> I charged the ball the way I thought I could play it best. If Martin feels I didn't hustle, I feel sorry for him. You know, in this game, the manager is always right. I'm just a player.
>
> It makes me cry the way they treat me on this team. They treat me like a nigger. The Yankee pinstripes are Ruth and Gehrig and DiMaggio and Mantle. The Yankee Hall of Famers have all been white. I'm just a black man to them, who doesn't know how to be subservient. I'm a black man with an IQ of 160 making $600,000 a year and they treat me like dirt. They've never had anyone like me on their team before.[68]

Jackson went on to theorize that his closeness with Steinbrenner created jealousy on the team. And he was right. Early in spring training, George had invited him to a birthday party at which no other players were welcome. They were insulted that the freshman got in while men who had been with the Yankees a decade (Roy White), since the '50s (Billy Martin), and since 1969 (captain of the team Munson), didn't. They probably wouldn't have wanted to go, of course, but such respect should have been earned by then. Reggie stated further that he did not care anymore about his teammates' feelings. "I'm going to play the best I can for the rest of the year, help this team win if I can, and then I'm going to get out of here!"[69]

Steinbrenner had watched the whole dugout scene on television and stood firmly behind Jackson. "Did you see him?" George shouted at Gabe Paul over the phone, in reference to Martin. "He was ready to kill him. What kind of example is that to set for America's youth?"[70] George leaked to Milt Richman of the Associated Press that night that Martin would be fired and succeeded by Yogi Berra. When Nettles and Munson heard this, they found George to tell him that if Billy was let go, they would quit immediately. Instead, a meeting was scheduled between Martin and Jackson in Paul's suite that night. It solved nothing.

For the record, Boston won on the 18th, 10–4. On the 19th, Figueroa took the match 11–1, and Jackson saw his 14-game hitting streak snapped. The club then flew to Detroit in the night.

The next morning, Steinbrenner flew in to assess the damage. The press knew he was coming, thus the players knew he was coming. Waiting in the lobby at the Motor City's Ponchartain Hotel, reporters interviewed anyone who wanted to talk. It was a zoo. Through the early hours of the afternoon, each man voiced his own opinions. When George arrived, Reggie offered his opinion, to talk him out of firing Billy. "I appreciate you talking to me this candidly," the Boss assured, "and I'll think about everything you said, but my decision has already been made."[71]

Steinbrenner met with Martin in the afternoon. Though George vowed he would let Paul make the final decision, "As far as I'm concerned, you're gone." Men named the Boss don't let others make those decisions. Gabe had pleaded with him to keep Martin, and eventually Steinbrenner gave in. Naturally, he boasted that he had saved the manager's job through his own magnanimous concession. Of course, George is the man Billy was saved *from*.

At about four o'clock, Steinbrenner called Jackson up to the hotel room where he and Martin waited. "Can you play for Billy Martin?" George asked.

"Sure."

Steinbrenner turned to Martin. "Can you get along with Reggie?"

"Yes."

"Then you two meet in the lobby downstairs in a little while and ride out to the ballpark together and go beat the Tigers."[72] Meeting shortly, they split a cab to Tiger Stadium. They discussed the team, but not personal differences. It was a relatively calm ride.

When Martin and Jackson showed up together, it was a shock, and it was a shock that Billy was even around at all. Steinbrenner came later and gave a speech to the team promoting unity, tactful consideration of the club in the media, and the reaffirmation that Martin would be in command for all of 1977. He also held a press conference, going over Billy's contract and restrictions, plus the agreement that Jackson be used flexibly. Steinbrenner ordered more frequent meetings of him and his manager, to include the studying of charts, graphs, and various statistics. Martin was to arrive earlier at the park and submit less (or, preferably, no) criticism to the press.

The ballgame in Detroit was televised on ABC's "Monday Night Baseball," which meant notorious broadcaster Howard Cosell was on duty, a frequent symbol of impending dramatics. It had all the earmarks of another blowup. Yet there wasn't much to speak of. Jackson made a crucial error when he lost the ball in the lights. Martin took his side this time, agreeing that the lighting was difficult. The team lost the ballgame.

On Friday, June 24, the Yankees began a three-game set against the Red Sox. The sweep by Boston a week before had put them at a five-game advantage over New York by this series in the Bronx. Fifty-five thousand fans were on hand to give Billy Martin a standing ovation upon his presentation of the lineup card. It was the first time they had seen him in the flesh since his near-firing. Cat was back on the mound, but he had made no significant improvement and allowed three home runs. But Boston failed to bust the game open at any point, and the score stood only 5–3, in their favor, after eight and a half. The fans were disappointed; they had expected a victorious rebirth. They would be obliged.

Two were out, and Willie Randolph was on base with a triple. Ninth inning, last chance. Bill Campbell was on the mound trying to silence Roy White. But instead White slugged a home run to tie the game up. In the bottom of the 11th, Reggie Jackson laced a pinch-hit single to win it. Reggie was thrilled, and the team celebrated in unison. It was the game that turned 1977 around.

New York completed the sweep by winning its next two; the last game was won on a dramatic Paul Blair single in the ninth inning. The losses sent Boston into a downward spiral of ten games, but more important they pulled the Yankees to within two. At one point in July, the Sox lost nine straight. It was all about the Yankees now.

Having spent only a couple of weeks with the Bronx club, Cliff Johnson bombed three home runs in one game off of the Toronto Blue Jays, two of them in the eighth inning. Despite Baltimore's winning 14 of 16, the Yankees were in first place by the second of July.

Billy Martin was miserable, though. At one point in the season, Steinbrenner called on the dugout phone. After a moment, Billy yanked it out of the wall as George was in the middle of a sentence. One day Munson found him silent on the bench before a game. "Are you all right?" Thurman asked.

Billy nodded. "Yeah."

Thurm was well aware of what was transpiring. "Boy, I wish they'd leave you alone."[73]

Eventually, Martin overcame his silence. He was sick of being threatened with firings, losing money through trivial clauses, and being issued his team's batting orders. "As we spoke," Munson wrote, "tears welled up in his eyes. To avoid having anybody see him so upset, we took a walk around the block until he could clear the air a little. I felt very close to Billy that day."[74]

Munson couldn't stand to be silent, so on July 10 a commentary of his appeared in the papers under the cover of "a prominent Yankee." "George doesn't care about anybody's feelings," he told Steve Jacobson and *New York Times* sportswriter Murray Chass. "He treats everybody like that. He's done something to everybody. He's destroyed Billy. He's made him nothing. Not a single guy on the club is happy, except Randolph."[75] Randolph's happiness, incidentally, was more characteristic than conditional. After making those quotes, Munson[76] then criticized Steinbrenner for making managerial decisions.

Steinbrenner emphatically denied the allegations. "It's a lie. And any player who says it isn't is a liar…. Billy hasn't had one iota of pressure from me about his lineup." He called Martin and ordered a press conference for Billy to unequivocally corroborate George's defense.

Steinbrenner attributed the anonymous quotes to Carlos May, who at the time was entwined in contract struggles and registering above the playing weight. Thurm stepped up to insist it was he who had made the comments. "Carlos wasn't the man! I was! I gave out those quotes, and I believe they're accurate. So stop picking on Carlos."[77] He left thinking it a dead issue.

Lou Piniella was having drink one evening at the Milwaukee Pfister Hotel — or at a lakeside restaurant called Sally's, by Munson's account — on July 12 when Thurman sat down to join him. The two discussed their general disappointment in the club and fear that they couldn't grab the pennant. Fran Healy had just told the two that Jackson was unhappy not to be in the cleanup spot, which Steinbrenner now opposed permitting.

"Why is it so important to him?" Munson wondered.

"Who knows," responded Piniella. "Who can figure that guy?"

"But it is."

"It sure is."

By this time it was 12:30, and they were sipping a new set of drinks. Thurm turned to Lou. "Let's go upstairs to see George." Steinbrenner had flown in specially for the series and was staying at the team hotel.

"I don't think that's our business," said Piniella. "Let things happen the way they are going to happen."

"Lou, George likes you. If you come with me, he'll listen. I think we can help the ballclub. We're not winning, all the guys are angry. Why not discuss it with George? Maybe we can help."

The exchange went on awhile before Piniella relented. "Let's do it."[78]

One of the two knocked on the door of Steinbrenner's eighth-floor suite. He greeted them sleepily in silk pajamas. "C'mon in. Let me get my bathrobe."[79] Munson and Piniella, especially the former, championed inserting Reggie in the four spot. George was receptive throughout. Mulling over the suggestion, he wheeled a blackboard over to his two players. "Rivers, Randolph, Piniella, Jackson," he wrote, "Rivers, Randolph, White, Jackson ... Rivers, White, Chambliss, Jackson." Assessing the possibilities brought out through the insertion of Jackson's bat, he agreed.

Piniella then contended that the club was better than it looked and that Martin was handling it adequately; he just needed to be left alone and not badmouthed in the press. "You've got to get off Billy's back," said Munson. "You're driving him crazy. If you're going to fire him, then fire him. If you're not, leave him alone and let him manage."[80]

Just as he said that, Martin was returning (in the wee hours of the morning) from a long night out. Of course, he was notorious for his excessive consumption of alcohol. In his 1980 autobiography, *Number One*, he steadfastly denied being an alcoholic, but it was common knowledge that such a contention was indisputably false. According to Piniella, Billy was with Art Fowler, his traveling pitching coach who was not to be hired by the Yankees for four more weeks. When Billy heard the secret Yankee conversation as he walked to his room, which was next to Steinbrenner's, he began to pound furiously on the door. "I know you're in there plotting against me."

George looked to his players. "Go in the bathroom, you two. There might be trouble.... I'll take care of the problem."

Billy pushed his way in. "Take your job!" he hollered at Steinbrenner. Storming, he continued over to the bathroom and flung open the door. "Two traitors!"[81]

After awhile, Martin cooled down enough for the four to discuss the team for an hour. Steinbrenner again took to the blackboard, and now wrote the lineups of New York, Baltimore, and Boston to compare batting averages. "Well, what's wrong with the team?" he asked.

"You, George, you're what's wrong with the team." Martin probably so out of it after one of his storied nights on the town that his account of bold bravery, from his aforementioned book, can hardly be taken as gospel. "You're meddling all the time, you're creating problems leaking out stories in the newspapers. When you get mad at a player, you call the newspaper and leak out a story on him. You're the problem. That isn't like the New York Yankees. We don't leak stories and do things like that. That's unlike any Yankee I ever saw in my life."[82]

In a goodwill gesture, Steinbrenner removed the restrictive clauses from Martin's contract; it was a fine and desired reaction. Four hours past midnight, Billy looked over at George. "If you want it, I'll bat Reggie fourth." Wrote Piniella, "We all shook hands and decided finally to call it a night or a day or whatever it was by now."[83]

The following day, Steinbrenner held a press conference to announce he had met with his nemesis and "Billy Martin will manage this club for the rest of the year." He would make the same promise in later years to Gene Michael, Bob Lemon, Michael a second time, Lemon a second time, Clyde King, Billy Martin again, and Yogi Berra. All got early walking papers.

At the next stop, in Kansas City, Steinbrenner held a clubhouse meeting, "a 'pep talk' to get us up for the second half of the season," wrote Munson:

> But it didn't work out that way. He lectured us and threatened us, and finally he jumped on anonymous players who leak things to the press.
>
> Here I had gone to the man on my own and told him I had made the statement. My teammates knew I had done that to get Carlos off the hook. And now, right in front of me and all my teammates, he was making me look like a liar — as though no one had confessed to the quotes! I was stunned.[84]

Munson kept his mental edge despite such soap operas, and by June he felt that he was in line for another MVP. In a close race, Fisk narrowly managed to secure the nomination as starting catcher for the American League All-Star squad. Fisk also beat him in final statistics by a narrow margin: batting average (.315–.308), RBI (102–100), and home runs (26–18). This was not Munson's only frustration. "I really couldn't care anymore," he wrote of his emotional rollercoaster:

> By now, I was more determined than ever to get out of New York.
> The problems at the ballpark made me feel closer to Diana and the
> children, and seek more gratification from my business interests.
> It all added up to my wanting to go home, where I could play ball
> in peace and attend to the things in life that matter to me.
>   I'm not a controversial person. I don't go popping off to the
> press, I don't look for publicity, and I don't create trouble. I'm the
> guy Steinbrenner would turn to when he needed an intermediary
> to settle a dispute with a player. I'm the guy called upon to
> represent the players at the Gullett and Jackson signings. Now,
> suddenly, I'm in the middle of this whole mess.[85]

Alleviating his aggravation, Munson got in as a backup for his sixth
midsummer classic appearance, set for July 19 at Yankee Stadium. Nettles,
Jackson, Lyle, and Randolph also made it, Martin was manager, Monahan
cotrainer, and Ellie Howard and Dick Howser batting practice pitchers; it
was a Yankee affair. The New York fans were rowdy, though the American
League was being easily set down. In the ninth inning, Boston's George
"Boomer" Scott hit a two-run homer to pull the junior circuit close. The
fans even gave him, a Red Sox star, a standing ovation. Munson came in
to pinch-hit for Sparky Lyle, with two out and the Americans' last chance.
With the count 1–2, he made an awkward half swing on a high inside fastball. He had turned with the bat still halfway, by home plate umpire Bill
Kunkel's perspective, in an attempt to obstruct his view. The ump shot
his fist up confidently and rung Munson up. Thurm twirled his bat and
had some words with Kunkel, who remained adamant.

Later that week, Steinbrenner called Munson to express concern over
the wildness taking place on Billy's watch. He didn't think the Yankees
could be a consistent winner under their manager. "Hey," Thurman
answered, "what do you want me to say? It's up to you. Do what you want."
In key foreshadowing, George then asked what, in his opinion as captain,
the players would do if Martin were fired. Thurm envisioned no revolt.
The two agreed to keep the matter confidential. Thurm told only Piniella,
who quickly phoned George with a few choice words.

Steinbrenner first called Walt Alston, legendary Dodger manager, to
offer him the job, but to no avail. Paul called Howard Cosell next to tell
him to wait for a big scoop. The next day Paul turned to Dick Howser,
third-base coach for the club since 1969. Loyally, Dick turned the job down
with a simple "No." Gabe called back Cossell and told him to never mind.
But there were still undercurrents worth great copy, such as a possible
Dick Williams hiring.

Martin found out quickly about Howser's refusal; he could sense his days were numbered. Before the team, he gave a teary speech on the pride and tradition of the Yankees. Most everyone believed it was to be his last address. The club responded with a shutout win. The next day, Billy didn't even bother to dress in uniform. "I feel like those guys on death row," he told the press. "I need a reprieve from the governor."[86] Soon the phone rang. Gabe asked to see Billy in his office; it seemed to be all over. With finality in his countenance, Martin spoke with the writers for a half hour, mostly to complain about Steinbrenner's interference.

After the session, he trudged over to Paul's office. "Am I fired?" he asked, point-blank.

"You're here, aren't you?" Gabe replied.

"But what about tomorrow, next month?"

"You'll still be here. You're the manager."[87] While Billy was relieved, Gabe proceeded to warn him about criticizing Steinbrenner in the press. Of course, he had just spent the previous 30 or so minutes doing just that, and he couldn't keep the comments from being printed. The quotes, the story, it all came out, and two days later George held a press conference. "We have come to a time," he announced, "when for his own good we must demand an accountability of what Martin does and says."[88] The edict came in the form of seven guidelines to gauge the quality of Billy's performance:

1. Does he win?
2. Does he work hard enough?
3. Is he emotionally equipped to lead men?
4. Is he organized?
5. Does he understand human nature?
6. Is he prepared for each game?
7. Is he honorable?

Truthfully, these were a criteria for hiring — not firing — a manager, set up by Gabe Paul in 1973, after Ralph Houk departed. Number seven was the only one added by Steinbrenner to assess Billy more completely.

Munson was disgusted by what he called "public scorekeeping." "I don't like being laughed at," he told a reporter. "When a manager gets seven rules thrown at him, people laugh. The Yankee uniform stands for more than that."[89] The fact that the fans and media could now judge Martin by the same specified standards as management shocked Thurman, and it was even worse that Billy would take it.

Before a late–July series with Baltimore finished, Phil Pepe of the *Daily News* called Munson to ask about a scoop he had just gotten. Apparently,

Steinbrenner had told him of the July 12 meeting, except the Boss—for whatever reason—claimed that Thurm and Piniella had met to *encourage* George to fire Billy. Munson was infuriated.

On the 28th, Senior Citizen Day at the stadium, the Yankees put on a hitting clinic. Torrez started a streak with his 14–2 win over Rudy May. Munson collected three hits in the game, most notably the 100th home run of his career. In apology for the Pepe story, Steinbrenner sent down a magnum of champagne. Thurm thought it was sent because George was afraid of how he would react in the press. With the champagne before him, Martin offered a beer. Thurm opted for the latter.

Steinbrenner called Munson that night to deny that he gave such a story to Pepe. Thurm didn't really believe George and was growing weary of the team's merry-go-round. It was difficult to handle the physical strain of playing and the emotional strain of the Bronx Zoo. Fortunately, it paid off.

Earlier in the season, Marty Appel—Yankee PR director for several years who had just quit to enter a company, along with former Yankee employee Joe Garagiola, Jr. in the business of representing athletes' interests—had approached Munson about writing a book. The idea was clever: he wouldn't open up to a sportswriter, so why not a competent friend? Thurman was hardly enthusiastic. "I'm thirty years old. That's too young for an autobiography. Who'd want to read it anyway?"[90]

Appel contended that the market for a player's story was larger than Thurman thought, and that 30 was by no means young for an athlete. The subject was still not convinced. Then Appel clinched it:

> Look, when you play in New York, when you win an MVP award, when you star in a World Series, feud with Reggie Jackson, fight with George Steinbrenner, and hate Carlton Fisk, someone is going to write a book about you. It will be an unauthorized biography, based on newsclips and conversations with other people. You will have no say in it, you will make no money from it, and it will live forever in libraries as the definitive story of Thurman Munson. If you write your own story, you can look at it as an insurance policy. Once word gets out that you're doing it, no publisher will do a biography to compete with it. You can make it all come out just the way you want it.[91]

(Unfortunately, the book did not turn out to be as definitive as advertised, as will be described later.)

So Appel and Munson spent ten weeks that summer negotiating his life over a tape recorder. Meanwhile, Tracy, Kelly, and Michael ran about the new Munson home in Norwood, New Jersey. The family was finally moved into the mammoth custom-built home, which cost $300,000, made possible through Thurman's contracts and, primarily, his business dealings. Cat, whose nearby house in Norwood was only a fraction of the size of Thurm's, asked why he needed so much room. "Well, I might stay here all year 'round."

"No way, all your business is in Canton."

"I don't know," Munson replied comfortably. "I'm going to make it big enough to do either one."[92]

The following episodes all occurred during one week in August 1977, encapsulating the essence of the Bronx Zoo:

— Cat Hunter and Mike Torrez went on an Oakland radio station to criticize Martin for not establishing a firm and set pitching rotation. Of course, Cat was still having arm trouble, and Gullett and Figueroa were seeing a Los Angeles doctor to have their arms checked out.

— Holtzman called Steinbrenner a fool for paying him so much to let him rot in the bullpen.

— Boston won 11 straight and 17 out of 19, to take over first place by five.

— Billy was rumored to be losing his job in favor of Frank Robinson.

— Gabe Paul issued a statement to the players calling for their attention to seriousness and to play good baseball.

— Steinbrenner publicly apologized to the citizens of New York for the team's losing ways.

— Jackson was exonerated of an assault charge at the All-Star game.

— Munson's average for August held at about .100 with less than ten RBI.

These were all in the same time period. But the week-long headline? The beard.

"Let this walrus off at Sea World," Piniella used to joke about Thurman on the team bus. Back in 1975, Thurm had grown a beard and nobody cared. He liked beards, but Diane detested them, so often on road trips he allowed some stubble. But on this sojourn to the West, he gradually permitted it to grow into a full beard. Instantly, it became a headline, for facial hair was seen as a gesture of open rebellion against Steinbrenner and his policies. Munson rejected such a notion, but in a reported exchange with Gabe Paul, it seems to be true after all. "Thurman, what is all this stuff?" Paul begged.

"He isn't going to tell me what to do."

"All you're making is a lot of turmoil for everybody. For me and Billy, would you do me a favor and get your beard cut off?!"[93]

In addition, Lyle, Martin, Jackson, and Nettles all wrote in their respective autobiographies that they believed this to be a revolt of some magnitude, and with any knowledge of who Thurman was and how he operated, it is doubtful that this did not factor in.

The press was all over the beard "situation." Munson found the media obsession amusing at times, and yet equally enraging. Some speculated that he was doing it in order to frustrate Steinbrenner so much that he'd peddle him to Cleveland. It was annoying the team as well. Billy was talking to *Newsday*'s Joe Donnely and Henry Hecht and got the core question off his chest. "Why is this so big?"

"People want to know about the Yankees."

Like an echo that had reverberated through every distraction of the hectic decade, Martin responded classically, "Why can't you guys just write about baseball games anymore?"[94]

Before the final Seattle game on the seventh, Munson claimed he was all set to shave clean when Bobby Cox, his freshman coach, reminded him that if he did so, the skin would be irritated underneath his catcher's mask. So Thurman decided he would shave for the next day's annual Syracuse exhibition game. After the series finale that Sunday, Billy relayed an order from the top that Munson needed to shave the beard or his skipper would be "in trouble." It especially stung him that the employment of a professional manager hinged on the status of his facial hair. Of course, it truly hinged on principle, but the consequences seemed excessive. A rebel who despised being told what to do, he reversed his prior plans and kept the beard.

Upon arrival in Syracuse, New York, Munson had the aforementioned exchange with Gabe Paul. Reportedly, he told Gabe, "I'll do it for you," in reference to shaving. "But I ain't gonna do it for anyone else."[95] On the other hand, according to Thurman himself, it was a conversation with Diane that was the clincher. "In Syracuse, I talked to my wife on the phone," he wrote. "She was crying. All the stories about my defying Steinbrenner had gotten to her. Diana and the kids are my weakness—if it had moved her to tears, it was time to take it off."[96]

Thurman asked a friend to buy some blades at the hotel lobby. Inevitably, the sportswriters, who shrewdly calculated its recipient, overheard the friend as he bought them. Following up to Munson's room, the scribes asked for permission to watch him shave. It was the final straw. Thurman couldn't believe it. For the rest of 1977, and for that matter '78, his stock reply for nearly all media questions was "I'm just happy to be here." And he was happier, happier than he'd ever been, under the protection of relative silence.

Munson showed up for the game with only his mustache and immediately sought out Martin. "I'm not going to talk to the press anymore," Thurman said.

"Okay," Billy replied, "you don't have to talk to them if you don't want to. Just treat them politely."[97]

"I will."

One of Munson's first remarks to a reporter that day was clear: "Don't even bother coming to my locker."[98]

Martin got great news before the game on August 8. Steinbrenner called him into the office to offer a two-year contract with a raised salary. In camaraderie, Billy even allowed George to choose and write in the figure, which was $90,000. Martin was granted permission to pick up Art Fowler, quite possibly his best friend, as pitching coach. Fowler was a former pitcher who once — while coaching with Billy in Denver — put himself on the mound and surprised all by winning nine games and saving 15 — at 48 years old. He could have easily been named Most Valuable Player of the minor league band, but insisted it be given to a young man. His efforts for the Yankees were undeniable. Guidry went on a winning streak to end up 16–7 as a fill-in. Torrez threw six straight complete games, and Tidrow won five at a time when his elbow was suffering from bone chips. Bottom line, the Yankees won 40 of 50 from the time Fowler joined.

That day, Martin volunteered to bat Jackson at cleanup and play Piniella regularly. After an off-day, the club resumed with a night game against Oakland at Yankee Stadium, where the alterations were executed. Reggie didn't know why the change happened, but was nevertheless pleased that it did. By the time he took over for Chambliss, he had hit fourth but ten times that year. After his permanent insertion, New York won 39 of 49 games played with Jackson in that slot. "As long as he keeps swinging the bat good, he'll stay there," Martin affirmed.[99] Jackson stayed for the rest of the stellar season; he hit .286, smacked 39 doubles and 32 home runs, drove in 110, and scored 93 runs.

A week later on the 16th, brighter stars were shining. Up 9–4 on the White Sox, Guidry and Lyle — an unlikely combination for failure — allowed six runs. But Chambliss burned Chicago with a two-point shot that led New York to an 11–10 victory. Two weeks later, Chris came back with a pinch-hit clout for three runs to beat Kansas City 5–3 in a makeup game. The next match was won on a Mickey Rivers ninth-inning yard job, and Nettles subsequently followed with the same. On August 23, Torrez pitched his seventh consecutive complete game to win the Yankees their

Thurman Munson and Reggie Jackson
in the on-deck circle at Yankee Stadium.
(Courtesy Louis Requena)

sixth of seven away. Overwhelmingly, they swiped first place out of Boston's grasp. The championship looked realistic, controversies were dying down, and Jackson was feeling comfortable.

In addition, Munson's regressive August was wearing off, and he was steadily working toward his goals of a .300 average and 100 runs driven in. Down the stretch run, he went 27–54 (a .500 average) to raise his season mark 20 points from .288 to .308. In that period, he had ten games of two or more hits, plus a hitting streak of 13.

It seemed like a do-or-die situation when the second-place Red Sox came to town on Tuesday, September 13. Fifty-five thousand showed up for the first two games, in which the opener was won by Guidry, 4–2. New York now had a 2½ game lead on its nemesis. That evening, Steinbrenner and Jackson spent some time at "Clarke's" restaurant discussing the team. George looked him in the eye confidently. "I'm telling you right now that you're going to win the game for me…. Have I ever lied to you?"[100]

Come game time, New York City's pulse came straight out of Yankee Stadium: the fans, the press, the citizens. It was a see-saw game. At times, Boston looked as though it had a rally, at times New York appeared to. The threats were just an aberration. A scoreless deadlock through eight was largely in debt to Reggie Jackson, who made two superior catches in right, one off George Scott and the other off Dwight Evans.

Reggie Cleveland pitched a masterful game for the Red Sox and remained on the hill for the ninth. Munson was to lead off the inning and Jackson to follow. Together they stood in the on-deck circle, no media to overhear their conversation, no personal relationships relevant. Their discussion was of baseball.

Munson was glaring moundward. "I'm going to single between short and third."

"Huh?" Reggie said, caught off guard.

Thurman's eyes stayed locked on Cleveland. "I'm going to single between short and third, and then you get me home."[101]

"Deal."

Munson stepped to the plate and cracked a single between short and third. Third-base coach Dick Howser called time to beckon Reggie over. "We may have you bunt," Howser said. "But watch me after every pitch 'cause Billy might change his mind, depending on the count."

"Let me get this straight," Jackson replied in understandable confusion. "You guys want me to *bunt*?!"

"I just give the signs, Reggie. Where's the best place for you to lay one down?"

"I have no idea."

Howser could not repress a smile. "When was the last time you bunted?"

Reggie paused a moment. "1972."[102]

Jackson returned to the plate and quickly drew a 1–1 count. He was given the bunt sign. Cleveland, with a shocked look on his face, delivered a ball. Two balls, one strike. After the sign was taken off, he ended up with a full count. The crowd was wild as Cleveland shot a fastball low. Reggie adjusted deftly to shoot a 430-foot bomb into right-center field, sealing the game at, 2–0. As he ran the base paths, Jackson felt that he'd finally proven the hype and exhibited his true value. Of all the things to be said of him, for certain, he was one of the best to ever perform in the clutch. The crowd was ecstatic, the whole park electrically charged.

Munson was waiting as Jackson crossed home plate. "You done good," Thurman congratulated.

Reggie smiled. "Just following orders."[103]

Though Boston won the final game of the series, New York had clinched the division. According to many, in the closing weeks of the season, starting in mid–August, Billy Martin put on one of the most classic managerial clinics in history, making all the right moves at precisely the right times. The plaguing kinks in the Yankee system were eased out.

With those distractions gone, New York could focus on business. After all, the Yankees had still not closed the race. Munson was getting frustrated, for he believed the club contained too much talent not to make the postseason, regardless of circumstance.

On October 1, Fan Appreciation Day, the skies opened up with rain. The three other divisions had been decided, so the Yankees took the stormy opportunity to watch Baltimore play the Red Sox. Elliot Maddox, now an Oriole, made the game-ending catch to knock Boston out of the race and clinch the decision for New York. With only one more day left in the season, the team was concerned about the regulars, who hadn't much time to rest. That had been the case the previous year, and they had been swept in the World Series.

Kansas City was the repeat opponent in the American League Championship series, having won the West with 102 season wins. The Yankees had proven victorious in but two less, beating the Orioles and Red Sox by 2½. New York's pitching was strong as usual: Gullett (14–4), Torrez (17–13), and Guidry (16–7); the Royal aces were Dennis Leonard (20–12) and Paul Splittorf (16–6). Billy Martin and Larry Gura were still having words, the former suggesting that the latter find protection for his way to Yankee Stadium. A single game makeup in September bothered the Royals, as did, of course, the tough loss of '76. The hype was easily assembled.

October 5 was a beautiful autumn afternoon at the House that Ruth Built, with pennants flapping proudly in the breeze. Many doubted the Yankees in light of their tight squeeze by KC to make it to the World Series the year before, but the club remained confident. Splittorf was effective in his start for the Royals, while Gullett allowed a home run by Hal McRae and left the game after two innings with arm trouble. Tidrow relieved but then surrendered a couple of four-baggers, to John Mayberry and Al Cowens. Munson tried to battle back by continuing his fall excellence with a two-run shot of his own, but those were all the tallies New York could muster in a 7–2 loss.

Gid performed superbly on the mound for game 2, giving up only three hits and striking out seven. In the sixth, Hal McRae broke up a double play at second base with a blatant body block on Willie Randolph. There was a small fight between them as the ball settled in the dust several feet away. With Randolph's attention diverted, McRae flapped his arm violently, encouraging Freddie Patek ahead of him to scurry home. The diminutive, 5'5", 148-pound shortstop hustled to the plate to establish the score at 2–2.

When the Yanks received their turn in the inning, vengeance was theirs. On a close play at third, Munson rose his spikes to the view of hot corner tenant George Brett, precipitating a staredown as the two "looked at each other menacingly," according to writer Bill Gutman.[104] "I slid late just to let him know I was there," Thurm said later. "If I'd have wanted to hit him, I'd have hit him. My argument isn't with George Brett. The guy I want to get is McRae. He better stay away from me. I told him so. He's been trying to hurt people for eight years."[105]

The pair of fouls set the standard for the series as a rough and dirty battle. The Yankees took umbrage with Kansas City's aggression and used this as motivation to push across three runs for a 6–2 win. While New York had ten hits—three by Munson—Guidry permitted only one batter to reach first after the sixth inning. Kansas City manager Whitey Herzog was impressed. "I knew the way the kid was pitching, it was going to be tough to score."[106]

On Friday, the series shifted to Kansas City, Missouri, where three more games—contingent on necessity—were to be played. Dennis Leonard pitched an easy four-hit, one-walk game. Roy White touched him for a couple of doubles, but Munson was shut down, 0–4, and his teammates failed to fare much better. With the Yankees down two games to one, they would have to win two consecutively on the road, in front of an electric citywide opposition that spat on the big-market Yankees in the first place. On top of that, it seemed the pitching was wearing thin.

Ten or twelve of the Yankees got together that evening at Trader Vic's, located in the Crown Center Hotel. Late that night (or in the early morning), Piniella turned to Munson with a fresh perspective. "We're bigger, stronger, more powerful," he reveled.

Thurm agreed. "We have to show some muscle."

"We have to play hard-nose baseball ... do what has to be done to win this thing."

"Let's use our power," Nettles added, "on the bases and at bat."

"This isn't baseball tomorrow," said Piniella dramatically. "This is survival. Whatever needs to be done on that baseball field tomorrow, let's do it. Let's not spare our bodies now."

"Let's show that we are stronger," Thurman proclaimed.

"Let's do it," Piniella concluded victoriously. "We're the New York Yankees!"[107]

The game started early in the afternoon to accommodate a football broadcast. The Royals opened by plating three runs off Ed Figueroa in the first before star catcher Darrell Porter came to bat with the bases packed. He drove the ball a long way to center field, where Mickey Rivers leaped a mile for the inning-ending capture. The outstanding grab saved the Yankees from a dramatic early deficit. Larry Gura was on the mound for Kansas City and Billy handled him perfectly, playing head games with the pitcher so that he wasn't just hungry to win, but desperate. Gura's hopes did not materialize, for the Yankees touched him for four runs on six hits, and he was gone after two innings.

Figgy was relieved in the fourth, and then Tidrow faced three batters but he could not stop the Royals. To most who watched, the series appeared to be over, for the Yankees were out of pitchers. It would be quite strange to bring in the closer in the fourth inning, of course. But since when was Sparky Lyle conventional? Lyle's season was arguably the best by a relief pitcher ever, 13–5, 26 saves, a 2.17 ERA, and nearly two innings logged for each of his league-leading 72 appearances. While warming up in the bullpen, Art Fowler asked the pen catcher, Fred Stanley, how Lyle looked. "Sparky ain't got nothing, Art." Billy called for him anyway, and Sparky warmed. As he did so, the slider finally kicked in. But others were worried for different reasons. Said his batterymate, Munson, "I was kind of afraid after I drove in the sixth run, because Sparky doesn't know what to do with a two-run lead. He gets flustered out there."[108]

Lyle ended up stepping to the mound with a 5–4 score. He shut down the Royals on only two hits, no walks, and no runs over five and a third innings. Fifteen of 16 batters were retired. Mary Lyle followed up on Thurman's theory with a breathless joke to her husband. "I knew you weren't going to lose that game. You only had a one run lead."[109] New York prevailed 6–4. Now it was deja vu all over again, as coach Berra remarked.

Billy was musing in the clubhouse, talking to Steinbrenner, when Cat Hunter crossed by. "Can Reggie hit Splittorf?" Martin asked.

"Not with a paddle," he snorted.

Steinbrenner looked hard at his manager. "You do it, but if it doesn't work, you're going to have to suffer the consequences."

"Fine, as long as if it works, I get the credit."[110]

Jackson was sitting before his locker when Fran Healy bestowed the news that he would be sitting out game 5. Reggie was furious. He felt that his prior clutch performances—despite a 1–14 series—superseded his deficiency against lefties. Holtzie and Catfish, his former teammates, both agreed that Reggie could not hit Splittorf well, while Paul Blair, his replacement, hit about .400 off the pitcher and had a superior glove. Swarmed by the press, Jackson gave a speech that Healy had earlier coached him on. He handled the news like a true professional and was more than cooperative during the game in maintaining a steady cheer from the bench. At one point in the night, he spoke with Martin, who was impressed with Reggie enough to promise him an everyday spot in the lineup should the Yankees advance past Kansas City.

Gid started the game for New York on only two days of rest. Billy was not afraid to pull out all the stops, for he feared that this would be his last game as the team's manager if defeated. Guidry was touched for a couple of runs in the first, but the Yanks had a knack for turning such situations around. The tensions that had mounted between the two clubs came to a head in a play at third base, reminiscent of Munson's earlier run-in of that series, in which Nettles and George Brett engaged in a scuffle. Puff kicked and shoved while the benches cleared and each player picked a "sparring partner." It didn't last long.

The Bombers scored in the third, but Guidry gave up his third run and met the quick hook. Torrez, also with only one day's rest, came on in relief to shut the Royals down through seven frames. A classic outing, but he couldn't have done it without the famously important defense up the middle. Rivers made a long, running stab; Randolph executed a pair of fine plays; and Munson gunned down a potential base thief.

Randolph singled against Splittorf in the eighth to justify the pitcher's removal after seven masterful innings. Munson was up next with the opportunity to do the most serious damage, for he ended up with a .286 mark and team highs of six hits, five RBI, a homer, and three runs in the series. Righthanded relief specialist Doug Bird was called in to assassinate a prospective rally. And so he did — with a strikeout of Munson. Yet he was promptly exchanged for Steve Mingori, who responded by giving up a single. Suddenly, Martin called out, "Reggie, hit for Cliff." Jackson was relieved to appear and desperately wanted a home run. However, he had to settle for driving in Randolph with a single to shave the Royal lead to 3–2.

Mingori was not entrusted with the ninth, so game 3 starter Dennis Leonard took the mound and promptly gave up a single to Paul Blair. White pinch-hit for Dent and walked, which was as good as anything at that point. In desperation, Larry Gura continued the parade of relievers. It was probably the worst way to go about the ninth inning of a pennant clincher, making moves out of desperation. The more sure a manager can be, the more rhythmically he works as the game progresses, the more fluent a team's play and collective disposition. Whitey Herzog did not have that luxury. As the first batter against Gura with men on first and second, Rivers was given the bunt sign, only to foul it off. Billy, remembering how Mickey had refused bunting lessons from Rizzuto in spring training, took off the sign and was rewarded with a hit to tie game 5, 3–3. The Yankee bench cheered enthusiastically. Mark Littell completed the bullpen nexus, still with no outs recorded. Randolph hit a sac fly to drive in White with the go-ahead run. George Brett then made a throwing error to increase the lead by two.

The night before, a writer had asked Lyle if he could pitch for game 5. "Only four or five innings," Sparky laughed. "After that, I might start getting tired."[111] He came on with two out in the eighth inning, and continued through the ninth. Jamie Quirk was retired easily in that frame, but second baseman Frank White reached on a single. As the crowd got rowdy for Freddy Patek, Munson gave the sign for a slider. It was returned as a one-hopper to Nettles. Graig's only notion was to catch it at the chest and throw to Randolph for a double play. It worked. Lyle leaped from the ground with his hands extended high in the air as Munson ran out to embrace him in a hug. The American League champions swarmed him.

Emotions had exhausted them, but the thought of World Series redemption brought Munson and the Yankees back onto the ballfield. They had two days to rest before beginning the World Series with Los Angeles, a powerhouse of a club that had defeated Philadelphia handily in four games. The '77 Dodgers were the only team in history to accrue 30 home runs from four different players— Dusty Baker, Steve Garvey, Reggie Smith, and Ron Cey. Thurm had hoped that Cincinnati would be his opponent in the series, but the Big Red Machine didn't even make the playoffs.

Gullett was a surprise starter for the Yankees, considering his early exit and sore shoulder in game 1 against the Royals. There was no designated hitter in the World Series that year, so Piniella manned left field. Jackson was in right, with Roy White relegated to the bench. Gullett was more excited than necessary, and consequently overthrew at first. The Dodgers took advantage to score two runs, and Tidrow was told to warm up in the bullpen. Munson went out to talk to his pitcher. Confident as he was, Gullett calmed down quickly after the conference, to Thurman's satisfaction.

Munson cracked a single in the bottom of the first, to establish a new World Series record of seven straight hits. Chambliss drove him in with a single of his own to keep the score close. The game was still through five when one of the more important moments of the matchup came. Steve Garvey raced home to score on a close play, but was tagged out by Munson according to Hall of Fame umpire Nestor Chylak. "He was wrong," the Dodger first baseman contended in his autobiography, *Garvey*. "I was safe; Chylak was out of position and could not possibly have seen."[112]

On the hill for Los Angeles was a slick, confident future Cooperstown member, Don Sutton. He was cruising fairly smoothly until Munson doubled to tie the game at 2–2. Sutton was subsequently taken out before New York tacked on a run. Gullett had calmed down considerably and threw eight strong innings before Lyle was called in for the ninth. Lee Lacy singled in a run to even the score, 3–3. Sparky was disturbed by his performance, despite pitching with now-extinct relief durability through the 10th, 11th, and 12th, shutting the Dodgers down all the way. In the bottom of the 12th, Randolph doubled and Munson reached via an intentional walk. Now Paul Blair came to the plate, a man of subdued batting skills but much postseason experience. He had come in for Jackson under defensive considerations and replaced him aptly with a single through shortstop to left field. Game over, a dramatic win.

The story of game 2 was not how the Yankees finished, but who they started. Catfish hadn't pitched in a month and was not in good condition to work the game. The other starters, however, were injured and tired, so Billy made the move to start Hunter. It seems he considered that second game expendable. The writers were all over it with headlines and negative stories. As if that weren't enough, Jackson contributed his two cents with a criticism of Martin to which its subject took offense. Apparently, Cat wasn't too confident himself. "Make sure you watch the first inning," he told his son, "because I may be gone by the second."[113]

Unfortunately for Hunter, he was nearly correct. To highlight the first, Reggie Smith shot a double into right-center field, then Cey followed with a home run to the bullpen in left. An inning later, Steve Yeager hit one to the same general area to make the ballgame 3–0. In the third, Bill Russell, the shortstop, singled before Reggie Smith scored him with a mammoth right-center field bomb. New York had little chance to make up the distance and so they fell, 6–1. It would seem that Martin had failed to trump the Dodgers with a surprise move, but to most, in retrospect, it was another stroke of genius. Heading to Los Angeles for two games, the pitchers were well rested and in a positive mindset.

Prior to the third game, during batting practice, a writer brought up Jackson's scrutiny of Martin for pitching Hunter. Munson responded sarcastically that "Billy probably just doesn't realize Reggie is Mr. October. If I was hitting .167, I wouldn't be second-guessing the manager. And I'm going to stop talking because the more I talk the madder I get."[114] Thurm had just unwittingly birthed Jackson's greatest place in history, as the incomparable "Mr. October."

Torrez, who had spoken excitedly on the plane of signing with Boston in the off-season, put Beantown out of his mind long enough to cruise through nine fluent innings. The Yankees scored five runs off nine hits at the expense of Tommy John through six, and there the score stayed for a 5–3 final. Torrez allowed only seven hits but was not done for the series. Los Angeles was under a lot of pressure, for now it had only four opportunities to win three games.

Doug Rau started for the Dodgers, a quality southpaw who would be lost to rotator cuff surgery in 1979. He was a clever moundsman with a healthy variety of pitches that precipitated a 14–8 record with a 3.44 ERA that season. New York was hitting him all around the ballpark by the second inning, when "Cut me open and I'll bleed Dodger Blue!" manager Tommy Lasorda elected to remove him. But Rau didn't want to leave. "There's a lefthanded hitter coming up," he argued. "I can strike this guy out!"

Lasorda was insulted to be having this disagreement in front of a massive World Series crowd. "Yeah?" he challenged. "Then how come the three runners on base are all lefthanded hitters?"[115] With that, he called in Rick Rhoden. The new hurler threw the rest of the game, but he could not match the opponent. Gid, after some well-needed rest, yielded only four hits. Reggie homered to contribute to a 4–2 win.

Afterwards, the team was savoring a surge of confidence. Munson roamed about the clubhouse singing like a green rookie. "Did I ever say I wanted to be traded to Cleveland?"[116] he laughed. The whole Yankee club was excited, anxious to win game 5 and thus the series, with room to pigpile or reach home plate free of streaming fans to obstruct the celebration.

The Battle of the Dons—it sounds more like a mafia flick than a pitchers' duel. It turns out that the fifth game between Sutton and Gullett was neither one. The Yankee youngster was hit hard and pitched erratically, beginning when fleet Dodger second baseman Davey Lopes led off the game with a triple, and Bill Russell completed the thought with a single.

Entering the seventh, Los Angeles had a 10–0 lead. The Yankees bounced back somewhat to put two runs across in the top of the inning. Reggie Jackson homered in the eighth, and Munson followed with one of his own. As he circled the base paths, Sutton yelled out, "Is that as hard as you can hit it?" Thurman had to laugh; Don was just kidding with him. The two had a mutual, competitive respect. In passing, it must be noted that Reggie's first pitch homer, a steady drive, seemed to be inconsequential at the time, and with all sentiment aside it was. The fans just did not know at the time that this was merely the first act in a historical masterpiece.

Munson sat the ninth, his first inning off in the postseason. Whether he was willing to concede it or not, he was hurting, and the rest would prove valuable. The final score read 10–4 and sent the fall classic back to its most frequented house, a few thousand miles away, in the Bronx.

October 18 was a chilly, serene evening. Reggie Jackson had earlier concluded a McGwiresque exhibition in batting practice. Players and writers stopped to watch in awe as a dozen or two balls were deposited over Yankee Stadium's outfield fences. "Would you do us all a favor," Randolph cackled, "and maybe *save* a little of that?"

Reggie laughed. "There's more where that came from."[117]

A knuckle-curving righthander, Burt "Happy" Hooton, of the same type of moniker as a fat man called "Tiny," was an intense competitor who struck out 19 in a Pacific Coast League game once to match a 66-year-old record. He had also no-hit Philadelphia in only his fourth start with the Cubs in 1971. His opposition that do-or-die World Series night was Mike Torrez, who grudgingly permitted two runs to Los Angeles in the first. The Yankees bounced back when Jackson drew a walk, and they scored two of their own.

LA was up 3–2 through the middle of four. Munson led off with a quick, sailing single toward the left field line at Hooton's expense, extending a string of ten straight World Series games with a base hit. Jackson stepped to the plate. The fans were excitable, their chants in full swing: "REG-gie! REG-gie! REG-gie!" Hooton's opening pitch was up and inside, but the muscular recipient adjusted and brought the business end of his ash club to connect. The ball sailed smoothly on a tight arc to the lower base of the short right field porch for a home run. He jogged the bases confidently and slowed down as he approached home plate. Munson was waiting there with a two-handed slap. He smiled brightly at Jackson, who returned the gesture, and Thurm casually waved him back to the dugout.

After another RBI that inning, New York had cemented a 5–3 edge.

Hooton was relieved in the fourth in favor of Elias Sosa Martinez, a journeyman bullpen worker better known without his surname. With Rivers on first, Munson drove a shallow lineout to center field before Jackson came to bat. After a throw to first base, Sosa shot a fastball over the heart of the plate for the first pitch. Reggie swung and drove another home run to the right side of the outfield. Initially, it didn't look to be much of a power drive, maybe a single or double, although a remarkably solid one at that. Everyone in the ballpark, save Los Angeles, loved the moment. Reggie was mobbed once inside the dugout as teammates clamored to show their gratitude. Munson, already sporting his backwards Yankees cap and trademark orange chest protector, whacked him on the shoulders and shouted congratulations through an unguarded grin.

The stage was set again during New York's side of the eighth inning. The ageless stalwart Charlie Hough was on the mound, at an early stage of his lengthy career. His bread-and-butter pitch was the knuckleball; it was Reggie's favorite too. As was now customary, Jackson was looking for the first pitch. The ball came so that it was not before him but even with his body. Reggie unleashed a lightning-quick cut. He drove the baseball deep into the night, navigating toward the seats of center field, a sector that had been reached just once since the renovation. The crowd was ecstatic. As Jackson reached first base he detected a clap inside the tenant's mitt. Looking up, a smile was on Steve Garvey's face.

"REG-gie! REG-gie!" cheered the patrons, devoted community chanting the pulse of its hometown hero. Overwhelmed with an 11-month exhale, Jackson glided around the diamond, deft as Mercury. Nettles took the on-deck circle in duty, waving his helmet as though the great throng was glorifying him. Like everyone else, he couldn't hold it in; eventually Graig kneeled down to honor Reggie Jackson and his amazing sixth-game classic.

As chaos reigned around him, Jackson returned to the dugout to again be mobbed by the men who had just seen their championship aspirations locked in by his heroics. Amidst the raging waves of "REG-gie!" chants, he leaped to the top step of the dugout, doffed his helmet to the surging crowd, and spun back to his side of the dugout. Behind the midnight blue Yankee helmet he held, the scoreboard read 8–3.

Fans were still wild for the ninth as those in right field sat with their legs dangling over the blue wall. Some threw firecrackers onto the field, forcing Reggie to stop the show again by trotting in for a batting helmet. But the Yankees were so confident in their fate that they had already stored all the equipment inside. Once Jackson retook the field, Mike Torrez caught a soft pop-up for the final out. Munson ran out wildly to hug him before the fans chased the players into the clubhouse. It was the price paid for a world championship.

If anything, the Jackson crescendo healed the wounds that had developed in the previous year, mostly out of appreciation. When Ray Negron pushed Reggie out for a curtain call after completion of the trifecta, his teammates were just as honored to be a part of it as any fan in any row of Yankee Stadium. Back in the clubhouse, Munson put his arm around Mr. October. "See, I knew what I was doing when I gave you the nickname, you big coon."[118] This time Reggie accepted the joke; the relationship between New York's star and New York's captain had finally reached a comfort zone.

The celebration was a mob scene. ABC and Yankee broadcaster Bill White pushed through the crowd to interview Jackson. "How do you feel?" White asked.

"Great — but I'd like to thank all the people who stuck by me the whole year, friends in New York, Arizona, and Oakland. And I want to thank God for everything that happened tonight."

"Now come on, Reggie," prodded White. "Quit with the commercials and tell us how you really feel."[119] Munson did not believe White was fair in his line of questioning either, for the future league president interrupted Thurm's ecstasy to ask for comment on a possible trade to Cleveland. He declined and went on celebrating.

Reggie dove into Martin's office where the two, oil and water, compromised and drank some champagne. As famous as Billy's managerial career was, this proved to be his first and last World Series championship as skipper. In fact, Jackson was the only regular who had previously recorded one. For team members Roy White and Thurm Munson, 22 years of pinstriped service between them, nirvana had been a long time coming.

9

KEEPERS OF THE FLAME

Baseball is 90 percent mental. The other half is physical.
— Yogi Berra

Munson, if anything, had improved on his 1976 season. He had bested his MVP year in nearly every substantial category, save decreases from 186 hits to 183, 105 ribbies to 100, and 14 stolen bases to five. His defense was noticeably better; less errors, less past balls, 111 more putouts. His handling of the pitching staff was textbook, despite the difficulties of dealing with an ever-changing, injury-plagued staff. Ron Guidry's successful entry into the rotation was a pleasant surprise, and he would often give credit to Thurman for making him such an effective moundsman. In addition to his 18 home runs, Munson's .308 batting mark and 100 runs driven in made for three years straight of .300/100. That had not been done by any American Leaguer of any position since 1954.

Thurm batted .320 against the Dodgers, with eight hits, a homer, three batted in, and four scored. He might not have been the straw that stirred the drink, but he sure was an ingredient. His importance to the Yankees seemed unquestionable. But what of Thurm's leadership? Wrote Roger Angell in his classic baseball rhapsody, *Late Innings:*

> I visited the Yankees after many games last summer, but I rarely stayed long, because it was the most joyless clubhouse I had ever been in. In time, I became sorry for them all, and it even occurred to me that this rich and favored team was terribly unlucky, because it didn't seem to have a true leader — one carefree or charismatic veteran who could laugh at all this once in a while and suggest to the other players that they were young, after all, and that what they

171

were engaged in was, for them if not their glum employers, still a game.[1]

Munson, in fact, could not create that facade. Despite his championship and all the season's treasures, he was miserable in the New York stable. "I can't go through another year like this, no way," he exhaled in October. "The Series is going to hit me in a couple of days. But I was happier when we won the playoffs, just because of all the stuff we've been through and being under the gun all the time. I'm tired now. I'm happy it's over."[2]

In some ways, though, the game was only just beginning. November 21 has forever been a historic day in baseball: the one on which Stan Musial and Ken Griffey, Jr., were born (a half century apart, both in Donora, Pennsylvania), and the one on which New York Giants' teammates Carl Hubbell and Mel Ott died. For the Yankees in 1977 it was a day to celebrate the signing of Rich "Goose" Gossage. Goose was a fireballing All-Star who spent the 1972, '73, and '74 seasons with the White Sox, posting an altogether nondescript performance. In 1975, Chicago gave him his first real chance and he responded in kind with nine wins and 26 saves. The Sox got overly exuberant at the sight of his talent by placing the young find in the starting rotation. He failed with a 9–17 record, and had started his last game. Converted to a full-time closer after being traded to Pittsburgh in 1976, a sparkling 1.62 ERA helped him to 26 saves and 11 wins against nine losses. Goose capitalized on that by going the free agent route and collecting $2.75 million over six years from the Yankees.

Lyle felt betrayed. After he unexpectedly won the Cy Young Award, Steinbrenner had signed him to a contract extension that, for him, was usually negotiated in the spring. It was now obvious to him that his early signing (which was held off until spring training) and volunteered pay raise was a ploy to get him under contract before he felt unwanted by Gossage's addition. Goose was a rising star in his midtwenties; Sparky was 34 and the defending Cy Young Award winner. Something had to give. Logically, there was no way both of them could get satisfactory work. "That's baseball," Lyle told his wife. "They can do with you anything they want."[3]

New York paid $100,000 in mid–December for the right to sign Atlanta's Andy Messersmith. The previous season he had been inked to a three-year, $1 million pact after throwing 20-win performances with the Dodgers. In 1976, though, he was victorious in 11 before sustaining an injury at midseason. For the Yankees, he dazzled the club in spring training, but ended up injuring his shoulder. Messersmith made only six appearances in '78, before trying, unsuccessfully, for a comeback with the

'79 Dodgers. His signing came on the heels of Rawly Eastwick's, a wacky reliever from the Cincinnati Reds. The latter acquisition, for $1.1 million, was beginning to annoy the proven Yankees making far less money. Summarily, the bullpen began to feel rather cramped, and tension in the Yankee camp was growing.

As the Yankees continued with their additions, there seemed to be significant subtractions on the horizon. Back in Canton, the house that Thurman and Diane had been building for years was completed. "My three children are in school here," he once said of Canton, "they have their friends and my wife and I have our friends here. This is where I grew up. I'd like to be here as much as possible."[4] Thurm hoped the new year-round home would provide stability for his family, a secure and rooted foundation. In order for such an atmosphere for him and his family to be complete, Munson wanted to play for the Indians of nearby Cleveland. "Cleveland was an attractive place for me to play ball," he wrote in his autobiography, on which he and Marty Appel finished collaboration early in 1978. "I don't need to play in a glamour city. I don't seek publicity and, in fact, haven't received it. I care about my family, I care about business interests, which provide security for my family, and I care about getting a good contract from my baseball employer."[5]

But such a transfer seemed implausible. Commented Gabe Paul when asked of it by a reporter, "I understand his desire to be near his home. But we would not entertain any thought of trading Thurman Munson unless the Yankees could benefit from such a transaction. It would be pretty hard to do that."[6]

Many mocked Munson for electing to play for Cleveland, a depressive pit of baseball failure at the time. He wanted not only to be close to home, but also to get away from the stress of New York, as a city and as a baseball club. Thurm knew the Yankees wouldn't let him go. At one point in the year, a rumor was hot around the league that he would be traded to Pittsburgh for burly slugger Dave Parker. Steinbrenner took a look at it, but Martin told him frankly, "George, there's no way we can part with Munson."[7] It was apparent that New York had no plans to relinquish Thurman, and over the winter he considered whether to quit or go back. Some thought it was all a ploy for extra money, but if so he would have been volunteering himself for months of repetitive questioning by the media, which is quite inconceivable.

The method worked, slowly but eventually. By March, Munson decided to charge forward as a Yankee, and so in spring training he and George came to an agreement on an exceptional contract. Thurman was pleased with the owner, and went so far as to declare that the good handling he received superseded all prior contractual misgivings. The pact ensured that he would be a Yankee player through 1981 unless any unforeseen occurrence — trade or otherwise — took place.

In order to compensate for Munson's continued service in New York, away from home, he studied for and earned a pilot's license over the winter. He took flying lessons throughout spring training in Fort Lauderdale, and flew all over the state. At times Lou Piniella came along, and he took note of how impressed the flight instructor seemed to be with Munson's skill, a result of diligent practice and many hours at his locker poring over aviation magazines. By applying the same vigor to flying as he did to baseball and business, he soon began piloting Piper props before purchasing a twin-engine, six-seater Beechcraft Duke. Using this, Thurm could now fly from New York to Canton in the same time as fighting the gridlock back to Jersey, an hour or so. Taking that route became a habit throughout the year. Fortunately, he was cautious about flying. Whereas usually he had a few beers with Nettles after the game, Thurm would not touch alcohol before taking off. Soft drinks sufficed. Diane hated the idea of flying, no matter what precautions were taken. "I tried to get him to stop flying," she later said. "I was frightened. It just wasn't worth it."[8]

Reggie Jackson owned a plane, too, more for business than for recreational purposes. He and Munson often found a common ground in discussing this. Reggie saw nothing wrong with owning an aircraft, but as for operating it, he used to tell Thurman jokingly, "Get yourself an old World War II pilot. Make sure he's wearing a leather flight jacket. Buy him a white scarf. Just check him out first and make sure he's learned to fly everything since Wilbur and Orville." With a smirk glimmering brightly, Thurm laughed, "I like to fly myself."[9]

There are plenty of reasons why Munson flew: he was a thrill-seeker, enjoyed expensive possessions, wanted to see his family more often. But in the end, it was all as simple as what he told Catfish Hunter: "You get up there and nobody asks you any questions."[10]

For years Munson had forsaken an extended career by sacrificing his body in order to help the team. By the spring of 1978, the noble choice had caught up with him. His feet, legs, and knees chronically plagued him, making his receiving role increasingly difficult to pursue.

Munson, along with his fellow catchers and the pitchers, arrived for spring training on February 21, and if Thurm thought that he had it rough, imagine when he saw the pitching staff. Gid was weak from a bad bout with bronchitis over the winter months; Cat was still reeling from an explosion in his hometown of Hertford, North Carolina, which nearly killed him; and Holtzie had a miserable spring. Steinbrenner wanted to trade him, but

Kenny's no-trade clause allowed only for transfers to Milwaukee or Chicago. The staff was shaky, needless to say, and there were as many unsure spots as steady ones. Tidrow, Hunter, Figueroa, and rookies Ken Clay and Jim Beattie were all possible starters. Gullett was a wait-and-see situation because of his bum arm. At least Gossage was around to pick up the slack if the early pitchers faltered.

For those who haven't looked it up yet, the man who was the last American Leaguer before Thurman Munson to hit .300 and bat in 100 runs for three consecutive seasons was Cleveland's Al Rosen (1952, '53, and '54). He was also the man who replaced Gabe Paul in New York.

In the winter of 1977–78, Gabe had planned to retire after logging his first championship in October, when his friend Steve O'Neil, who was preparing to buy the Indians, vowed that he would not go through with his purchase unless Paul was there to direct the organization and receive partial ownership. He accepted reluctantly to embark on a tenure in Cleveland that was to last through the bleak mid–1980s. Martin told the writers in spring training, "Gabe just got in the way. I won't have any problems with George anymore because I can deal with Al Rosen. He's a baseball man. He understands me. Gabe didn't understand me."[11] True to character, Gabe did not retaliate nor mute his support of Martin as manager.

Support was not contagious among former Yankees that season, as Thurm Munson discovered when he opened the newspaper on March 7. Mike Torrez, who had signed with Boston in the off-season for $2 million, had told writers that when Munson was in a slump, he lagged behind the plate. Hurt and insulted, Thurman asked Cat if he were doing poorly, "You would have told me to my face, wouldn't you?"[12] Hunter seemed to avoid the question, but gave no heed to Torrez's stab. Lyle dismissed the theory as well.

After a spring in which the Yankees as a whole were lagging, the club opened on April 8 in Arlington. Over seven innings, Gid gave up a single run, but his club could only match that. Gossage entered in relief in the eighth and an inning later faced Richie Zisk, a muscular slugger renowned as the "Polish King of Baseball." Two fastballs blew by for strikes before Goose inserted a slider, which Zisk jacked out of the park to beat New York.

Later that week, Holtzman pitched beautifully and held Milwaukee to one run. Gossage, either oddly sentimental or unadvisedly habitual, put two strikes on Larry Hisle with heaters only to surrender a home run on the slider. Lyle sat in the bullpen all the while, his grumblings increasing. "Tell them to trade me back for Danny Cater," he told the press.[13]

Before Reggie had come to New York, he was asked how he would fare in an alternate location. "If I played in New York," he responded, "they'd name a candy bar for me."[14] The quote became so well known that by the Yankee home opener on April 13, 1978, Standard Brands had patented the Reggie Bar. The profits from the sales were to benefit children, in part to buy them seats at Yankee Stadium.

Forty thousand were present that day in the Bronx when each fan was given a free Reggie Bar at the gates. Jackson came up in the first with two men on and pulled a liner to right that cleared the fence. As he circuited the bases, a couple of Reggie Bars—in round, orange wrappers—crossed the white of the plate before Reggie himself. Taking a moment to let that sink in, soon orange saucers flew from all corners of the stadium, littering the field. Time out was called as groundskeepers picked them up and ten or so kids hopped over the barriers to grab handfuls at a 25-cent profit for every one. Some even found their way into the bullpen. Holtzman picked one up and almost spat it out at the taste.

"It must be a great tasting candy bar if they throw it instead of eating it," laughed genial Chicago skipper Bob Lemon. "They should advertise it as the candy bar to throw."[15]

Joked Catfish that day, "When you unwrap a Reggie Bar, it tells you how good it is."[16]

They were done laughing the next afternoon when Steinbrenner volunteered his players for a charity luncheon on what was their off-day. As legitimate and commendable the cause, the ballplayers had few gaps in which to spend time with their families over the course of a hectic schedule. In Nettles's case, his wife was pregnant and had to be rushed to the doctor. He, Lyle, Munson, and Rivers all skipped the mandatory occasion. When the reasons came before Rosen, he was anything but receptive. Instead, each of the four were fined $500.

Rivers was so discouraged that he went on an angry tirade. "There's always something hanging over this team," Mickey complained, "and it's the front office. They wonder why we can't win with all this stuff."[17] Munson and Nettles were especially incensed. Both agreed not to play in the April 15 contest against Chicago. Thurman could back it up—he had a disturbing cyst behind his left leg that intensified when he squatted to catch. Puff just said he had the flu. "I've played when I'm sick," he lamented, "but they think so little of me now, why should I play when I don't feel good?"[18] Munson and Nettles did not reveal why they truly missed the game, for if they did, Steinbrenner would surely blame Billy for not controlling his men.

Rivers drove in two and scored one off the White Sox, accounting for all the Yankee runs in a 3–2 win. Nettles retained his biting humor after the game. He told the writers, "If they want someone to play third base,

I'm ready. If they want an entertainer, they can hire Georgie Jessel." (The next day, he received a telegram from Jessel. "Thanks for getting my name in the paper," it read.) As he sat with Lyle, Graig warned, "You better not talk to me any longer. You're liable to catch the flu."[19]

The pitching staff seemed to have contracted a case of mediocrity, especially Hunter. Cat had been shelled in his first start of the season (six runs, six hits over two innings, though his arm was allegedly fine). In his second, the line differed minimally: five runs, six hits, 4⅓ innings. Gossage came on for his third appearance and gave up a homer to Baltimore third baseman Doug DeCinces. The next batter was Rick Dempsey, whose head avoided Goose's mean heater by a matter of inches. He fell, encouraging manager Earl Weaver to put forth his best impression of a sprint to get out there. He wanted a warning for Gossage, but the umpire refused. Munson stood to the side, detached from the argument. Eventually, Weaver turned to him to promise, inexplicably, "I'm going to get you."[20] Apparently, he thought Thurm had called for the brushback.

When Martin heard the threat he rushed out to scream his unedited opinion, and in doing so, flipped Weaver his middle finger. Earl had to be restrained by Frank Robinson. Had it not been for Robbie, there would have been quite a fight. As far as Billy was concerned, that offer was still on the table if the Orioles retaliated.

Martin was still steaming a few days later in New York, upset now with the failing club. He held a meeting to air his complaints. "When I was playing, no one was making the money you guys are making, but whatever we were playing for, we enjoyed playing." Billy threatened that if the team did not improve, restrictions would be so tight that they'd be living on the edge. He felt the players were not particularly moved by losses and fooled around afterwards. "If you have anything to get off your chest, do it now. If you don't like me, it's tough. If you don't agree with what I'm doing, if you don't want to play, I'll make it miserable for you." The warning soon evolved to an agonizing point of anger. "I'll fight one of you," Billy screamed, "I'll fight all of you!" Wisely, no one responded. They heard the crack in his voice, his ultimate sign of fury.[21]

The next night, Billy was asked if the speech had helped. "I guess so. We only left eighteen men on base."[22]

The frustration continued with a 3–1 loss to Minnesota on April 29. At one point, an impatient fan almost provoked Thurman into a fist fight over an autograph. It was an odd twist on normalcy, for Munson had a rather solid relationship with the patrons, at least in New York. However, there was a home game in '76 when he mistakenly hurled the ball into center field to allow Don Baylor to score. After a strikeout the following inning, fans near the dugout were brutal. In a weak moment, Thurman made the infamous "obscene gesture" (so perfectly executed by Martin above) in the direction of the group. He came to regret that absence of class and was greatly surprised when he stepped into the batter's box the next day to receive a grand ovation. Whether or not the people agreed, they understood and forgave him.

Martin was still in an ornery mood by mid–May after having to chew out Johnson for jawing with an umpire behind the plate and scolding Rivers for not running out a groundball on consecutive days. "I want a guy out there who tries," Billy complained. "Mickey says his leg hurts, so until he tells me he can play, he'll sit on the bench."[23] That promise was retracted quickly, for Rivers was in on the 14th to lazily jog after a fly ball with the score 9–9 toward the end of the game. He made a lackluster flip of the ball instead of trying to gun the runner down.

While walking up the runway, Piniella caught up with Martin. "Why don't you bench him," Lou said, according to Billy, "so we can win this thing?! We don't need a guy like that playing."[24] While Billy mulled that over, he also took the opportunity to hold a punishing meeting in the club-house. He was sick of seeing the low effort that in his heyday could only be excused by paralysis. "Yeah, you guys sit in the back of the bus and play your tape recorders and laugh" he screamed wildly, "ha, ha, ha, ha..."

That night, the Yanks took a commercial flight to Chicago for a set. In Billy's autobiography, he claimed that a flight attendant told him that some of his players—as it turns out Piniella and Rivers—were causing a ruckus in the aisle. Martin went to straighten them out, and parted with a harsh glance at Piniella. "Why don't you tell [Rivers] what you told me going up that runway?"

At that point Munson came up to inquire of Piniella, "Is Billy mad at me? You mad at me, too, Skippy?"[25] And nothing more amounted of that but a small fit of tense voices. If that is the case, then Sparky Lyle has one inordinately erratic imagination. His account of the incident—written presumably within hours of it in his diary of the 1978 season, *Bronx Zoo*—contradicts Martin's:

According to Lyle, Holtzie, Chambliss, Piniella, and Rivers were playing cards in the back of the plane of about 200 passengers when Billy stormed over to Lou. "You're always going on about how this should be done and that should be done," Martin snapped, "and then you turn around and sit and play cards with the guy who is screwing up."

"Billy, I didn't do anything," Piniella responded. "I didn't lose the game."[26] To the players it was obvious that Billy's anger was being directed at the wrong person, that he was just waiting for Rivers to jump in so Billy could get out his frustration on the man with whom he was really upset. When Mickey held his tongue, Martin headed back in disgust.

The players were fed up themselves. They felt that if Billy had something to say to Rivers, why make a big scene chewing out Piniella?

The coaches all sat in first class, while the players rode in coach. Munson relaxed in the front of his section playing his tape recorder, which traveling secretary Gerry Murphy had specifically prohibited. Thurm kept pulling the earphone in and out so the music could blast for a few seconds and then be silent. It's unclear whether he was doing this to be rebellious because of the injustice of Martin's actions and the ban on tape recorders or just to kid around with his occasionally playful manager. With Thurman it could easily be either one.

When the plane landed, Munson rose to get off. Billy stopped him to rant about him acting as a better influence. The two argued until Thurm shouted, "The only reason you're saying this stuff now is that there are nine guys between us." It came off wrong. He had only meant to point out that Billy's drinking, which had grown increasingly harmful, was making him say things he didn't mean and wouldn't commit to. Billy took it to be antagonistic and went for blood. As coaches restrained him, Thurman just shook his head, laughing at what had happened. Again, his actions may have been misplaced, for this only ignited Martin's temper further.

After stepping off the plane, nobody knew what to expect. Fortunately, the coaches took Martin in a taxi while the players caught the bus.

Munson was indignant the next day in Chicago. He was so upset that he didn't even want to play. "Screw it," Thurm spat. "I'm not going to do it anymore if that's all the man thinks of me about what I've done…. Hey, if the man doesn't think enough of me to give me a little respect, when I don't feel like playing from now on, I'm not going to. Just because he's in the sauce doesn't mean I have to listen to him yell at me."

Martin had been in the sauce as of late and was showing up more and more often with large sunglasses to hide the redness of his eyes. During better times, when Thurman saw Billy with them on, he'd exclaim, "Here comes our little Martian!" Now the same cast did not have the same sense of humor.

That Monday in Chicago, Billy called Munson in to apologize. According to Martin's recollections, Thurm started it off. "Skip, I wasn't trying to yell at you."

"I know it, Thurman, but your timing was wrong. I was mad at somebody else, and you come up agitating me. That has nothing to do with you."

"I wouldn't do anything in the world to hurt you," Munson said. "You know how I feel about you."

"I love you, too, pal, but your timing was off, that's all."

Munson in one of his more relaxed stances in the dugout at Yankee Stadium as he prepares to put on the tools of his trade. (Courtesy Louis Requena)

The Yankees' collective timing wasn't too great. Cat had a terribly sore arm, Tidrow hurt his thumb, and Gullett was still on the DL. Injuries abounded, but the worst was Billy Martin's. He was seriously ill and nearly passed out during a game. Doctors tried to get him to the hospital, for they were concerned that he suffered from heart problems. But Billy foolishly refused. He was not speaking to the team. He was reclusive and weak. The fellows knew something was wrong, though not until May 20 did it really hit.

When the players walked into the clubhouse and passed by the trainer's office, they could easily see Billy as he lay on the table, half dead. He was developing ulcerlike sores because of his drinking, and later revealed to Nettles in confidence that a test had shown a spot on his liver. The players were concerned, especially because they knew that the excessive drinking was largely due to the pennant race, in which Boston was beating the Yanks handily. New York was playing well, though, and not many games separated them from the Red Sox.

One important reason for their success was the improved pitching; Gid had struck out 11 and defeated Cleveland to go 6–0 on the season, 16–1 dating back to a point in 1977. But then Catfish hit the disabled list again. A month later he was throwing the ball around with his son, Todd, in the backyard when his wife Helen suggested, "Why don't I pitch and you go and play the outfield?"

"Why?"

"Cause I throw harder than you now."[27]

Cat knew where the lines were drawn. The next day he had his shoulder manipulated by a doctor. It worked unexpectedly well, so he entered the rotation as July rolled around, then went 10–3 from that point on.

Despite all the injuries, feuds, and general chaos the Yanks were only three games down in the division after a 23–7 month. In a game on the final day of the month, May 31, Nettles booted a grounder, and the batter went on to steal second. Figgy bounced one wild pitch, then another. As the runner came in to score, Munson strained his knee badly while chasing after the ball and was expected to be out for a couple of days.

Throughout the tumultuous season, what kept the Yankees breathing were Hunter, Gossage, and Guidry. All three separately gave credit, though, to Munson as the pulse. He was like a father figure to the team. In fact, during the month of May, he was awarded the Baseball Father of the Year honor. But the season had a mounting group of negatives. Late in May, he had only hit one home run, and nearly all of his stats were far off pace.

Munson had said that if he became a handicap to the team, he would ask to be removed. That time seemed to be impending. As he eased out of his prime, Thurman had horrible pain, but rarely spoke of it. The fans knew; some were sensitive, while others yelled out jeers that he was old. That really disturbed Thurm. No matter how much his body ached, Munson still ran out every groundball, even at times when he could scarcely bend. Calmly, wearily, he'd rest his knees in the dugout and slowly take off his catching equipment.

On the positive side, Munson was finally getting along with the press. It's not that the two sides finally agreed or even liked one another — "I'm just happy to be here" was still the stock quote he gave the writers. But they communicated, even if it were exclusively through pleasantries and light conversation. That's how it stayed, and Thurman was so happy with the new arrangement that he didn't mind staying in New York a few more years. No more questions, less controversy; Thurm was actually enjoying baseball again.

Early in the year Munson was asked to star in a commercial for Williams' 'Lectric Shave, which boasted the slogan "Not just another pretty face." According to attorney Bob Woolf, Thurm was ecstatic to be playing a national role. "It was the first one he had ever done and he was proud about it," Woolf remembered. "He'd found out all the times it was going to be on and called all his friends to tell them to watch."[28]

So excited was Munson that he named a chapter in his book "Eat

Your Heart Out, Fisk!" in reference to having finally done a commercial as Carlton Fisk had done. The book's final proofs were pored over in July and came out later in the year. Entitled simply *Thurman Munson*, it was a nice book, not a terribly detailed one in many areas, not flashy or exaggerated, almost nondescript, as was Thurman's way. It wasn't just a "dumb jock" book, which was vital to him. It was important to him to be remembered as a 1970s player, for Munson saw that as the decade when athletes first brought their images out of a stereotyped shell and asserted themselves as intelligent professionals, independent, industrious, successful. His last paragraph in the book read:

> If I can be remembered as a "player of the '70s," I'll be proud. I'd like to think that today's players have left the ranks of the dumb jocks and become well-respected individuals, able to fend for themselves in the free enterprise system.[29]

Other chapter titles are "A Mike Garcia Autograph," "On the Road: The Saga of a Season," and "The Talented Mr. Bench." He was evasive in several areas, particularly his childhood. When Marty Appel was at the Munson home, Diane told him of random incidents, such as the day Thurman signed with the Yankees. Thurm's unguarded venture into that subject didn't come until the last chapter:

> When I was a boy and my father was gone a lot, we didn't have the closest of families. I didn't realize at the time that his absence bothered me, but today I'm sure a lot [of] my feelings for a close family stem from those early years. I know I'm not the only guy in the world whose occupation keeps him away from home, but I can't help it if it bothers me more than others.[30]

An old spring training quote of Billy's came out in the *New York Times* on June 1, criticizing the big-money free agents he dubbed "George's boys." Steinbrenner told Martin's agent, "If Billy made these comments about me, he's gone. And if Chass wrote these comments out of context just to antagonize me, we're going to ban him from the clubhouse."[31] After a couple of weeks, an article came out from a "reliable source," one of Steinbrenner's constant covers, complaining that the Yankees were falling apart under Martin's tutelage. It was not all Billy's fault, since the club was racked with destructive injuries.

The DL started to unload in June, though. White, Jackson, Messersmith, and Gullett returned from injuries. With those four back on the roster, some had to go. Holtzman, though healthy, was put on the disabled list to clear room. He was so livid he threatened a lawsuit. That same day

Rivers tried to attack Reggie over a misunderstanding. As is not difficult to imagine, the team did not have its focus and lost the game. Boston won to raise its lead to 4½ over New York.

On June 10 in Anaheim, Munson braved a foul tip off his throat and was forced to leave the game. Rookie Mike Heath — a strong, anxious bull of a catcher — was then dazed by a couple of collisions in the game. New York was being hit from all sides. Their offense was suicidal: they got on base but died on the base paths. For the three-game series against the Angels, the Yankees stranded 27 men, one for each inning. The distance from Boston grew to six games and there was talk of deals, including one involving a starter and two young pitchers for Minnesota's Rod Carew.

A day before the trading deadline, some deals actually went through, such as Rawly Eastwick to Philadelphia for the equally wacky Jay Johnstone. Del Alston and Mickey Klutts were shipped to Oakland for Gary Thomasson. After all, the Yankees were short on lefties; they only had Nettles, Rivers, Jackson, Johnstone, Brian Doyle, and Jim Spencer! Roy White was to be sent to Oakland had he not used the ten-and-5 rule, a veto power given to ten-year veterans who have spent 5 years with their current team. Holtzman finally got his transfer, returning to the Cubs for Ron Davis, a future star reliever for New York. In the wake of Holtzie's departure, a new player rep had to be elected, and it was Reggie Jackson.

Amidst all the commotion, the Yankees were a bigger story on the ballfield. Gid was on fire when he scorched the Angels on June 17 at the stadium. Before the game, he told Lyle he had nothing and looked to be correct when California led off with a double. The number two hitter went down with a strikeout. The next man was barely retired and Guidry Ked another batter to end the inning.

Five had been mowed down on strikes when Joe Rudi came to bat and registered two misses. Gator rang him up on a 96-mile-per-hour fastball to the fans' ballistic response. As they grew stronger, so did Guidry. He struck out the side in the fourth, fifth, and sixth. The 15th came against Brian Downing to close the seventh inning and tie Bob Shawkey's 59-year-old Yankee record, which was broken with the eighth frame's leadoff victim. By inning nine, Gid was shooting to tie Steve Carlton, Nolan Ryan, and Tom Seaver for the major league one-game record. To do so, he'd have to K the side again.

With 16 to his credit, Guidry took care of Rudi once more and another for 18. Don Baylor lined a single to center field, then Ron Jackson stepped to bat. He shot the ball toward third. Tough luck. Nettles snapped his body over and stabbed it for the final out.

Munson had been kidding Guidry earlier in the week that he shook

Thurm off just to show who was boss. After the 18-strikeout performance, Thurman wasn't so sure who the boss was. Gid was a bit dejected not to have caught a 19th victim. "That's all right," Munson comforted, "you can't do everything in one night; you have to save something for next time."[32]

"He'll strike out more than nineteen," Martin assured confidently. "I'm sure of it. It's just a matter of time."[33]

Nolan Ryan was watching the whole show from his perch in the California dugout. Remarked the eventual Hall of Famer, "The entire bench was laughing because we felt we were overmatched."[34]

During the game, Phil Rizzuto noticed a sign calling Guidry "Louisiana Lightning." Scooter kept up the nickname and soon it became Gid's standard moniker. His fame in New York came to the point where on every two-strike count, the audience would stand on their feet and cheer madly; if he failed, they booed mercilessly. That tradition lasted until the end of the twentieth century in ballparks across America.

After losing two straight to Boston, the Yanks were at a crossroads in the season. "I know we're playing bad and we have a lot of injuries and our pitching staff is hurting," Martin said at a team meeting in Detroit. One could just feel the optimism swell as his inspiration poured forth. "Just go out there and play as aggressively as you can, and let whatever will be."[35]

Munson appeared to have taken Billy's exhortation on aggressiveness to heart. Umpire Jim McKean rung him up on strikes at one point in the game, so Thurman bumped him in anger. It incurred a suspension, which didn't kick in until June 28, six days later. In the face of his loss, Jay Johnstone took it upon himself to procure a watermelon, draw on facial features and sideburns, put on a hat, and round it out by fitting "Thurman" for a pair of spikes. Placed next to Munson's uniform shirt and mitt, the players marveled in laughter at their new teammate.

The Yankees swiped three out of four games in the Motor City, yet lost a game in the standings. "We're 29 games over .500, and that means we could play .500 ball the rest of the season and still have 95 wins," Don Zimmer remarked, manager of a Boston team that was in the process of winning 14 of 16 games. "Maybe that won't be enough, but I guarantee you we won't play .500 ball the rest of the way either."[36]

Zimmer and his Sox came to the Bronx on June 26. It was a last breath chance to dispel the Red Sox after racking up an eight-game deficit. Once play started, Butch Hobson reached on a middle infield error, and Jim Rice knocked his opponents out with a booming home run.

The powerful outfielder did that a league-leading 46 times that year.

He reached a .315 batting average on 213 base knocks, plus had 139 runs batted in, 406 total bases, a .600 slugging percentage, 214 runs, and even 15 triples. It was one of the most impressive campaigns that a baseball fan's eyes have ever wondered at. Only he stood between Guidry and an easily earned MVP plaque.

Gid failed to register a victory against Boston, albeit a no-decision. He held the BoSox at bay until giving way to Gossage early, in the sixth. Goose pitched even longer than his predecessor, through the 12th, when Lyle took over. Sparky had his best stuff of the year as he shut the Sox down for three frames. In the bottom of the 14th, Nettles won it at the expense of reliever Dick Drago. Puff would hit 27 homers in 1978 and score 93, while his defense was customarily stellar. Inspiration such as Puff lent, though scarcely given its due in history's blurred eyes, was often one of the largest differences between a quality Yankee team and a playoff Yankee team.

On the third of July Munson was back in the lineup, only to tweak his knee on the bases during the sixth inning. It didn't seem to be anything serious, but the injuries were destroying the potential of his season. He coughed, cleared his throat, and went on playing. But Thurm did not want to stop catching and switch positions, not just to extend his career. He stuck true to the statement of not serving as a liability to the team.

In July, Martin moved Thurm to the outfield because the pain was hindering his catching so badly. His RBI were far off, though the clutch hitting was as good as ever and his handling of the pitchers golden. Munson understood the shift but didn't feel comfortable; his defense was subpar in the outfield. Injured as much as he was, he managed to appear in a remarkable 154 games. Though selected for the All-Star game, Thurman was in such pain that he couldn't make it. He'd never have another chance.

When Gid was hit for his first loss courtesy of Milwaukee on July 7, the benefactor Brewers surpassed New York in the standings, ten games short of Boston. The Yankees were now third in the East, and Steinbrenner visited Martin's office the day that the second half opened.

Billy emerged first. "Will you gather round here, pl —"

"Can I have your attention?!" George boomed. "Can I have your attention?!" He turned to Martin momentarily. "We've done it your way for the first half of the season and it didn't work, and now we're going to do it my way. I still believe we can win the pennant, but we're going to have to try harder." He turned to the assembled players:

> I've had a talk with Billy, and there are going to be some changes made, and if you don't like them, come and see me, and I'll try to accommodate you.

> There are going to be some changes made in the lineup, some players aren't going to be playing as much, but there's no sense in getting mad. This is the way it's going to be. It's my ball club. I sign the checks and I'll do what I want.[37]

Steinbrenner proceeded to dictate the new positioning. Munson was shifted to right where his bat could stay in the lineup; however, he'd now be a liability in the outfield, ambling about on tortured legs. Why not let him DH? Not many people liked the idea of losing him behind the plate, especially the pitchers. Cliff Johnson had been catching in his stead, but now George ordered rookie Mike Heath to take over.

Clyde King was also called to work with the moundsmen. Art Fowler was still the pitching coach, but his job was anything but stable. Steinbrenner had tried to fire him, but Billy had stepped in and threatened to quit if that went through. So King was grandfathered in to dethrone Fowler, a logical choice as a former relief star and manager, primarily of the San Francisco Giants. He'd end up directing the Yankees from many posts throughout the 1980s.

Roy White was relegated to the bench. George had long had a problem with White, which was inexplicable to most. Reggie became the designated hitter, a position he detested, and Piniella also spelled him there at times. The former would face righthanders and the latter southpaws. With the new batting order, Munson's bat was now a tempest in the three slot, and he was followed by Chambliss, Nettles, and Jackson.

The meeting did not last long. Martin concluded it by reiterating the rules and regulations of the Yankee club, plus made a promise to crack down on infractions. The players were not happy with what they heard. "George shouldn't be messing with a team that won the World Championship," Rivers said. "It ain't right to panic. All Steinbrenner had to do is wait until the hurting guys get healthy. Then we would have started to win."[38]

Nevertheless, New York was uninspired, losing eight of ten games to set them 13 back of Boston by July 16. The next evening, about 45 minutes before their game with Kansas City, Steinbrenner held a meeting in his office with Jackson and Martin. The conference was originally slated to address Billy's batting of Reggie low in the order, but by the end he was chewing out his star player. "You better get your head on straight, boy!" George hollered. "I mean it! You better get your head on straight, boy!"[39] Reggie was so insulted that he wouldn't leave the office, so George was forced to exit himself — from his own office.

Jackson's temper was high. He told Martin to stop communicating with signals, as they'd customarily done. "One day I won't play," Reggie lamented to the press before the game. "The next day I'm the cleanup hitter." That night he was hitting cleanup and serving as designated hitter.[40] As previously mentioned, he despised DHing and not playing consistently. "I'm not talking anymore," he informed writers disgustedly at one point.[41]

New York led the Royals going into the top of the ninth inning at Yankee Stadium. But Gossage gave up a couple of runs to send the two teams into extra innings. In the top of the tenth, Munson led off with a single. As Jackson headed up the dugout steps, Billy stopped him, having noticed the first and third basemen playing deep. "Can you bunt?"

"Bunt?" Reggie asked curiously. "Yeah, I guess so!"[42]

Al Hrabosky, the "Mad Hungarian," was on the mound. The thick southpaw, who had been traded for Mark Littell, threw his first pitch high and in for a ball. Reggie had been given the sign, but did not bite. The corners drew in and the signal was thus repealed. The batter had little interest; he didn't want to check. The second throw was bunted foul. Third-base coach Howser called a timeout as he moved down the line. "Billy wants you to hit away."

"I was told to bunt — I'm bunting!"

"Reggie, he wants you to hit away."

"Listen, Dick. Nothing against you, but when I left the dugout he told me to bunt, and I'm going to bunt. I'm gonna get the runner over and Piniella will come up and knock the run in, and we'll win. I'm a real team guy, right?"

"I hope you know what you're doing," admonished Howser.[43]

Jackson personally claimed in his book that this was payback for the incident in Boston 13 months prior. He tried to bunt twice more, but fouled both for a strikeout. "Billy wants you to go inside," Gene Michael told Reggie upon his return to the bench, "and take a shower."[44] He refused and took a seat. The dugout was dead silent.

In the 11th, Munson dropped a flyball in right. The bases were soon loaded and it was two out on a full count to fleet center fielder Willie Wilson. Gossage pitched one that seemed so sure to be a strike that he and Heath began to walk off the field. Umpire Marty Springstead dictated differently, and the runner walked in to score. Goose was so enraged that he was ejected. Three more runs were tacked on by Kansas City to outbalance the Yankees by two for a 9–7 loss.

Back in the locker room, Martin shut his office door to suppress the sound as he shredded the inside to fragments. Berra came in to warn him to stay away from Jackson. Billy instead picked up the phone and called Al Rosen to threaten that if Reggie was not fined, he'd quit. "He defied me," Billy ranted, "and there's no way he can get away with that. If he does, the game's crooked, and I don't want any part of it. Let him get away with that, and you might as well forget the ballclub; might as well make Reggie the manager."[15] Billy wanted a full season's suspension of Jackson. Rosen countered with five days, and Martin accepted.

One of the cruel quirks of the situation was Sparky Lyle's departure. He had been brought in to pitch the fourth and fifth, but after that decided he had his full share of misuse and said to the manager, "I've had enough. I'm going home."[16] Billy considered it to be no big deal. To Reggie that was racism, though favoritism does not seem far off. Though both had let down their comrades and asserted their own egos above the welfare of a failing team, Lyle was not punished.

The team's reaction to Jackson's suspension was apathetic. Rivers was the only one angered, because he felt the Yankees needed the bat. Paul Blair summed the consensus up best. "If Reggie's here, fine. If he's not, fine."[47]

On July 18, New York was 47–42, 14 games back of Boston, and most players had written the club off. Interestingly, Munson had predicted in his autobiography a good pennant race, and as Marty Appel read that over in July before publishing, he was tempted to delete it, but ultimately figured, "It was, after all, his book, and he said to leave it in."[48]

The clubhouse was inconspicuous in the ensuing few days. The Yankees got back to little ball. Scribes wrote of the on-field games. The team won four straight in Reggie's absence before he returned on July 23, late to the clubhouse. He had been tardy to board the bus so Billy ordered its departure without him. The writers huddled at Jackson's locker for a soundbite. "For the way they interpret the offense," he declaimed, "I guess an apology is in order. The way I interpret it, you know, I haven't done anything wrong."[49] The interview took so long that he missed batting practice and remained rusty.

Steinbrenner called Martin at his office. "You play that boy," the order came. "He's been working out."[50] Billy had Dick Howser go to check if Reggie was in fact in shape. Surprisingly, Jackson said he hadn't touched a bat since the suspension. Billy was livid not only over *that*, but also the press interview. "We're winning without you," he told Reggie. "We don't need you coming in and making these comments."[51] Later, Martin told the writers, "We got a good thing going and I don't need him and his big mouth coming along and breaking it up…. It's like a guy getting out of jail and saying he's innocent after he kills someone."[52]

Jackson countered that Billy hadn't communicated with him for a year and a half. "It's a flat-out lie," Martin returned.[53]

Reggie sat the bench that night as the Yankees won their fifth in a row over Chicago at Comiskey Park.

The night before, Billy had downed some drinks at Comiskey's Bard Room with White Sox owner Bill Veeck, the incorrigible maverick whose fearless stunts—such as batting midget Eddie Gaedel to bring publicity to his dead St. Louis Browns—made baseball infamy. Pushing 65 years of age, he was as strong and crafty as ever. "Did you know that we almost got you to manage the White Sox?" he asked Billy.

"What do you mean?"

It was no surprise. Back on June 16, a day past the trading deadline, an anonymous Yankee employee had announced to the papers, "We're going to trade managers. Billy's going to Chicago and Lemon's coming here."

Nevertheless, Veeck proceeded to reveal, "About a month ago Steinbrenner called to propose trading you to the White Sox for our manager, Bob Lemon."

Martin was stubbornly surprised. "You're not kidding me, are you, Bill?"

"No, Billy. George wanted to trade you for Lemon."[54]

Veeck's role has been questioned in this situation, as the sneaky enemy of Steinbrenner and the Yankee titans. He was a grappler who had dealt with low-budget, embarrassing outfits in St. Louis, Milwaukee, and Chicago on different levels. Coupled with his antiestablishment nature, he was not a man to ignore an opportunity for a shakeup in the Bronx. The next night, that of Reggie's return, Veeck and Martin met under the same circumstances.

At one point in the session, writer Jack Lang crossed by. Billy stopped him to ask what Jackson had submitted for comment that day, so Lang showed him the earlier quote by Reggie claiming that he had not "done anything wrong." "Ick," Billy responded.

Lang looked up. "Is that a comment on my story?"

"No, on him."[55]

Soon, Martin boarded the bus to O'Hare airport. As it neared, he asked Murray Chass for a talk in the terminal. Instead, Billy ended up at the bar, where Chass tracked him down. The conversation came to a reference to Billy's contract clauses, and he asked rhetorically, "Jackson's refusal to admit he was wrong, is that conduct detrimental to the Yankees...? I'm saying shut up, Reggie Jackson. If he doesn't shut up, he won't play. I don't care what George says. He can replace me right now."

Chass was not sure if that was off the record. "No sir," Martin assured, "it's on."[56] And it was.

Chass called his editor just as Henry Hecht of the *Post* picked up on the story. Instead of stopping, Billy only continued with a barrage of examples of Jackson's preferential treatment by Steinbrenner. As the flight was called, Billy asked Chass, "Did you get that in the paper?" He answered yes.

"I ran him out today and he'll get the same thing tomorrow," Martin continued. Anger swelled inside him as he mulled over Steinbrenner and Jackson, who had tormented him for two grueling years. An old Graig Nettles line flashed in his head. "The two of them deserve each other," Billy spat. "One's a born liar, and the other's convicted."[57]

Drunk as he might have been, foolish as he may have seemed, Martin knew what he was doing. Number one, Murray Chass flat out did not like him. And he worked for the *New York Times*, through which word would obviously end up prominently circulated. Billy had finally vocalized his most basic emotions just as he felt them. He had tested the water before; this day he dove in.

True to form, Chass immediately phoned Steinbrenner for comment. George's first reaction was one of experience. "Was he drinking?" Now, the logical response is clearly yes, but apparently the sharp, reeking odor of alcohol filling Martin's breath and the bravado with which he spoke did not faze Chass. He responded that he had not *seen* Billy drinking. "I've got to believe no boss in his right mind would take that," Steinbrenner said calmly.

Some saw Hecht as the villain in this saga, a writer who the players generally despised. Traveling secretary Bill Kane firmly believed that Chass was the only one with Billy at the time of his famous quote. "Murray didn't have the guts to go with it himself," Kane claimed, "so he told Hecht, knowing Henry would print it because he hated Billy so much. Then Murray made sure Billy would get fired. He called George to tell him what Billy had said."[58]

Cedric Tallis was the highest ranking organization man in Kansas City for the road trip, so Rosen sent him to see Billy. He was drinking with the coaches when Tallis came in. "Did you say it?"

"No," Martin assured. He tended to stick to that. He now did not want to lose his job, despite the heartache and pain such perseverance would inevitably incur. But his quotes had been too assertive to ignore. Steinbrenner called Doug Newton, Martin's agent, to tell him that if his client wanted to be paid, he would have to quit and not be fired. Money talks.

The difference between re-signing and resigning is as slight as the line of a hyphen; Billy Martin had crossed it one too many times. Cigar in one hand, speech in the other, dark glasses to block out the last hours, the address was to be given. But no questions. Billy explained that his health was the reason for quitting. He wished the team good fortune, then apologized to Steinbrenner. He had no harsh words. "That means now and forever, because I am a Yankee and Yankees do not talk or throw rocks."[59] He was shaking, rocking, unstable. The words were choked out painfully.

Reggie Jackson, a man who forever begged to be understood, cackled with cruel hypocrisy at the episode. "I wanted to laugh," he remembered in his book. "I didn't know, of course, that George and all Yankees fans everywhere were eating that up like it was ice cream."[60]

With tears running down his gruff face, Martin stammered, "I'd like to thank the Yankee management, the press and news media, my coaches, my players ... and most of all ... the fans."[61] With that, he ceased to make sense; he barely managed to make a quote. Phil Rizzuto, hardly a great friend of Billy's but at least a compassionate Yankee, threw his arm around the trembling shoulders, and the two strolled down the hallway toward the exit sign.

Martin advanced down the street with another friend to a bar. Country music flowed through the air. The press was nowhere to be found.

Thousands of calls lit up the switchboard at Yankee headquarters the next day. Shortly after receiving multiple threats on Steinbrenner's life, the operators shut down at noon. Five separate offers had been made to buy the franchise so Martin could manage it again.

"I never took the game home with me," he once said. "I always left it in a bar along the way."[62]

"I drink after wins, I drink after losses, and I drink after rain-outs."[63]

No, those aren't the words of Billy Martin; they are the famed quotes of Yankee manager Bob Lemon.

The late Robert Granville Lemon was calm and reclusive, a man who once said after a win, "This is the way I like it. You guys play and I sit in the dugout and enjoy."[64] He was an ordinary-looking, fair-haired, 57-year-old Californian with a bulb of a nose. Late in the 1978 season, the team bus pulled over before a Detroit night game. Someone in the back asked what the problem was. "No problem," Nettles answered. "We're just stopping to get batteries for Lem's nose."[65]

Lemon had a storied career as a star pitcher for the 1940s and '50s Cleveland Indians. At one point, he won 20 games in seven out of nine seasons, on top of two American League pennants. His achievements were impressive enough to merit election to the Baseball Hall of Fame in 1976. After winning the Manager of the Year Award in 1977, Lemon was fired by the Chicago White Sox in mid–1978. It took but a few weeks to be contacted by George Steinbrenner.

While the team awaited Lem's arrival from the West Coast in Kansas City on July 24, Dick Howser served as interim manager. New York was up 2–0 in the bottom of the seventh. With two on and two out, Steve Braun lined to Munson in right. He paused, caught the ball, but then dropped it. And stepped on it. And booted it. It was embarrassingly clear that Thurman was ill suited for the outfield. Braun's hit was counted for a double that drove in two runs. The Yankees laughed, but lost.

Lem arrived the next day and laid down the ground rules. "When I played, I played the game as best I could. I hustled, and that's all I ask you people. If you can't hustle, come and see me, and I'll take you out of the lineup. When you're ready to hustle again, tell me, and I'll put you back in again."[66]

The attitude of Lemon, the example he set, instilled a new atmosphere on the team. About a month earlier, Piniella had said, "If I was rich, I'd quit. I used to love playing baseball. Now I hate it. I just hate everything about it. I especially hate the garbage that goes with it."[67] The residue of that sentiment had certainly not been scrubbed away, but at least it had finally subsided. Controversies died down, and the players were generally comfortable. They were also more responsible, accountable, and even communicative. The Yankees shot out of the gate with the breath of fresh air, won 10 of 12, then at different stretches 12 of 15 and a dozen out of 14. Ultimately, the club went 48–20 from the time of Lemon's arrival. But the players spoke little of a divisional comeback; they just played hard daily.

Back at the stadium on July 27, Reggie returned to right field and the lineup to launch a home run. Munson consequently shifted back to catcher. He had felt distant away from the plate and detested manning right. Thurm had also been surprised to find that the outfield put even more strain on his legs than receiving due to all the running involved.

Behind the scenes, Billy Martin and his agent, Doug Newton, were invited to Steinbrenner's suite at the Carlyle Hotel. One night earlier at the home of *Tampa Tribune* columnist Tom McEwan, George looked at Howser on the bench and mumbled dimly at the television, "That's Billy's job."[68] He called Newton to set up the meeting. Billy had rejected a number of other offers in order to keep a return open. When he arrived at the Carlyle, George offered the job for 1979. "If things were very different, I would," Martin replied.

Steinbrenner persisted. "If both of us could give a little, I don't think we'll have any problem at all."

"You're right, George, because you're really not a bad guy."

"Actually, you're not either."

By now, the two were developing toothaches from the lies being pushed through their pearly whites. "One of the problems is that you and I didn't talk to each other." Steinbrenner echoed that and listened carefully as Martin disapproved of a system in which players could bypass him and talk directly with the owner about team affairs.

Steinbrenner was receptive. "If you promise to do a couple of things and if I promise to do a couple of things, I don't think we have a problem."

"If we both keep our word," Martin said, "we won't have a problem."[69]

The problem started on July 27, the day after the meeting. Rosen found out about the confidential conversation and staked his job in getting Lemon more time to prove himself — or even disprove himself, as long as he received a fair shot — as manager. Steinbrenner did not want to lose Rosen, and so it was agreed that Billy would not take over as field general until 1980, instead of '79 as originally planned. He would scout in the meantime, at $100,000, free of contract restrictions.

It was Old-Timers Day, Saturday, July 29. Ford, DiMaggio, and Mantle had already been called to the field. Annually, Joe D. was the crescendo. But the formalities were not done yet. The dignified tone of Bob Sheppard hit the multitudes. "May I please have your attention, ladies and gentlemen, I have an announcement to make. In 1980 Bob Lemon will become general manager. And now, the manager for 1980 and hopefully for many years to come, number one." The crowd's roar drowned out the name that followed, but they didn't need to hear the words voiced. New York had its icon back.

A press conference was held after Martin's appearance, no questions to be asked. The biggest question was whether the plan was truly to be brought to fruition. Was it Steinbrenner's ploy to get the fans off his back? to get the issue of Billy Martin to die down? Billy himself would wonder in the coming months.

George explained his motives as compassionate:

> What kind of man would I be if I let a guy go for saying something that was true? I'm the leader of this team. I had to be able to take the heat. I knew he said it. I also knew it was true. He had made a mistake. I had made a mistake. The only guy who never made a mistake was the guy with long hair, the guy who walked on water. I kept thinking about that all night long.[70]

Martin's only restrictive clause was that if he did not take care of himself physically to Steinbrenner's satisfaction, his contract could be terminated.

On August 2, Boston came to the Bronx and took two games from New York. Only a couple of days before, Dent's return from an injury marked the first time since June 10 that the 1977 Yankees' World Series lineup was together on the field. With the Red Sox suffering injuries to Boomer Scott and Jim Rice, the team lost 12 of 15 through the end of July to whittle the fortnight-old 14-game lead on New York down to 6½.

After an up-and-down August, New York still had 6½ games to make up in the division on September 1. Munson was well aware of it. "I looked at the schedule," he told Piniella. "If we can pick up two and a half games this week, we can go into Boston only four down."[71] And they would.

The Boston Red Sox versus New York Yankees rivalry had one of its most vital matchups beginning September 7 with a four-game series at Fenway Park. The BoSox came in hurting. Fisk had cracked ribs, and Evans was still fuzzy after a week-old hit by a pitch. In addition, Fred Lynn was rumored to be jealous of Rice, and Rice held a grudge against Lynn for having been brought up earlier than him back in 1975. Don Zimmer was being called a poor manager, and Boomer Scott was overweight.

Who did these guys think they were, the New York Yankees?

Urban Shocker sounds more like a fearful socioeconomic term than a crafty moundsman, but his demeanor was not much less serious. Originally a catcher when his career began in the 1910s, he had acquired a permanent crook in his ring finger from stabbing at a foul. But this improvement of his grip coupled with Shocker's astute and intense study of the pitcher's art allowed him to enjoy a 13-year career without a single losing season. Signed initially by the Yankees, he was exiled to obscurity to the St. Louis Browns, by way of a rare misdiagnosis of talent by manager Miller Huggins in 1916. Eight years later, Shocker returned to star at the stadium until death felled him in 1928. A year before passing prematurely of an overexerted "athlete's heart," Shocker was in failing health and discounted as a viable arm for the Yankees.

This was the 1927 Yankees, Murderers Row, a lethal lineup sure to strike fear in the hearts of all of its opponents. Fortunately, Shocker was clever enough to use his skill to play on their heralded reputation. In batting practice before the World Series, the opposing Pittsburgh Pirates sat in the bleachers to watch the Yankees swing. By his pinpoint control, Urban served up meatballs one after another, which his team's sluggers clobbered over the fences. So intimidated were the Bucs that they practically rolled over and died in a series sweep.

A half century later, the Yanks were up to old tricks. Devoid of crooked pitchers (either in morality or finger jointings), the Bombers' clouts rang like trolley bells through Fenway's greens. "We could see the tension in the faces of the Red Sox players as we took batting practice," Lou Piniella later wrote in his book:

They hung around to watch us plaster the wall. They knew it was slipping away. They had had a first place lead of eight and a half games as late as August 21, and now it was only four. We couldn't wait for the games to begin.[72]

The Bombers were in prime form. Mike Torrez started for Boston, but went only two innings before being succeeded by Andy Hassler, Dick Drago, and Bill Campbell. The Yankees scored two in the first, three in the second, then two and five. Every starter had at least one hit. Jackson and Piniella homered, and White, Randolph, and Munson collected three base knocks each. Thurm's performance was in spite of a beaning by Drago. He hit the dirt completely still, but eventually picked himself up, to the team's great relief. Once inside the clubhouse, Thurm assured all that he was fine. In the third, Hunter also became a casualty, the victim of a pulled groin. Of course, he wasn't around long enough to rack up the win, which came by an astronomical 15–3 score.

The second game was a painful replay for Boston. Evans dropped a flyball; Fisk committed two throwing errors; Rick Burleson booted a ball; pitcher Tom Burgmeier threw a ball away. The Sox's fumbling cost two runs in the first and six in the second. Jim Beattie took the cushion and ran. He went all the way to the ninth, with two out. Catcher Mike Heath lost a pop foul from Fisk. Redeemed in the same at-bat, he slapped a homer for two RBI. Bob Davis relieved for the final out of a 13–2 romp.

Bill Lee, still a bitter opponent of the Yankees and their ethics, wrote a scathing newspaper article during that series in which he cast Steinbrenner as an Adolf Hitler, Martin as Hermann Göring, and the New York team as storm troopers. He opined that all of the Yankee players were washed-up derelicts. Still angry over the fight in which Nettles handicapped him, Lee was also hanging onto an incident earlier in the year in which Billy planted a dead mackerel in his locker. George posted the clipping on the clubhouse wall, provoking such a deep sting of insult that the Yanks sought to slaughter Lee.

The truth is he was intimidated to death. "No team ever looked more intense than they did," Lee wrote in his autobiography:

> Getting on the field with them was akin to stepping into a wading pool with Jaws. Every time we made a move, they would bite off another limb. It was terrifying to watch. We had expected at least to split with them in our own ballpark. That's what everyone said and wrote, "All we need is a split and we're in good shape." That was the wrong attitude to have. The Yankees weren't thinking split. You could see that in their eyes. They came in thinking sweep.[73]

In the fourth inning of game 3, Chambliss doubled, Nettles received a free pass, and Piniella drove one home with a two-bagger. Now there were two outs and the game was close. But it was soon to be ripped apart. White was granted an intentional walk and Dent batted an RBI single. Yastrzemski booted the ball, allowing Bucky an extra base. Rivers's single drove in two and Munson provided an RBI single. Burgmeier replaced Dennis Eckersley, only to throw a wild pitch that plated Randolph. It was an incredible run; the whole lineup had passed before one out could be recorded. Three outstanding mistakes were committed. It was painfully clear to Beantown — the Red Sox were running scared. Wrote Lee:

> After they beat us the first two games, we were finished. We spent the final two games waiting for something to go wrong, and it invariably did. By the time the Yankees left Fenway, we were walking around in a daze. It was as if the entire team had just returned from Cambodia.[74]

The Red Sox were a team in fear, playing in fear. Defeated before it stepped on the field, Boston left itself without a chance to win. It was impossible to win on empty fuel; victory is birthed by elitism.

On Sunday, September 10, the hit parade continued. The Yankees had 18 safeties for the game to put them up 5–0 by the second inning. Summing the series up, New York recorded 67 hits and outscored the Red Sox 42–9. Most blamed Boston's submission on their rash of injuries, though the Yankees had worked through the same dilemma. But one point was clear: whatever confidence the BoSox came into September with was now shattered. The series became known as "The Boston Massacre."

	Wins	Losses	Winning Percentage	Games Back
Boston	86	56	.610	—
New York	86	56	.610	—

Reggie turned to Piniella Sunday night in awe. "Well, what do we do now? We're in first place, you know?"

Lou paused a moment and smiled peacefully. "I know we're in first. What I'm wondering is how we got here."[75]

The Yankees were anything but overconfident. They remained solemn and focused, aware that their authoritative position could vanish on any day. They played as Billy had taught them, going for the jugular as the opponent gasped for air. Through stolen bases and advanced runners, they were finding ways to cross the plate. While Boston panicked, even Rivers and Jackson were relaxed. Morale was upbeat.

On Friday, September 15, the Yankees and Red Sox met again, but this time in the Bronx. The former rolled on with a 4–0 win, courtesy of home runs by Chambliss and Nettles, who also sparkled defensively. Before a crowd of 50,000, Guidry won yet another game, while allowing only two hits.

In game 2 Rivers led off the next game's bottom of the ninth dead-locked at 2–2. Yastrzemski and Lynn played him unadvisedly shallow, so Mickey shot one over their heads and wheeled around for a triple. Munson followed with a screamer that Jim Rice snared, though Boston was unable to prevent Rivers's run. Jackson hit safely in three out of four for two RBI that day. As Reggie knelt in the on-deck circle, Munson burned a foul that Jackson attempted to block with his hand. The ball stripped his thumbnail off, and he was forced to DH because of the injury.

In game 3 Boston led 3–1 when Lyle entered the eighth inning against Carlton Fisk. After walking Pudge, Frank Duffy singled. Boomer Scott came up. He was still battling to stay in playing shape, but kept a good humor over it. "I got Dunlop Disease," he'd say. "My belly done lopped over my belt."[76] He showed bunt a couple of times, and when that didn't work, drove a two-run double.

After taking two of three from Boston, New York split a two-game set at home with Milwaukee. Piniella complained that Brewers pitcher Mike Caldwell was throwing spitballs; if he did, it was worth the risk. Caldwell won 22 that year. Milwaukee was quite a compelling story that season as well. It led the major leagues in runs (804), home runs (173), batting average (.276), slugging percentage (.432), and on-base percentage (.342), yet finished 6½ back at third place in the Eastern Division.

Steinbrenner felt the heat of such a competitive pennant race. At a series in Cleveland, he told Guidry that he did not have any guts, nor did he strike out enough men. As the crowning fallacy, Gid was told that he would never be a major leaguer. He was 22–3 at this point but was being told he'd never be a major leaguer. While George's uniform was being tailored, the weakened Guidry started on three days' rest, with four games left on the regular season docket. He struck out nine and won his 24th of the season. But Boston kept pace with its fifth consecutive win. As great as the Yankee comeback had been, the victims would mount a spectacular resurrection of their own. It was to be a great race.

The Yankees went into the last game of September short their second baseman and number two hitter, Willie Randolph, who had just pulled a hamstring. Figgy was on the mound trying to become the first Puerto Rican player ever to register 20 wins, and he did it. Despite this, the Yankees' sixth straight win, they could not clinch the division.

The last scheduled game of the regular season was on October 1 in New York. In the opening frame, Munson was on first when a single to the outfield sent him sprinting. Hobbling around the base paths as fast as he could, Thurm beat the throw to home in an incredible signature moment of dedication. "It was the first run of the game," Marty Appel wrote, "and had it been the only run, it would have won a division title and been remembered as one of the great plays in baseball's history."[77] The glaring difference, unfortunately, between that and Enos Slaughter's great first-to-home dash of the 1946 World Series was the welfare of the hero's team. Whereas Slaughter's Cardinals proved victorious, Munson's Yankees did not. Catfish Hunter, who entered with a 12–5 record, was shelled for home runs by Wayne Cage and Gary Alexander, then yanked early. Tidrow, Rajsich, McCall, and Lindblad relieved, but to no avail. Cleveland pitcher Rick Waits shut New York down on five hits. Piniella kidded Catfish afterward, "That's what we get for trying to win a pennant with a soy bean farmer from North Carolina."[78]

Boston defeated Toronto in a shutout that day — their eighth straight win — and thus there would be a one-game playoff to determine the East champion at Fenway Park, as designated by a coin toss a few weeks prior. Surprisingly, the Yankee reaction was an immediate sense of justice, for the race would not be called by a winning (or losing) streak, but by a single nine-inning match, ancestral nemeses one on one. Piniella looked at Munson. "I think it's destiny that we should end this thing head to head."

"I would rather have settled it today," Thurman admitted.

"If we lose we can blame it on George," added Nettles. "He lost the coin toss."

"You guys won all four up there and only two out of three here this month," Steinbrenner explained profoundly. "That's why I lost the flip."[79]

That night, October 1, Thurman Munson, Graig Nettles, Lou Piniella, Sparky Lyle, and Goose Gossage all prepared for the most famous game of their collective careers by relaxing at Daisy Buchanan's bar just down the street from the team hotel, the Sheraton Boston. Unified, they were calm and confident, determined not to treat this playoff game differently from any other. The wives were not there; the attitudes were nonchalant; it was to be just another game.

George Steinbrenner had once marveled, "There is no greater rivalry anywhere in the world of sport than the Yankees and Red Sox."[80] That was true. Throughout the 1970s the matchup was uncannily similar. Over the decade, the Red Sox achieved a .556 winning percentage. The Yankees were .001 behind. The 1978 lineups read:

	Yankees	Red Sox
Catcher	Munson, .297	Fisk, .284
First Baseman	Chambliss, .274	Scott, .233
Second Baseman	Randolph, .279	Remy, .278
Third Baseman	Nettles, .276	Hobson, .250
Shortstop	Dent, .243	Burleson, .248
Left Field	Piniella, .314	Rice, .315
Center Field	Rivers, .265	Lynn, .298
Right Field	Jackson, .274	Evans, .247
Designated Hitter	White, .269	Yastrzemski, .277

The matchup gave every indication of being a classic.

Just before the Yankees left for Boston, Guidry had walked into Lemon's office and told him, "I'll take the ball." Though it would be on only three days' rest again, Lem had no problem with that. The players weren't sure Guidry would end up being able to go, but they hoped desperately to be surprised. His season was one of the best off the mound in history. Gid went 25–3 (.893 winning percentage, highest ever for a 20-game winner), with team victories in 30 of his 35 starts. He was the stopper after losses 15 times and won 12 of his final 14, with a 1.28 ERA over that period. Ron's season earned run average ran at an anemic 1.74, second all-time for a southpaw, behind only Dutch Leonard of Boston, who maintained a 1.01 rate in 1914. While holding opponents to a .193 average, Guidry had eight games of ten or more strikeouts. Among the Yankee records he set or tied were most consecutive wins to start a season (13), most strikeouts in a game (18), and most strikeouts over a season (248). The latter stat beat "Happy" Jack Chesbro's 239 in 1904, the season he won a modern era record 41 games. Gator also tossed nine shutouts (best in the majors), the most since Babe Ruth in 1916. Unanimously, he won the Cy Young Award and fell only 61 votes short of American League Most Valuable Player. All of his accolades and records, however, could not buy an edge against the Red Sox.

The crisp, perfect autumn afternoon was the top subject of conversation on October 2, save the baseball game. The players showed up early at Fenway to take an intense round of batting practice. The Bombers did little fooling around, less flippant and confident than at Daisy Buchanan's the previous evening. Looking over at the formidable Bostons, Piniella whispered softly to Munson, "They look more relaxed."

The Yanks were feeling the pressure. "A playoff like that is totally different from the divisional playoffs or the World Series," said Gossage later. "If you make those, you've already been a winner because you've won something. You lose a playoff, and you've won nothing. Nothing. Then make it the Red Sox and Yankees after all we went through and I was more nervous pitching in that game than I was at any other time in my career."[81]

Nervous as the Yankees were, the Red Sox fans were even more so, scared to say a word. Frozen in a trancelike state, they cheered in relief when Mike Torrez's first pitch to Mickey Rivers tailed in for a strike. Immediately, they fell silent again. Despite Boston's mini-comeback, there was a sense of fear in the team and its patrons, as though their fortune to come so far was liable to run its course at any moment. There was still popular belief in the fabled "curse of the bambino," dating back to the sale of Babe Ruth to the Yankees. Among the portents involved was the order of Boston's retired uniform numbers. Lined up chronologically on a balcony wall, the digits read 9, 4, 1, 8. No one thought anything of it until one year a fan noticed that 9–4–18 was the date the Red Sox had last won a World Championship (the season having been shortened a full month by World War I).

Fenway was an ill suited park for a lefty such as Ron Guidry. Facing icon Carl Yastrzemski in the second inning, he cruised a ball high and tight. Yaz took an awkward, tomahawk swing, and somehow the ball carried out for a home run and early lead. The fans finally unleashed a wild, surging cheer. They were back in the game.

Guidry's slider began to lose its zip rather early, so to compensate, Munson, Piniella, and Gator himself discussed the problem and decided Lou should play for the pull, over toward the line to an extreme. That became crucial in the sixth. Rick Burleson led off with a strong double, a sacrifice pushed him to third, and a Jim Rice single scored the shortstop. After recording an out and an intentional walk, Fred Lynn came up. Two outs, two base runners. He cranked a slider into the corner, but Piniella — hugging the line as earlier agreed — was there to catch it and leave the runners stranded. "It was a ridiculous place for him to be," Lynn said, "about twenty yards out of position toward the corner, a hundred-to-one shot. There wasn't any reason to that, just a hunch. The man's a gambler."[82]

Torrez's strength had a tendency to waver late in the game. That could be seen in Don Zimmer's grim expression and by the two relievers warming up in the bullpen while Chambliss capitalized with a single, then White did the same. The score stood 2–0 when Bucky Dent came to bat. Valuable for his defense, he had scraped together a .243 average with just four home runs that season. For two years he had been regularly pinch-hit for late in the game. But with Randolph out due to his injury and second baseman Brian Doyle having been replaced by Fred Stanley, there was not a bench player capable of taking over at shortstop in such a game. Lemon reluctantly permitted Dent his at-bat. Seeing the number 9 hitter up, the

Boston defense was not worried. To Lou Piniella, though, the rich possibilities registered. Reservedly, he told Munson, "If we blow this, we're in trouble."[83]

A tight slider came in to Dent at which he took a defensive cut, fouling the baseball off his instep. He hit the ground and hobbled over to Dick Howser, coaching third. The trainer rushed to spray on ethyl chloride, a potent pain killer. As Torrez paced the mound nervously, Dent looked up at Howser. "If [he] comes in there again with that pitch, I'm going to take him into the net."[84]

"He cracked his bat," Mickey Rivers said, focused intently. "What?" someone asked. "He cracked his bat," Rivers repeated and called Dent and the batboy over.[85] Handing his bat to Dent, Mickey said, "Here, use this. I feel it will be lucky for you."[86]

Torrez's 1–1 pitch was a meatball of a slider. Dent swung easily and lifted a fly to left. Yastrzemski thought he had a routine flyball to catch. "The way he hit the next pitch," the Hall of Famer wrote in his autobiography, "high, with not much on it, I could have expected it to come down to me on the warning track — on any other day of the year, in any other inning of the year. Except on that fall day."[87] Yaz shuffled back in the direction of the left field line, awaiting the ball's inevitable descent. Looking up at the sky, he could not see it falling, and his knees buckled sharply. With an aggressive wind that had redirected from its former inward course and was now blowing into left, the ball carried seven inches over Fenway's Green Monster for a home run.

Dent circled the bases to a deathly silence. The cruelty of fate, the curse of the bambino, the invincibility of the Yankees— they had all crushed Boston once again. Wrote Lou Piniella, "Bucky Dent had turned Fenway Park into the world's largest morgue."[88]

Rivers ironically got no use out of his club in the succeeding at-bat, earning a walk from the hapless Torrez. When Zimmer emerged to yank him, the Boston crowd finally came alive — to boo their manager. Rivers quickly swiped second from new pitcher Bob Stanley. Munson came to the plate, off a hot September that had brought his injury-filled season to a nearly .300 average. He ripped an RBI double to make the score 4–2. Piniella's flyball ended the historic rally and inning.

Butch Hobson led off the seventh with a strikeout, then George Scott, in his next-to-last year in the big show, lined one to the second baseman who, playing at normal positioning, would have been caught. Lemon came out to check on Guidry, who did not want to come out of the game. "Lem, I'm still strong." But Lemon was a former pitcher, one who worked well with the current stock, and called in Gossage from the bullpen. Gid went in to ice his arm in the clubhouse while Goose took over. Having led the league in saves with 27, Gossage would record more than 150 in his six seasons with the Yanks. Uncompromisingly, he blew the ball past the hitters and worked easily out of the seventh.

In an oft-forgotten saving heroic, Reggie Jackson took a fastball down Broadway to straightaway center field off of Bob Stanley in the eighth inning. So excited was Reggie that he even gave Steinbrenner a high five in his seat beside the dugout. "It's nice to be in the game!!" Jackson roared.[89]

In the bottom of the eighth, with the score 5–2, Boston mounted a rally. Jerry Remy doubled, and Yaz drove him in with a one-bagger. Fisk singled, Lynn singled, and all of a sudden the game was 5–4 New York. The sun had been stinging right field so dramatically that before taking his position there that inning, Piniella mused, "I sure hope nobody hits a ball to me. I can't see out there."[90] In the bottom of the ninth, that situation would come up.

Rick Burleson reached first with one out before Jerry Remy came to bat. The light-hitting, 155-pound second baseman sent a high drifter to Piniella. Almost immediately, Lou lost it in the sun that shone from behind the roof, but brilliantly he decoyed, pretending as though he had it all the way. Third-base coach Eddie Yost knew better and hollered for Burleson to go forward. But the runner was so unsure that he held up between first and second to see if Remy's fly would be caught. The baseball hit the grass about three yards before Piniella, who stuck out his glove instinctively. By some miracle, he stabbed the ball; it had leaped right into his mitt. In savvy reaction, Lou regrouped and rifled to Nettles what he'd later declare to be the best throw of his career. With Burleson restricted to second and Remy at first, Jim Rice dug in. Big Jim Rice. It seemed whatever he'd lay ash on would be good for a win. However, the MVP flew a ball to Piniella which, this time, was easily handled for a catch. Theoretically, Burleson would have scored on the play had he not been fooled. "He is so smart, I couldn't help but think that he might be decoying me," Burleson said afterward of Piniella's play. "I couldn't be doubled off first base to end the game."[91]

With two outs in the bottom of the ninth, Carl Yastrzemski, one of Boston's all-time favorites, stepped to bat. Wrote Peter Gammons, "The 1978 season came down to Gossage, the premier power reliever of his generation, and Yastrzemski, perhaps his generation's premier fastball hitter."[92] By script, it seemed only right that he'd save his club and procure the win. Gossage sought to test that. King of the heater, he was just what old number 8 wanted.

"I had always hit Gossage well," wrote Yaz in his biography:

I loved the fastball, after all. That year Goose's fastball exploded on the hitter. It really moved. If it was up, it would rise. If it was down, you wouldn't know what it would do. It could sink or it could come in on you. I was thinking of the at-bat before, when I got the base hit to center field, the pitch was out over the plate. Now I had a different situation. I had a runner on first. I made up my mind. I don't know whether it was the right way to think, but I said to myself, *I'm going to go to the hole. I'm going to look for an inside pitch, just to tie the score.*[93]

As 32,925 Boston diehards rose to their feet, Gossage wound up and fired a tight heater along the border of Yastrzemski's knees. He seemed to have a chance until the ball neared and accelerated. Yaz couldn't catch up with it and reacted with an undercut. The ball spun and sailed to the third-base coach's box, where Nettles drifted to make the play. "I was thinking, 'pop him up,'" Nettles remembered. "Yaz did and I said, 'Jeez, not me.'"[94] The ball dropped gently into Nettles's glove for an out, and he thrust his arm high in the air. Steinbrenner charged the field and embraced Al Rosen, then Lemon. Gossage stood on the mound with his arms flailing, muttering to himself, "My God, it's over, we've done it."[95] Munson sprinted out to him and jumped into his arms like a Little League kid.

Afterward, the two parties were anything but bitter. When Jackson came to the Boston clubhouse to pay his respects, he told Yastrzemski, "You are the greatest."

"Please," said Yaz, "win it all. For us. We are the two best teams in baseball."[96]

The Yankee players were exhausted by the flight to Kansas City that Monday night. Thurman took to the back to negotiate with Steinbrenner for a trade to Cleveland. Desperately, he suggested to George a deal of him for Dennis Eckersley and Fred Kendall. "No," Steinbrenner said. "They wouldn't give Eckersley for you. I can get Frank Duffy and John Lowenstein. If they throw in Tom Buskey, I'll make the deal."[97]

The Royals were as formidable as ever, but the Yankees just handled them better this time. A crowd of 41,143 showed up in Kansas City for game 1 of the ALCS. Jim Beattie and Ken Clay shut the opposition down on two hits and but one run. New York, on the other hand, was red hot. Their 16 hits and seven runs were highlighted by Jackson's homer off Al Hrabosky in a three-run eighth inning. In the second game, roles reversed. Kansas City amassed 16 base knocks of their own and plated ten. The series headed for the Bronx tied at one.

Cat started the third game and had few problems, save for George Brett. He had his third home run of the game by the fifth inning, all solo shots. Yet the score was only tied after Brett's trifecta, 3–3. Losing by a run, Munson came to bat, ragged from his dogging injuries. Despite that, he hit .278 for the series, playing all four games. Often he asked Piniella over that period, "Lou, can I still hit?" The answer was proven to be yes. Facing reliever Doug Bird, Thurman plowed his bat through the strike zone and crushed a ball into the left field bullpen, near the famed monuments. A 440-foot clout, it was the longest he'd hit in his distinguished career. More important to Munson, it gave him the winning run of that vital game.

The fourth match was a pitcher's duel. Dennis Leonard went the full nine, while Guidry surrendered a run in the first inning. But that was it. The score 1–1 on a Nettles homer, Roy White shot a death blow over the outfield wall in the sixth inning. To shut off any margin for error, Gossage was brought on in the final and clinching frame. On to the World Series, it would again be the Yankees and Dodgers for the 11th time in their histories.

Los Angeles had just given Danny Ozark's Philadelphia Phillies their annual beating, hinged on a Bill Russell extra-inning RBI single. The old New York rivals would now be facing each other in a return World Series match, the first time that had occurred since 1957–58, between the Yanks and Milwaukee Braves.

Dodger coach and former star Junior Gilliam died just before the series, which the team subsequently dedicated to him. Aside from that, they could no longer hold together the family act that had been perpetuated throughout the decade. A clubhouse scuffle between flashy superstar Steve Garvey and durable hurler Don Sutton displayed the lack of cohesion that often plagued the team. The Dodger image became jaded but was deflected by heated criticism of New York: its team, fans, city, and atmosphere. It was like a set of 25 John Rockers. Used to the relaxed life in LA, they resented the hustled, angry attitude of the Big Apple. But their objections worked against the Dodgers in public opinion.

Figueroa took the mound before three shy of 56,000 in the Los Angeles Coliseum. He was beaten mainly by Dodger second baseman Davey Lopes, who swatted two home runs for five RBI in the third and fifth innings. Rounding the base paths, he gave the Yankees an inflammatory "We're number one!" salute. The Yankees, incensed by his bravado, scoffed at the act as "bush."

Jackson led off the seventh with a home run, the first of two in the series. He'd also hit .391 and drove in eight. Though New York inched closer with four late runs, they lost game 1, 11–5, to 17-game-winning southpaw Tommy John.

Game 2 came down to Bob Welch versus Reggie Jackson, with two outs in the ninth. Though the Yankees had plated the opening runs, a Ron Cey three-point clout had picked the Dodgers up for a 4–3 lead when Reggie stepped to bat. Welch, a strong, firearmed freshman righthander a month shy of his 22nd birthday, came in for Terry Forster with an out recorded. Dent had just singled and advanced on a grounder. He induced Munson into a lineout, setting the table for Jackson, who already had a double and three RBI to his credit. With the count 1–2, Reggie fouled off a couple, eyed a ball wisely, and fouled another. Welch then made it a full count. The Los Angeles crowd overcame its usual complacency to peak in an excited roar. Welch unwound with a pernicious heater. It took nine pitches and some violent cuts, but on this last one Jackson was distracted by Dent's break for third and missed. He returned to the dugout flinging his bat against the wall. Lemon scolded him and he calmed. Later Reggie conceded, "Give him credit. He beat me."[98] Welch gained plenty of notoriety at an early point in his career for the strikeout, for many admirers apparently gave him as much credit as his victim did.

As the series shifted to New York on October 13, so did the momentum. Guidry's start betrayed his dominance by allowing the Dodgers eight hits and seven walks. The positive byproduct of his erraticism, and the prime factor for stranded runners, was the legendary defensive show by Graig Nettles. Sparky Lyle, who sat out games 1 and 2 with an injury, once told Graig's wife, Ginger, "Let's take out a life insurance policy on Graig, and make you and me the beneficiaries, because one of these days when I'm pitching, he's gonna get killed."[99] On a Davey Lopes liner, he dove and grabbed it. He then cut down a Reggie Smith smash, jumped to his feet, and gunned him down. Nettles haunted Smith on a later single by blocking it to cancel extra bases. The next batter, Steve Garvey, had led the National League with 202 hits but was held to a .208 average in 24 at-bats in the series. He sent a ball down the third-base line. Nettles snapped his body over, spun, set, and fired to force out Smith at second. Having scored early on a Roy White home run, the Yankees easily won 5–1. Afterward, Lemon marveled, "I don't think anyone has ever played third base any better than Graig did tonight."[100]

Tommy John and Ed Figueroa dueled scoreless into the fifth inning of game 4, when the latter permitted a three-run homer to Reggie Smith. An inning and a half later, Reggie Jackson singled in Roy White. One was out, and Munson stood on second when Piniella drove a weak liner in the direction of shortstop. Bill Russell had a bead on the ball, then lost it. Reggie had held up in fear that the orb would be caught. But once Russell recovered and headed for the forceout at second, Jackson continued on his way. The throw to first deflected off his hip and trickled into right field. Piniella pulled in safely and Munson, having stopped and started, hustled easily into home. The Dodgers argued vehemently with the umpires over what was soon called the "Sacrifice Thigh." Lasorda, Garvey, and John all claimed it was interference because the runner had deliberately offered his leg to block the throw. Reggie did not buy it but conceded perhaps a twitch. Later he'd kid, "I was just walking down the street, and this baseball came up and bit me in the leg."[101]

When he got back on the mound, John turned to umpiring crew chief Ed Vargo. "You know where we screwed up on that play? Russell should have taken that ball and thrown it with all his might at Reggie's head, and then see if he wanted to stand in front of the ball."[102]

Munson tied the game with a double in the eighth. With two out in the first frame of extra innings, Lou Piniella singled White home with the winning run on a drive to center field. The series evened at two apiece. On the way to Los Angeles, Piniella joked to Munson, "All that has to happen is for the plane to get us there and we're world champions."[103]

Thurman validated up his teammate's theory by having a stellar game 5 in which he collected five RBI on three hits. He excelled in yet another fine series with a .320 batting average, three doubles, and seven RBI. Burt Hooton, who had picked up the win in game 2, was thrashed in a New York bombardment in game 5. But it was not a bombing. Though the Yankees scored a dozen runs, nary a homer was smashed. The Yankees, however, did rack up a World Series record 16 hits, as well as a couple of doubles.

Prior to the sixth game, in Los Angeles, Hunter found out the day before hunting season opened that his father had lung cancer. Distraught, he picked up an airplane ticket. He didn't care whether a seventh game was to be played or not; he figured it would be his last hunting season with his father. Piniella was furious that Cat allowed himself to be so distracted, but Lou probably did not know the circumstances. "Why don't we all take a twelve o'clock flight?" he asked sarcastically.[104]

The wear showed in Cat when he gave up a home run to Davey Lopes on only his third pitch of the game. In the third inning, Reggie Smith was at bat with two men on base. Munson trekked to the mound. "Well, Catfish," he said, "you better make sure you hit my glove exactly where I put it because you ain't got diddly squat tonight."[105]

Hunter didn't feel like negotiating. "Hey Captain Bad Body," Cat responded, using one of Thurman's kidding monikers. "Just get back on behind the plate and catch it after I throw it. I'm in a hurry to get home."[106] He nailed Smith with a double play to end the inning, and only six hits came against him in seven innings.

New York took the lead in the second, spurred on by the most unlikely of heroes. Bucky Dent and Brian Doyle (replacing of the injured Randolph) combined for six hits and five RBI in the game from the bottom of the order. Doyle hit .438 to lead all batters in the series; this was a guy who hit .161 in 199 career regular season at-bats. Dent registered a .417 mark to earn the series MVP. By the time Reggie Jackson came up, with a .391 clip to his credit, there was little left to prove. The score was 5–2 New York, but a very distanced 5–2 lead at that. The pitcher was, poetically, Bob Welch. Jackson was issued a venomous fastball on the first pitch. He stroked a drive into the seats and doffed the taunting blue Yankee helmet to the Dodger faithful as he crossed home plate. Gossage came on with a 7–2 cushion and shut Los Angeles down easily. The Yankees had repeated as World Series champions.

Steinbrenner dedicated the victory to New York, the city the Dodgers detested. In doing so, he deemed the Big Apple's patrons "the greatest fans in baseball." After game 6, Thurm and Catfish drove to the team hotel where a party was being held for the Yanks. The two, close as ever, hopped out and shook George's hand. Cat hugged him. George invited both in, but Hunter declined. He had some hunting to do the next day with his father.

The Yankees went hunting as well. Their prime game was Tommy John. The amiable southpaw had come over to congratulate the Yankees after the World Series. While he was there, Munson and Howser wondered whether T. J. would turn free agent or re-sign with the Dodgers that off-season. "With your great sinker," Thurm reasoned, "and style of pitching and our fielding, Yankee Stadium is made for you."[107] Apparently, John had agreed.

The gracious opponent and his supreme accuracy (53 walks over 230 innings) entered the free agent sweepstakes after a 17–10 1978 season. New York procured the lefty to replace Don Gullett, who, plagued by arm troubles all season, registered only six decisions and called it quits at the tender age of 27. T. J. inked the deal for $2.8 million, to be paid partially through deferred payments. He cited Munson as the single most influential reason for joining.

A press conference was held to announce John's signing, but when the contract was put in writing, the two sides located some discrepancies. Al Rosen was vacationing on a remote Caribbean island with but a single phone, but he was tracked down and dragged back to New York to settle the matter. When it was resolved, John, the new Yankee, posted 21 victories, 276 innings, 17 complete games, and a 2.97 ERA in 1979.

On November 10, the more notorious pawn was advanced. Sparky

Lyle, Dave Rajsich, Larry McCall (the three comprised half of the bullpen), and flaunted prospect Domingo Ramos were traded to the Texas Rangers. In return, the Yankees admitted center fielder Juan Beringuez ($400,000) and four minor leaguers into the fold: infielder Greg Jemison and pitchers Paul Mirabella, Mike Griffin, and Dave Righetti. The latter proved reason enough for such a trade. "Rags" won 71 for New York over his first decade with the team before establishing himself as a superior relief pitcher. Nettles summed up the trade of his old buddy Lyle by saying, "He went from Cy Young to sayonara."[108]

Many Yankees were to bid farewell in 1979. While Luis Tiant, Bobby Brown, and Oscar Gamble came in, Paul Blair, Catfish Hunter, Roy White, Dick Tidrow, Cliff Johnson, Mickey Rivers, and Thurman Munson would spend their last seasons in pinstripes that year. It was the end of an era.

Munson felt secure, no matter the dealings around him. He worked out a rudimentary agreement with Steinbrenner about his aviation. Thurm was now regularly flying to Canton after home games, and on road swings a trustworthy friend would transport the plane, for accessibility. Thurm flew with such frequency that he didn't bother to rent a residence for the following season. The only times he didn't fly home were if he could find a roommate when he had to be in New York the next day. Since George wouldn't trade him to Cleveland, he was reluctantly permitted to fly as he pleased.

═══10═══

EARLY DESCENT

Even the strongest branch can be broken.
— Marty Schottenheimer

He died October 31, 1978. Four days earlier, the young man inexplicably lost control of his new Jeep and flipped over twice in an area just outside of Phoenix. The injuries sustained were enough to take away Jerry Lemon at 27 years of age. Bob Lemon, his father, was demoralized. He had been so close to his son that the death robbed him of his spirit. Throughout 1979, he could barely focus on his career, baseball; he was apathetic and oblivious to the deterioration surrounding him.

Munson's off-season was a serene intermission, as he savored his family, his business, and baseball supremacy. But the three were clashing. Michael, nearing four years of age, was having trouble settling in Canton. Thurm was disturbed to see this, and tried to give his son the attention he needed, painfully aware that it wasn't enough. His longing for family increased, and more and more that spring the discussion turned to the steps needed for postcareer security. He looked in wonder at the colleagues who played for 15 or 20 years, knowing that that was something he could not pull off. Said Jim Palmer, "I saw him early in spring training and he said he couldn't wait 'til the season was over. You know Thurman was joking, but you also knew how much his family meant to him."[1]

Munson flew his plane, a Beechcraft Baron, down to Fort Lauderdale for spring training. One afternoon, he and Piniella took it down to the Bahamas. Lou was greatly impressed by Thurman's navigation and understood the love he had for the sky. So affected was Piniella that he decided to take flying lessons himself that spring, but that prospect failed to materialize.

Thurm hounded his teammates, especially Jackson and Nettles, throughout 1979 to fly with him. Early in the season, he convinced Reggie and Piniella again after a game in Baltimore. Nearing Pennsylvania en route to New York, the three spotted thunderstorms and eventually lightning in the distance. Munson was cool about the whole thing, and contacted the control tower for a new flight plan. The two passengers, as had now become routine, were awed by his command. Perhaps they didn't realize how much stormy weather Thurm had already been through.

During the winter, Munson headlined a charity benefit in Ohio for men only. When a female reporter entered to interview him, Thurman expressly ordered her out. As much copy as the incident made, only a scarce few acknowledged the $70,000 he raised for charity that day.

Then in spring training, Munson was the victim of the attention-starved antics of Jim Bouton, a successful author and at the time a sports anchor for New York's Channel 2. Bouton caught up with him at the batting cage one day in search of an interview. When Thurm would not comply, he followed him around the cage and harassed the recalcitrant player, with cameras rolling all the while. Finally Munson shoved the microphone out of his way and belittled Bouton as the fool that he was being. Bouton in turn played the tape on the newscast that night, expecting an uproar over the player's arrogance. Instead, the fans united in compassion to champion Munson.

Lem was in a distracted state of mind that spring, but he failed to quench the mighty confidence of his team, a collective ego broadened by consecutive world championships. It was an easy training camp, lacking in requisite discipline. According to some, it was no more than a prolonged batting practice. There was little fielding, defensive strategizing, or basic defensive routines.

Steinbrenner, protecting his ticket sales, boasted that 1979's had been one of the greatest training camps the Yankees ever had. However, when the club lost its first six games, he became incensed and imposed a curfew; if broken, the violator would receive a harsh fine. To ensure obedience, a guard was stationed on every floor on which a player roomed. Munson, who was on the second floor, took his usual rebellious stance in response to such trivial handling. He, Nettles, and three young prospects including Chris Welsh and Tim Lollar, took a bedsheet and tied it to the railing of Thurm's balcony. As they climbed down, the venture happened to be in full view of Steinbrenner, dining in an adjacent restaurant. Mysteriously, Welsh and Lollar were added in a trade following the season.

Munson seemed to have a penchant for getting rookies into trouble that spring. A young pitcher up from Tacoma named Roger Lee Slagle, who would pitch only two innings in his big league career, was feeling well and throwing a smooth batting practice. Thurm was at the plate with an old minor league buddy of the pitcher behind it catching, Dennis Irwin. Thurm was shooting balls into the dirt to sting Irwin while the two laughed good-naturedly. "But then the catcher gives me the sign to flip him, you know, knock him down," Slagle remembered in an interesting retrospective by Tellis called *Once around the Bases: Bittersweet Memories of Only One Game in the Majors:*

> So, to protect my catcher, I tossed one in close to Munson, and all of a sudden, it tailed in. Munson couldn't get out of the way of it, and I thought it was gonna hit him right in the head. But luckily he stuck his hand up, and it hit him in the hand.
>
> Steinbrenner was sitting in the stands, and ... I just hit the Yankees' meal ticket and Steinbrenner saw it.... Fortunately, Munson was not hurt seriously.
>
> I went to Munson afterwards and apologized. I told him I didn't mean to hit him. He said "Forget it. You were only trying to protect your catcher, and I know you'd do the same for me. I like you more for that. And, besides, it gives me a few days off."[2]

Munson was back in time for the opener at home against Milwaukee, where Guidry was perfect through six. Yet somehow he was stuck with a loss for the beginning of a slide that brought him to 6–7 by the All-Star break. He tried to compensate by throwing harder but only strained his back. After Figueroa dropped the second game, the fans were hostile for the third, when Tommy John took the mound for his debut. He was intimidated by the howling Bronx crowd and started off with five straight balls. Pitching coach Tom Morgan came out to jumpstart his pitcher. "John, start throwing the ball over the plate. Listen to these fans. You're gonna get me fired!"

"Morg, what's my problem?"

"I don't know; you tell me."

"I think I'm overthrowing a bit," T. J. diagnosed.[3]

He must have guessed right because after giving up a run in the first inning, John kept Milwaukee still through seven. The game was an inspiration to him, one which propelled him to a tear through April, 4–0 with a 1.12 ERA. He'd be awarded the Pitcher of the Month honor and continue on a similar pace through May. Aided by some beautiful plays by Mickey Rivers, Goose Gossage came in to ice the first Yankee win of 1979.

On April 19, New York was 11 games into the season. The team had just been defeated by Jim Palmer that day, and Cliff Johnson was upset to have sat out. Relaxing in the clubhouse shortly afterward, Jackson ribbed him for not playing. Reggie was comfortable with the team by then, with the newness worn off and controversy quieted. By this point, he and Munson had become rather close, resolved to a mutual respect. After the game, Reg began talking to Heathcliff about Palmer's skill, that he didn't throw as hard as in earlier years, at least not with the speed of Gossage, who was in the sauna at the time. "Cliff," he kidded in reference to the two former National League opponents, "you must be awful glad you don't have to hit against Goose anymore."

Johnson dismissed it as ridiculous as he strolled to the bathroom and then to the shower. "I used to hit the big guy pretty good. *He's* lucky he don't have to face *me* anymore." Munson and Piniella howled, delighted. It was a normal clubhouse scene.

Soon Gossage returned to the news of Johnson's words. "He couldn't touch me," Goose scoffed. "I used to strike him out *all* the time."[4] The gallery again hooted.

When Johnson emerged from the shower, Jackson hollered over, "Hey, Cliff. Goose says you couldn't hit him with a broom."

"He couldn't hit what he couldn't see," Gossage added, and with that, Johnson flung a roll of tape at him. Reggie laughed and set off to the trainer's room, foreseeing no trouble. But Cliff took the exchange seriously. "Do you really believe I couldn't hit you?" he yelled.[5] Goose just laughed. Before the audience had a chance to realize what was truly transpiring, the argument had escalated into a shouting match. The two giants were nose to nose, and Johnson threw the first punch. They wrestled a bit, but by the time the fight was broken up, Gossage was clutching his pitching hand.

Some people hadn't even paid attention as the two scuffled, but when Goose yelped in frustration, holding his hand, they took concerned notice. The next day it was announced that he had torn ligaments in the right hand and was expected to be out through mid–July. Johnson was traded to Cleveland not long after.

With Gossage sidelined, Dick Tidrow took over in the closer role. He soon became overworked and in one stretch was called for on Friday, Saturday, and Sunday, each time to stop an opposing rally. In the latter contest's seventh inning, he halted the Angels before a 35-minute rain delay. Dirt's arm felt tight, so he suggested to Lemon that a reliever be brought in. Lem didn't think he had the arms available to do so and asked him to go back out. Dick consented, but asked that if the first two batters reached base he be yanked. The opening duo did in fact reach, and Tidrow looked to the bench. But Lemon wasn't there, not to reappear until Dirt had given up five consecutive hits. Then Tidrow was taken off the mound.

Steinbrenner was already incensed by that performance when Tidrow demanded a conference with the front office. "Get rid of him," George ordered. "Get him out of my sight."[6] He was traded to the Chicago Cubs for Ray Burris. While Tidrow was instrumental in the Cy Young season of Bruce Sutter, Burris was a predictably fruitless acquisition. Steinbrenner dodged responsibility. "Rosen made the deal with his buddy on the Cubs, Bob Kennedy."[7]

So during a nasty West Coast swing in one of the year's more crucial and telling periods, the Yankees were without a closer — twice. Guidry approached pitching coach Tom Morgan about assuming the role, and between him and Lemon, there was no opposition. Ron Guidry had just sailed through arguably the best pitching season in baseball's free agency era, earned the Cy Young, and led a world championship team. Now he volunteered to obscure himself in a much less profound position, costing fame and market dollars in order to pick up his falling club.

Gid's first game as closer came in Oakland after Catfish had thrown 61/3. With a man on third base, he induced an easy popup and the Yanks battled to a win on Jim Spencer's tenth-inning homer. That of course counted as a win for Gator. Besides that, he recorded only two saves. Upon Goose's return, Guidry yielded the post to reenter the rotation and converted his bleak record, ending up 18–8, along with a league-leading 2.78 ERA.

In the meantime, the bullpen was depleted. In an early May game in Anaheim, only a sole pitcher remained available, so Tommy John offered to go in, to Lemon's approval. Two outs in the ninth, base runners on second and third, Rod Carew at the plate. It was not an easy situation. Begrudgingly, T. J. threw a streak of curves, called for by Munson. As the game traveled into the 11th, tied, Thurm adjusted to fastballs and the Angels were held while New York scored four to escape with a victory.

As John packed ice on his hand after the win, he asked Munson why he had ordered such a slew of curveballs. "Well, when you warmed up," Thurm explained, "you had nothing. Your fastball was straight as a string. You throw one fastball and the game's over. We had a chance with you throwing curveballs, so what the heck. In the last two innings you found your rhythm, and it was safe to throw the fastball."[8]

The intelligence with which Thurm handled his pitchers was nearly flawless. Lyle, who often banged him up with sliders, considered Munson the best catcher in the league. Guidry named him as the chief reason for his accelerated success. A pitcher need not wonder what should be thrown under Munson's reign. He could take Thurm's sign and fire. And when it came down to a clutch game, that took a great deal of pressure off the hurler's laboring shoulder. Though that did not show up in the box scores or history books, it proved proportionately as important as any other achievement.

When Fran Healy had arrived in New York years earlier, he had readily admitted, "I can take it. I can take warming up pitchers all day because I know I'm not going to take that man's job away."[9]

In late April, Munson invited Piniella to venture to Canton for an upcoming Monday off-day. "We'll go out right after the game from Teterboro Airport and have dinner when we get there. I'll call Diane and tell her you're coming."[10]

"That sounds great," Lou smiled. "I'd like that."

That Sunday night, following the game, the two flew off to Canton. Proudly, Munson neared the house in his descent, buzzing it as a warning on approach. Nearly the whole drive from the airport to home, Thurman laughed about that.

Back at the ballpark, life was much less cheerful. Through the first two months of the 1979 season, the Yankees were strictly a .500 ballclub. They bounced from second place to third, repeated that, and then took atypical residence in fourth.

Amidst the struggles of mediocrity and adversity, Steinbrenner searched for a change. In early June, he secretly phoned and met with Billy Martin. The old manager had come to grips in his time off, but on November 28, 1978, there had been a rebirth of his uncontrollable image. As an invited guest to a college basketball game, he had been harassed by a young sportswriter. When the kid baited him with a challenge, Billy slugged him twice. The man pressed charges and made headlines nationwide. Steinbrenner, late already in sending Martin his contract, delayed it even further in response to the incident. Some thought now that his rehiring Billy was nothing but a publicity stunt. That would all change in the middle of June when George came along to supervise his ballclub on a swing through Missouri, Minnesota, and Texas.

Steinbrenner met with Martin on June 15, when the season was about 60 games old. "I don't think we have a chance to win this year," the owner said. "I'm going to make a change. I'm thinking of bringing Gene Michael in until next year."[11] Bob Lemon had not regained balance after his son's death. The club's atmosphere had grown heavy and morose in concert with the manager. One day Reggie went to speak with him in his office. Lem's eyes were weary and beaten. "Meat," he had said, a nickname used for virtually everyone he knew, "I just wonder if it's worth it anymore. It's different now. My heart's not into it."[12]

On the flight to Arlington after a loss to the Twins, the players got out of hand enjoying themselves. But Lemon did nothing. Steinbrenner had seen enough. "I knew right then and there a change had to be made," he said. The clincher had come in the meeting with Martin when the old Italian looked his nemesis in the eye and assured, "I think we can win it. I think I can do the job. I'd like to try."[13]

Back on June 2, at the stadium, Reggie had been breezing off the field in the ninth inning alongside Mickey Rivers when, inexplicably, he was hit by a strange, stabbing pop in his calf. It was expected to keep him out for a month.

Jackson was still on the shelf for the evening of the 17th, and was invited to sit with Steinbrenner in the stands. The Boss witnessed a disastrous loss and ranted his criticism of the team. The low point was a play in which Figueroa arrived late to first base on a ball to Willie Randolph. "I can't believe what's happening with this team," Steinbrenner fumed. "Mental mistakes. I won't tolerate mental mistakes."[14]

Reggie had not yet been told that Martin was returning early. He defended Lemon, but George persisted anxiously, hinting at the secret pressed heavily against his chest. "There's something very wrong with this team. There has been from the beginning of the season." Again Jackson defended; again Steinbrenner rebuffed.

Out of nowhere, George directed a question at his player. He mulled over the query, eyes fixed on the field. "Do you think I should fire Lemon?" It was said so nonchalantly that Jackson was caught off guard.

"You can't do that to the man after what he did for you last year," Jackson responded firmly. "You just can't. This is his last year anyway. You can't do that. Give him a little time. We've only played sixty games. Don't panic."[15]

Nevertheless, Lem was fired that night in 1979 after 65 games with a 34–31 record. Calls flooded the players, especially Jackson. He spoke with Lemon, who was by then a sullen shamble. "It's true, Meat," the old skipper said. "They're kicking me upstairs [to general manager]. Maybe it's best for everyone.... They're going to keep paying me, so I just take it like a man and keep my mouth shut."[16]

Al Rosen, who had brought his longtime friend and teammate Bob Lemon into the picture, considered this the last straw. Sick of public humiliation, disrespect, and Billy Martin, he quit in mid–July. Jackson was vocal on it to the point where a message was passed through Billy to have him shut up. Reggie showed more integrity. "George thinks he can buy everybody," he insisted. "Some guys have pride. You can't buy them."[17]

Steinbrenner felt he was in his finest hour in bringing Martin the icon back to Gotham. "I think Billy knows the conditions," he announced. "I think he understands the terms. I'm the leader here. I have to make the final decisions. My feeling is he has matured; he finally understands the meaning of responsibility. Billy has changed."[18] Indeed he had.

Martin was considerably more relaxed upon his return. Before games, players could now enjoy time with their families on the field or in the clubhouse, where they kicked back to watch "Jeopardy." The men were also allowed early dismissals from games more freely. Most surprisingly, Martin and Jackson began to share a mutual respect on the brink of a bond. Jackson made limited complaints and played hurt. But Steinbrenner warned his manager early. "He hates you, Billy. He really hates you. That boy is sick."[19]

Under the pressure of Steinbrenner's thumb, Martin was now almost completely controlled. He was forced to say and do things for George that he did not want to do, and he did them with little resistance. Slowly, the respect that his players once held for Billy withered away. He now knew his role. Before the press, he tried to look as unchanged and recalcitrant as ever. "The only difference is that now I have a mustache," the assurance came confidently.[20] Though 55–40 the rest of the way, he'd be fired and replaced by Dick Howser before the new decade hit.

Other matters were looking up. Munson's arm had regained its youthful thrust, forcing fear into potential base stealers. The old sportswriter Bugs Baer's quote rang true of the thieves: "He had larceny in his heart, but his feet were honest."[21] Obviously, Thurm's surgery had proven successful, but his legs were more unstable than ever. Unable to catch for elongated stretches, doubleheaders, or day games after a nightcap, he told Martin that he was not strengthening the team as catcher. Writers scoffed, said he would never play another game, but then he would be behind the plate the following day. However, his ravaged body could only handle so much.

Thurman's injuries were the fuel for Martin and Steinbrenner's first argument, a week or two after they linked again. George spoke to his manager one day after a game. "Billy, Thurman isn't producing like he should be. I want you to bat him eighth."

"There isn't any way I'm going to do that," Martin affirmed. "No way in the world I'd do that to Thurman." George did not like that.

"George, you promised me when I came back you wouldn't interfere with my managing, that you'd let me do my own thing."

"I admit I've been interfering too much," Steinbrenner conceded. "You're the manager. I'll leave you alone."[22]

Of course, George *did* have other wheels in motion. Late in June, New York purchased the contract of Bobby Murcer. After a disappointing run in San Francisco, Bobby was packaged in a five-player trade to the Cubs before the 1977 season. There he enjoyed his final superior campaign, with 27 homers and 84 RBI. Chicago was displeased with his subsequent performances, and so they swapped him for a minor league arm out of the Yankee organization. He joined the team in Toronto where Munson, Piniella, and Nettles were elated at the reunion. Thurm had kept in frequent contact with Murcer and was anxious to have a friendly ear around the clubhouse.

Shortly after Murcer returned, he, Piniella, and Munson were at a bar discussing flying. Unexpectedly, Thurm announced, "I'm buying a jet for a million and a half. A Cessna Citation. A real beauty."

"What do you need such a big plane for?" Murcer asked, stunned.

"I think it will be great. I'll be able to get home much faster. I expect delivery in a couple of weeks…. Now I'll have to play three or four more years to pay this thing off."

The response from Piniella was quiet. "You don't need it."[23]

Thurman just kept speaking of the plane, ecstatic with pride. The Cessna was a fine machine, a twin-engine, eight-seat passenger jet that cost $1.4 million. The plane was registered as "15NY" and had a New York Yankees logo plastered on the side. Utilizing the 350-knot cruising speed, he could now fly from New York to Canton in little more than an hour. Munson acquired the aircraft on July 6 and, according to Diane, from that day began battling trouble with it.

Teammates were concerned that Munson had jumped too hastily to a jet after relatively minimal experience with the two weaker planes, which he retained after purchasing the Cessna. They had ample reason to be cautious. Though he had only 30 hours of flight time in the jet, the Cessna Aircraft Company granted Munson his Citation rating, allowing him to fly without special training.

Often Thurman showed off the vehicle to teammates, who warned him incessantly of its dangers. He'd remind them of the proven safety as compared to automobiles, in which — of those Yankees— only Billy Martin would be killed. Billy had a problem with Thurm's flying, but a more savvy one. Since he demanded that all players be prompt for the team bus, was he making unfair allowances for Munson? Would he have tried to stop Reggie Jackson? He spoke with Thurman worriedly.

"Why are you flying this thing? Does George know you're flying?"

"Yeah," Munson said, "he gave me permission."[24]

"You gotta be kidding."

Thurm was undaunted by the objections, blinded by his pride in the grand new possession. One time he turned to Reggie with a serene smile

Munson in the dugout at Yankee Stadium. (National Baseball Hall of Fame Library, Cooperstown, N.Y.)

creasing his face. "Million dollar plane.... Not bad for an old catcher, huh?"[25]

Jackson and Nettles joined Munson for a flight on July 12. Heading to Anaheim from Seattle, the flight passed above Washington, Oregon, and California, amidst an illuminated evening highlighted by the clearly visible, purple, snow-capped mountains of the Pacific Northwest. Munson captained the controls with a flight instructor who had come for the trip by his side. The fluent cruise was interrupted by a sudden bang in the rear of the aircraft.

Sleeping in one of the back seats, Jackson was awakened by the tumbling oxygen mask. It had not been functioning properly, and Nettles joked to Reggie, "Thurman told me to make sure you sat in that seat." It was in reference to a recent alleged feud between the two. The instrument display was a blinking panel reminiscent of gold stars on a deep, clear night. "Nothing in this thing ever works completely right," Munson grumbled in the front.

Reggie was concerned that something was wrong. "Anything the matter, Captain?" he asked.

"The altimeter seems to be off. I think that's why the mask came down. I've got to get this whole thing checked out during the All-Star break." They were within a few miles of the Orange Country airport, but fog was damaging visibility and he decided it was necessary to make a second pass at the airport before descending to land.

Jackson felt secure enough to replace the oxygen mask and go back to sleep. When he awoke, he asked Munson what distance they had dropped to. "About 600 feet," he shrugged. "No problem."[26]

After landing, Reggie was picked up at the airport by a flight attendant he had been seeing. She was nearly scared to death when they converged. "Who was flying that thing?" she begged

"Thurman. You knew that."

"Well, why did he buzz the field as close as he did?"

Reggie had no idea what she meant. "What are you talking about? We were 600 feet up."

"Try a hundred," she stammered. "When he took it down the first time, he scared the daylights out of everyone."[27]

A few days later, Martin and friend Howard Wong left for a fishing trip in Kansas City and asked Munson to fly them. With Diane on board as well, they stopped in Albuquerque to refuel. Upon reentering the sky, their path led directly into an ice storm. When Billy looked out the window, he saw a flame came out of an engine. He looked up to say something, but caught a glimpse of Diane nearby and kept silent.

Upon their landing in Kansas City, Martin quickly sought Munson out. "You better check your engines. Did you see flames coming out of that right one?"

"Maybe that was when I switched on the deicer."

"No way," Billy affirmed. "I've never seen flames come out of an engine like that. You better check it out."[28]

In Chicago a couple of days later, Munson confirmed the fears. "You know we had to take another plane out of Kansas City after we dropped you off," he told Billy. "We had to stay overnight and take a commercial jet out."

"You're kidding me," gasped Martin.

"The rotors of the engine were all mashed in, bent," Thurm continued. "They must have put them in wrong when they built the plane."

Steinbrenner called Martin into his office that month, fuming over Munson's aviation. "George," Billy scowled, "you're the one who gave him permission to do it."

"Billy, I'd appreciate it if you'd talk to Thurman about it."[29]

Martin spoke with Munson, who assured him that it was not necessary to stop. Diane and he were preparing to move to New Jersey, according to Billy, so he wouldn't fly. "I think that's a good idea," responded Martin. "You'll be with your wife, you won't have to fly anymore, and it won't take so much out of you."[30] George remained wisely concerned.

According to sportscaster Keith Olberman, Munson braved so many near-accidents in the month in which he navigated the Cessna that Steinbrenner offered to allow a trade to Cleveland if Thurman would give up flying. Either the proposal failed to materialize or time simply ran out.

Ron Guidry's groan at the airport counter was loud; the misplacement of his ticket reservation was going to keep him from the big show, the All-Star game. Others wished they had a problem such as Guidry's. Thurm Munson — and Carlton Fisk — had been forsaken by the mid-summer classic in favor of Kansas City's Darrell Porter.

The power numbers were down for Thurman, and chronic injuries were eroding his optimism. Steinbrenner was angered at the slowed production and exhorted Martin over it. He was not receptive. "Don't you understand, George, his legs are killing him. He can't push off his legs to hit. The guy shouldn't even be playing right now.... He shouldn't be playing, but we don't have anyone else."[31] They had at least been trying.

The Yankees had sought a new catcher but could not attract a first-stringer. They made due with .211 lifetime hitter Jerry Narron in the meantime. Late in July, the club announced that he would start and Munson was to shift to first base in place of the injured Chris Chambliss. When Chambliss recovered, Thurman had no real place to go, since the outfield was typically full. Trade talks were in the air to get rid of Chambliss, thereby making room at first. At this point, Munson's career had hit a crossroads. If he was a liability to the team, then what was his purpose? as a leader? of what, a fourth-place ballclub?

New York now had an aging team. Jackson, Nettles, Piniella, Chambliss, Spencer, White, Hunter, and Munson were all on the decline. But as July closed, they were still red hot, though Baltimore was relentless. The Orioles recorded 102 wins that year, outdistancing the Brewers by eight. In all reality, the Bombers were fortunate to rank fourth.

The Yankees were a defeated ballclub and breaking down rapidly. Munson's knees were crippled, his muscles depleted and worn. He complained to few, but Piniella was one. "Why don't you quit," Sweet Lou would ask. "Why don't we both quit?"[32] Together, they laughingly agreed that they needed the money. Lou then turned serious to console Thurman. "They'll get another catcher. You won't have to catch so much. You'll have a better year next year."[33]

On July 29, the ballclub conceded its third straight defeat at the hands of Milwaukee, and afterwards Munson flew to Canton with Tony Dominick for Michael's fourth birthday. The next day, it was off to Chicago for a sweep of the White Sox. On the day of the series opener, Mickey Rivers was finally traded to Texas in order to recover Oscar Gamble. Mickey's time in the Bronx had alternated between up and down. The same could be said of his relationship with Steinbrenner. Rivers once said, "Oh, George understands me. Me and him and Billy, we're two of a kind."[34]

A three-run homer by Jim Spencer in the Windy City victoriously closed out July. That night, Munson, Piniella, and Murcer went back to Bobby's apartment, still under lease from his Chicago days. The three downed Scotch and held a long, deep discussion on baseball, friendship, and an emotional union of the two: Murcer's return to the team. Bobby expounded on the thrill of reclaiming Gotham, for he was one of the proudest Yankees to ever don the uniform. He had felt lost in San Francisco and Chicago, as the championship years sorrowfully passed him by. Eventually, he broke into tears.

With daybreak appearing on the horizon, the colloquy came around to what weighed heavily on the hearts of Munson's two teammates. "What did you get that jet for??" Murcer begged. "This isn't the same as the Beechcraft. This is a horse of another color. Are you sure you know what you are doing?"

Thurman was adamant in response:

> I am comfortable. I am confident. I know I can fly this plane.
> I'll tell you what. I have it out at a local airport. I'm flying home from here after Wednesday's game. I'll take you up tomorrow before the game. I'll show you I know what I'm doing.[35]

That appeared fair, and so the men agreed. They spoke a short time longer before all three retired for a period.

After minimal sleep, the trio awakened and, on Munson's insistence, Murcer drove them to the hangar where the Cessna resided. Thurman led the way inside. Gazing on the aircraft, the other two could not believe the colossal size and appearance. They climbed in, buckled up, and talked a bit. After a number of nervous moments, Murcer glanced anxiously at Piniella. "Let's do it some other time," he said uneasily. They unfastened their seat belts and Thurman let down the ladder. "Ahh," he chided, "There's no need to worry."[36]

From there, they drove to Comiskey Park to defeat the White Sox in Chicago's sixth straight loss. Munson was placed third in New York's batting order and stationed at first base to relieve his legs. He worked a base on balls in the first inning, lumbering down the line etched in pain. He looked weary that game. Slow. Beaten. Years of 140 games and reckless dedication had come back to taunt him. Reggie Jackson followed to the plate and eased Thurman's journey by slugging a home run.

It was 83° and clear at 9:15 P.M. in Chicago when number 15 stepped up for one more at-bat in the third inning. His aching limbs restricted every move. When he twisted his knee on the third strike, there was no muscle that could push further. He reached the gray concrete shelter of the dugout and shook his head, looking Billy Martin in the eye. "Skip, I'm done. Can't go anymore." According to some, it was the first time he had ever taken himself out of a baseball game. Munson hobbled back to the clubhouse, with the men left behind on his path frozen and quiet.

The Yankees soon filed in. Munson sat down to speak with Jackson in a long, reflective conversation. He spoke in golden pride of his plane and new pilot's license, which he pulled out of his wallet like a proud father. The Bombers had the next day, a Thursday, off before taking on Baltimore at home, so Munson took the opportunity to invite Murcer, Piniella, and Jackson to view some touch-and-go landings and take a ride in the plane. The former two declined in objection to his aviation. Bobby felt that by participating, he would be misconstrued as consenting or encouraging Thurman's flying. Reggie had additionally been asked to spend the day at Thurm's home and fly back to the Bronx on Friday. He had to turn it down because of a prior commitment to film a commercial in Connecticut, plus he had some plans with old buddies.

Munson's countenance soon grew serious. "This isn't fun anymore," he whispered. "Reggie, it hasn't been fun for a long time."[37] Jackson didn't know how to respond, how to console his teammate. It had been solemnly clear for a great stretch.

After the moment passed, Thurm again solicited Jackson to visit Canton, but the answer was a reluctant no. With that, Munson rose and said he'd see his teammates at Yankee Stadium on Friday. The self-proclaimed bad dresser, he strode away in a clean, white, pressed shirt the hue of a fresh league baseball. His slacks were a smooth charcoal, and a suit jacket hung over one shoulder.

Piniella crossed over to Jackson. "He may be hurting," Lou said, "but he looks good tonight, doesn't he?"

Reggie understood. "Always does when he's on his way to Canton."[38]

Stopping to tip the clubhouse boy, Munson walked out the door and hailed a taxi to the Midway airport.

Munson's plane touched safely in Canton at 3:00 A.M. August 2, 1979. His arrival at the house came shortly thereafter. Thurm drifted off to sleep for a few hours before awakening at 7:00 A.M. At that time, he sat for breakfast with Diane, then played with the children. Early in the afternoon, he and Diane met with her parents. Thurman mentioned to Tony Dominick that he had endured difficulties with the Cessna that morning and wanted to test it out. In addition to that, he needed to rack up hours for a jet license. Munson ate lunch in downtown Canton at a restaurant called Lucia's with some old friends. After he finished dining, he drove to the

Canton-Akron airport with two local men, David Hall and Jerry D. Anderson, licensed pilots of 32 and 31 years of age, respectively.

The weather was nondescript, generally excellent flying conditions. The three — Hall in the copilot's seat, Anderson in the passenger's, Munson at the helm — decided to try touch-and-go landings to identify the glitch. The plane departed to the left of the control tower at 2:45 P.M. They lightly toured the lovely Ohio countryside, circling the airport several times before Thurman radioed in for landing clearance. The reply was affirmative.

As Munson drew near, he dropped too slowly at 94 knots, or 108 miles, per hour. A safe descent would have been 104 knots, or 120 miles. Realizing what would later be deemed "pilot's error," he threw the throttle forward but got no response. A preliminary study would later cite a power failure. Anderson left his seat to kneel between the other two, in anticipation of the impending moment.

Descending at a rate that would place them 1,000 feet shy of Runway 19 and nearly 40 too low for the embankment concluding it, the plane dropped viciously. It swept some trees, and the wings were sheered off. The aircraft, uncontrollable at this point, skidded across the ground until it hit — miraculously for many bystanders— the only tree stump in the entire field. With that, the plane spun and flipped over a number of times before rolling a 500-foot distance to Greensburg Road, a two-lane highway 20 feet below the landing strip. Immediately, it was engulfed in flames.

Munson had truly made a pilot's error, a fatal error. Though he had buckled his seat belt across his waist before leaving, he had neglected to utilize the shoulder strap. As the jet crashed into the ground, his head bounced forward and struck an object in the cockpit with such a mighty force that he was instantly paralyzed from the neck down.

Hall and Anderson were relatively unscathed. The former kicked out a side door and dropped free to the earth, and Anderson struggled to follow. Instinctively, they looked for Thurman and noticed him still strapped in. Both men raced around the cockpit to save him. They found Thurm unable to move, though conscious, head jerked to the side due to his broken neck. From the exterior, Hall and Anderson tried desperately to unhook and release him for a long 30 seconds until the stored jet fuel exploded in a maniacal, roaring fire. The two were forced to scramble for their lives, clothes engulfed in flames as they ran.

Munson, 32 years old, husband, and father of three, held onto consciousness for three to four minutes. He passed away at 3:06 P.M. The official cause of death, as released by Summit County, Ohio, sheriff Anthony Gardarelli; was asphyxiation resulting from inhalation of superheated air and toxic substances. Simplified, it was a case of smoke inhalation.

By all accounts, Munson's last words were a betraying cry for such a strong, noble man. "Get me out of here," he pleaded. "Please get me out."

The first official on the scene was a man named Jeff Mashburn, the Summit County sheriff's deputy. "I saw an aircraft totally involved in flames," he reported. "Two subjects were running away from the plane."[39] Hall and Anderson managed to tell him there was a man still in the cockpit. At 3:07, Detective William Evans reached the site. He discovered Hall positioned against a tree nearby, eyes glassed over as he struggled for elusive breath. He had suffered burns on his hand, and his clothing was charred. Anderson too was breathless, lying on his back 90 yards from the plane with burns on his face, forearms, and neck. They would both be hospitalized in fair condition.

Mashburn rushed to the aircraft in light of the revelation that a victim was still in its cockpit. "I tried," he said, "but I couldn't come closer than thirty feet because of the intensity of the flames."[40] The body was found burned "beyond recognition."

As soon as Munson was identified, the police phoned Tony Dominick to break the news. He was asked to help the two officers and a detective tell Diane. When the group pulled up to the Munson house in Canton, the children were playing in the backyard, oblivious to what had transpired. Diane was alone in the house. She was understandably devastated by the news but held strong, at least strong enough to gather the children for an explanation. "Daddy has gone off to be with God," she whispered.

Michael, who was four years old, looked up at his mother and grandfather, their eyes filled with tears. "If my daddy's with God," he asked, "why is everybody crying?"[41]

It was 3:34 P.M. when Neal Callahan of the Chicago district office of the Federal Aviation Administration called Steinbrenner. George was tying up loose ends on the Oscar Gamble deal and had told his personal assistant, Gerry Murphy, to screen all calls with caution. Callahan anxiously insisted, "It's a matter of life and death."

Murphy told the Boss, "There's a man on the phone who won't identify himself, Mr. Steinbrenner. He just says he has to speak with you. He says it's a matter of life and death."

"Sure, put him on."

Quickly, Callahan identified himself and his position, then stated that a plane crash had occurred. "Your player, Thurman Munson, he's been killed."

George was blown away. He broke into a sweat. "Are you sure?" The confirmation was unequivocal. George regrouped to ask, "Does the family know?"[42] When that answer too was affirmative, he decided to call the veteran Yankees before they heard by way of the media. Cedric Tallis, the new general manager, would notify the remaining roster.

One of the first calls was to Hunter at his home in Norwood. Steinbrenner tried to be brief in order to be able to reach everyone before they heard it from an outside source. "You hear about Thurman?" he asked Cat.

"No."

"He's dead. He got killed in the worst way, crashed his plane and burned up." Having lost two close friends that year already, one being his father, Cat could not believe it. Neither did Nettles when Hunter crossed the street to notify him. Graig thought he was getting a rib. "Right. What's the joke?" he encouraged.

"No joke. Thurman's dead."[43] Suddenly, the phone rang. It was George. Nettles realized the truth.

Trudging back across the road, Cat explained to his son, Todd, what had happened. The young kid grabbed the mitt Munson had given him years before and placed it on the top shelf of his closet, never to be touched again.

The day was dark and dreary at Ron Guidry's New Jersey residence, where he relaxed with his wife, Bonnie, and her parents. "Ronnie, Thurman's dead," George informed him. "He crashed his plane."[44] The world went into slow motion for Guidry. Stepping softly to lower the volume on his television, he pulled up a rocking chair. There he sat quietly for five solid hours, uttering not a word.

One of the toughest to get to accept the news was Piniella. About 5:00 p.m. that afternoon, the phone rang. Hearing that it was Steinbrenner, he expected it was a consultation on team matters, as the two often exchanged. The weak voice that struggled to penetrate the telephone line suggested otherwise. George was a little slower this time in his explanation. "There's been a crash in Canton, Thurman's plane, very bad.... Thurman's passed away." Lou was confused and angry. First, he scorned Thurm for flying, then blamed himself for not having stopped him. He soon deposited the phone on its hook and choked out the words to his wife, Anita. "Thurman's dead. Killed in a crash."

Anita was hysterical. "Diane," she shrieked, "what about Diane?" She and Lou, and Bobby and Kay Murcer flew in to console Diane that day.

The story hit the wires as the clock read six. It made front-page copy from the East to West. The sportswriters who formerly had bathed Munson in scrutiny now lauded the depths of his story left overlooked. Most praise concerned his devotion to family and his classic heart.

Piniella was immediately phoned for comment. "I can't imagine the Yankees without Thurman. I can't imagine myself without Thurman. This is a death in the family."[45] That sentiment seemed to ring genuinely true throughout the baseball world. Accolades were spoken from every corner.

Commissioner Bowie Kuhn had never been close to Munson, but he knew the man's importance to the game. Kuhn regarded the death as "an almost indescribable loss. He was a wonderful, enormously likable guy, and a truly great ballplayer. As tough a competitor as he was on the field, he was a warm friend of baseball people and a loving family man. Baseball sends its heartfelt sympathy to his wife and children."[46]

Munson's attorney, Bob Woolf, was in Springfield, Massachusetts, where one of his clients, Larry Bird, was to accept an award. "It was an incredible shock to me," said Woolf. "It's inconceivable to me that we're here talking about it.... Thurman was such a vibrant person and a fine, young man.... He was much like Larry Bird. Both with dedication and a high code of ethics. They inherited the same Midwest culture."[47]

The eloquence of others came more subtly. Graig Nettles, the consummate humorist, could only mumble that he had expected to be a friend of Munson's for all of his life.

Early Friday morning, a hopeful crowd grew outside of Yankee Stadium. The denial in their hearts only increased at the sight of a bulky freight trailer delivering various baseball equipment. As though he would be there to wield them, a dozen new bats arrived bearing the name of Thurman Munson.

Not long after, George Steinbrenner stepped out of his vehicle. He had a pale, sickly complexion and dark glasses hiding the red, teary eyes of a night spent in disbelief. He managed to make a statement to the press:

> There is very little that I can say to adequately express my feeling at this moment. I've lost a dear friend, a pal and one of the greatest competitors ever known. We spent many hours together talking baseball and business. He loved his family. He was our leader.
>
> The great sport which made him so famous seems so very small and unimportant now. And therein lies a great lesson for all of us.[48]

There was some question as to whether the game would be played that night. Steinbrenner answered by explaining that Murcer had consulted Diane and she "said Thurman would want us to play, so we'll play."

It was announced that afternoon that Munson's number 15 was to be retired that day of August 3, 1979. He was only the ninth Yankee to ever be so honored. The company was truly fine: Babe Ruth (number 3), Lou Gehrig (4), Joe DiMaggio (5), Mickey Mantle (7), Yogi Berra and Bill

Dickey (8), Whitey Ford (16), and Casey Stengel (37). Today Munson is one of only four eligible Yankees with a retired uniform number not to be elected to the Hall of Fame, along with Billy Martin, Roger Maris, and Elston Howard. In fact, out of all the others that have reached Cooperstown, only Phil Rizzuto has had to wait for the Veterans' Committee to vote him in.

Additionally, a plaque was placed in Yankee Stadium's legendary Monument Park, which houses the likes of Ed Barrow, Jacob Ruppert, DiMaggio, Mantle, Stengel, Joe McCarthy, Ruth, Gehrig, and Miller Huggins.

Also retired that evening was Munson's locker. Twenty years later, Steinbrenner affirmed that it remained protected, nearly holy and unapproachable throughout the years. This certainly was the case that night as the players saw the eerie, empty sight. The uniform hung facing out, complimented by a Yankees hat, catcher's mask, and a pair of pants held on a hook for a stocky, grumpy backstop who would no longer make use of them.

In the clubhouse, the team met to discuss the proper tribute to their fallen teammate. The retired number and locker plus the plaque aside, they settled on donning black armbands for the remainder of the season. Among the other honors, memorial pins were made and a section of a street outside Yankee Stadium was renamed Thurman Munson Way.

A meeting was conducted by Billy Martin. Weak and derailed, he exhorted his men to progress, to hustle, and to perform with pride as their captain would have admonished. As he concluded, Steinbrenner entered, flanked by Cedric Tallis. Dressed in a blue suit, he stood by Munson's locker toward the back corner of the clubhouse. He expressed the impact of Thurman's contributions to the organization, not just the team, and that it took something of this magnitude to impress a true appreciation for life. "To be a Yankee player, to be the owner of the Yankees has always seemed so meaningful. Now it seems so meaningless in the light of all this."[49] Inevitably, he broke down. Then Piniella. Then Martin. The whole clubhouse fell into a silence that persisted throughout the day.

Across the field, in the visitors' clubhouse, the emotion was just as strong. Rick Dempsey, graduated now to Baltimore's regular catcher, respected Munson as much as any baseball man or most any other figure. "Our lives were a lot alike," he explained. "We had trouble with our fathers and our home lives."

Dempsey rhapsodized further in remembrance. "Last year I got a base hit, stole second, and scored on a close play in the ninth. Thurman was really mad 'cause he thought I was out. But in the bottom of the inning, he smiled at me from the dugout and flashed our special sign [an extension

Munson warms up on the sidelines at Yankee
Stadium, catcher's mitt on one hand and bat-
ting glove on the other. (National Baseball
Hall of Fame Library, Cooperstown, N.Y.)

of the thumb and pinky finger, with the middle three tucked inward]—it meant 'nice going, kid.'" Dempsey paused to scan the massive structure of Yankee Stadium. "Baseball will never be the same for me here. I'll miss talking to him and waving at him with our special sign. It's a tragedy because we have to stay here on earth and live without him."[50]

Game time came quickly. The Archbishop of New York, Terence Cardinal Cooke, canceled prior commitments to offer a prayer to the packed stadium for Thurman's family. As he spoke, both the New York and Baltimore clubs lined up on the top steps of their respective dugouts. Metropolitan Opera star Robert Merrill followed with a rendition of "America, the Beautiful." When he was through, there appeared on the center field screen a picture of Munson. Between the classic white facades, elevated in the higher reaches of the grand cathedral of baseball, stood the plain, gruff image of their spartan leader. A message ran, having been written by Steinbrenner earlier that day:

Our Captain and Leader has not left us—
Today, tomorrow, this year, next....
Our endeavors will reflect our love and admiration for him.

Eight men emerged, with the catcher's position left vacant in memorial as Jerry Narron waited in the dugout. The roaring assemblage was 51,151 people strong. As one body they stood, and cheered, and echoed for nine minutes. The applause shook Yankee Stadium as did the choking out chants of "Thurman ... Thurman ... Thurman...." Jackson lost control in right field, sobbing. An impossible bond had developed with Munson over the past year. The uproar naturally died down, but Piniella was riveted at his station. For a couple of minutes he stood motionless, just staring up at the distant picture.

The Yankees were defeated that Friday night by old farmhand Scott McGregor. The amount of persons who cared about the 1–0 loss equated roughly with the number of haircuts Munson endured in a year.

After the game, funeral arrangements were made for the following Monday morning, in possible conflict with a scheduled Baltimore game. "We'll go to the funeral," George Steinbrenner assured. "If we don't get back, we don't get back. We'll forfeit."[51]

By the governor's and mayor's decree, New York flags were flown at half staff.

One of the better quotes in the wake of Munson's death came from Carlton Fisk. Considering their relationship, it was a surprise. Considering his personality, it was nothing atypical. Clearing the air, he began:

There was no such thing as hatred or animosity between us. I had the utmost respect for him as a person....

> It was made out that there was a confrontation between us, but that wasn't justified in his eyes or mine. That was pure selfishness on the part of the owners and press to try to put more people in the ballpark.
>
> I think this shows you the vulnerabilities and frailties of this life we lead as ballplayers. This puts a dent in the fantasy that a major league player is important because some people think he leads a glamorous life. Baseball players are just human beings, as vulnerable to the fates and twists of life.
>
> I hope and pray the Lord looks down on his family and takes care of them.[52]

Early in Munson's career, he was a teammate of Lindy McDaniel. Besides the man's previously mentioned relief dominance, he also served as a lay preacher for the Church of Christ. Lindy hoped to convert many ballplayers and was quite successful in certain spots. But most people ignored his message and his monthly mailing of a newsletter entitled *Pitching for the Master*. Thurm could be counted among the rejecters. Yet mortality rarely fails in bringing the world closer to God for the guidance and comfort, as it did on Monday, August 6, 1979, when Munson was laid to rest in a Canton ceremony.

The Yankees, along with most of their wives, rose at five o'clock in the early morning to board a bus at Yankee Stadium. From there they arrived at the airport to fly to the Canton-Akron one. Once on the ground, the band collectively bused to the Canton Civic Center. The sight there was a remarkable testament. A thousand fans milled outside. Within, 500 attended. A mass of floral decorations covered the floor, including one in the shape of a baseball and another bearing the number 15. In the midst stood a gray casket draped with an American flag. White and blue flowers cascaded about it and several feet back a bright, vivid portrait of Munson was hung. Roughing a smile, he held his fist in his catcher's mitt before a soft blue background.

Diane was in the family waiting room, and wives flooded in to hug her warmly. Tracy and Kelly, nine and seven years of age, respectively, sat with their grandparents, the Dominicks, while Michael scurried about obliviously. He wore a miniature New York Yankees uniform, number 15.

Among those in attendance was Thurm's father, Darrell Munson. Back in 1975, when his wife suffered a stroke, he had left the family to live in Phoenix. It was one of the first times, if not *the* first time, he had seen his kin since the abandonment. They were not happy to reunite with him in the middle of the grief and anxiety already flourishing. Adding insult to injury, that Monday he assembled a press conference. "I was a better player than Thurman," he informed the scribes under the cover of a dark sombrero. "I never had the breaks he did, but I was a better player."[53]

When it came time to pay his final respects at the funeral, Darrell strode up to his son's casket, laughed, and walked away.

Diane, her children, and the Dominicks sat near the platform where Reverend J. Robert Coleman spoke. The pastor of St. Paul's Roman Catholic Church in Canton, he had married Thurman and Diane back in 1968. His complimentary oration was solemn and calm. Telegrams were read from Muhammad Ali (to whom Munson compared his confidence), Eleanor Gehrig (who nine years earlier had told John Ellis that Munson would be the one to replicate her husband's greatness), and Reggie Jackson (whose connection with Munson had evolved from bitter to bittersweet by its end). When Coleman finished, a hymn was sung, then players and close friends were invited to speak. Lou Piniella stepped out from the front row where his teammates and their wives sat.

Lou chose to first delve into Ecclesiastes and other selected scriptures. "We don't know why God took Thurman," he followed nervously, "but as long as we wear a Yankee uniform, Thurman won't be far from us. As a baseball player he was one of the best competitors. He played rough but fair. He was also a kind, affectionate, and friendly man."[54] Overwhelmed with emotion, Piniella stepped down.

Bobby Murcer took over. "He lived, he led, he loved," Murcer began in a eulogy that many remembered vividly years later:

Whatever he was to each of us—catcher, captain, competitor, husband, father, friend — he should be remembered as a man who valued and followed the basic principles of life....

As Lou Gehrig led the Yankees as the captain of the thirties, Thurman Munson captained the Yankees of the seventies. Someone someday should earn the right to lead this team, again, for that is how Thurm — Tugboat, as I called him — would want it. And that is how it will one day be —five years, ten years, whenever, if ever.... No greater honor could be bestowed on one man than to be the successor to this man, Thurman Munson, who wore the pinstripes with number fifteen. Number fifteen on the field, number fifteen for the records, number fifteen for the halls of Cooperstown.

But in living, loving, and legend, history will record Thurman as number one.[55]

Hundreds lined the five-mile route from the Canton Civic Center to the Sunset Hill Cemetery. The casket was carried by six of Munson's hometown buddies as pall bearers. Once at the gravesite, the Reverend Coleman prayed over the coffin. "Ashes to ashes," he whispered, "dust to dust." A few feet scuffed the grass, there came a silence, and the final prayers were uttered.

Departing on the team bus, the Yankee players were drowned in tears. As they pulled away from the cemetery, the vehicle drove past a strip of fast food restaurants. Nettles looked at it and laughed, "Only Thurman would get buried next to a Burger King and a pizza parlor."

Such coping was not an easy task; the thought of laughing while still considering Thurm's death seemed incomprehensible. Guidry was especially affected, yet struck by one echoing shadow of the past. Sifting through his emotions, Guidry drifted back to a game one year before. Martin had been headed for the mound to yank him, as Thurman stood by waiting. His countenance was rather quizzical, yet tranquil. "Gid, for the last half hour I've been watching those clouds in deep center field," Thurm droned, staring directly forward, deep into the morose sky. "They form and then suddenly break up, only to reform in a few minutes."[56] At the time, Guidry did not understand. In retrospect, his instincts were telling him to move on.

The Orioles volunteered to postpone the day's game to let the Yankees stay in Canton. But the players felt Thurman would want them to take the field. They returned comfortably in time for the night game.

Guidry manned the mound and by the seventh was losing 4–1 when Martin stepped out into the chilled evening to take him out. "I may lose this game," Ron told him sternly, "but I'm not going to come out until it's over. I have to win this one. This one's for Thurman."[57] Billy was impressed enough to accept it and let him continue. In the bottom of the inning, Murcer took Baltimore deep for a two-run bomb. He multiplied the feat two frames later. Almost single-handedly, he had lifted the Bombers to a sweet victory.

The players didn't leave Yankee Stadium until midnight. The win was an emotional lift and a splendid goodbye. But they failed to run with it. "The whole bottom fell out of the team," Billy Martin later said. "It was difficult from then on. Thurman's death took everything out of the club."[58] They quickly deteriorated to ineptitude. No longer could the club focus on baseball; it seemed a trivial, fictional story. Wrote Tommy John, "They could have cancelled the rest of the season. That's how bad we felt."[59] For an uncomfortable while they could not discuss Munson or even mention his name. Eventually, the team bus crossed by a heavyset man strolling along the sidewalk. "Hey, look at Thurman," someone howled. And that curbed the grief.

Finding a replacement for Munson on the field was more complicated than spotting one on the street. New York was demoralized behind the plate. The pitching had little confidence in the interim backstop. Not used to the added complication of minding their own pitch selection, they were thrown off noticeably. The team ERA rose a half point after his death. Guidry was the most affected, though he did recover quite well. He, as well as many others, resented the task of either shaking off a young catcher and diminishing his confidence or throwing a bad pitch to support him.

Rick Cerone was picked up from Toronto to inherit the role. The popular Jersey boy succeeded with a season in which he ranked seventh in the American League Most Valuable Player balloting. Before the clinching game of the 1981 World Series, however, he lashed back at George Steinbrenner for chewing out the team. (In all fairness to Steinbrenner, he would hire Cerone back as a broadcaster in 1997. The role was short-lived, though, as Rick soon moved on to ownership of an Independent League club.) But when injuries plagued him in '82 and '83, the door swung quickly for his exile to Atlanta. The Yankees never really did replace Munson at the catcher position.

Billy Martin's engagement in a hotel lobby scuffle earned an early termination of his contract after the season. Dick Howser took over and led the team to 103 wins and a divisional championship in 1980. A lost World Series in 1981 was the last hurrah for a short dynasty. It was often theorized that Munson spelled the 1980 and '81 championships for New York. And when times were so outlandish and unreal in the Bronx, he was noted as the sliver of class that kept the polish of the organization. Weathered, injured, unhappy, or not, he was the center of the Yankees.

No one was expected to hold the post of Yankee captain for a great while after Munson's death, just as Lou Gehrig's premature passing had left the position vacant. But in 1986, the heirs were crowned early. Guidry and Willie Randolph, by that time schooled veterans, were named cocaptains, the seventh and eighth in team history. The latter had broken out of his reserved shell. Now considerably vocal, he was known as the man who made newcomers to the team feel welcome, a trait he had learned from Thurman Munson. But not easily.

When Randolph came to the big leagues in 1976 he was treated every bit as badly by the Yankee veterans as rookies usually were. The elder statesmen of the House that Ruth Built, especially Munson, would order the rookies out of the cage during batting practice so they could take their cuts. When Randolph decided to take a stand, he went right to the heart of the clique, right for Munson. "Not knowing he'd probably kick my butt," Willie laughed to Tim Brown of the *Staten Island Advance* in 1999.[60]

After being told to leave the cage by Munson one afternoon, Randolph stared straight through his fear and into the steely eyes of his captain. "I'm not getting out," he spat confidently. "I put my pants on the same way you do." Years later he howled at the dead ring of his assertion, but at the time it was a leg to stand on. So Munson tried to hobble him.

"He jumped in my face," Randolph recalled, "kind of mocking, kind of looking like he was going to do something. I thought he was serious. I was like 'Uh-oh.'" Randolph clenched his fists and prepared for chaos, until Munson sneered at him.

"Hey, man," Thurm laughed. "Listen, if I didn't like you, I wouldn't mess with you."

Randolph was pleasantly surprised. "That was the first time I felt I belonged, that I was part of the group." Years later, he missed the man who had initiated him. "I was a young person. Thurman was a good friend of mine. When someone like that is taken away it's like having a family member taken away."[61]

That would be the atmosphere one year into Randolph's captaincy for the 1987 Old-Timers Day. Diane was called with an invitation to the event, and though she had returned only once since Thurman's death, she took the offer. The game was an exhibition of 1960s and 1970s Yankees, with the recurring theme of "One big team, present and past, together at last."

Kelly, by then seventeen years old, wrestled with the option of attending either the event or a vital state softball tournament. "I didn't want to force her to go to Yankee Stadium," Diane explained afterwards. Diane had remained energetic and active, spending the majority of her time between carpooling for high school and Little League. "That's not right," she continued in reference to forcing Kelly:

I wanted her to make her own choice. I said, "We're invited to
Yankee Stadium. I'm sure there'll be a lot of friends he played with,
plus I'm sure they'll mention your father. You decide what you
want to do, and I'll understand your decision and I'll support you."
She just drove herself crazy for four, five days deciding what to do.
Finally, she made the choice that she wanted to go to New York.
Her reasoning was that she didn't have that many memories of her
dad, and this was a time she thought she could hear some. I said,
'You know, Kelly, we're isolated from the Stadium, where they show
little tapes. People get to see his persona, and they get to be a part
of it every day at Yankee Stadium. But we don't. And we're there
so seldom that when we are there and they put those tapes on, and
the fans still get wild' and I'm getting choked up — it's still so
amazing for all of us. I think the kids should be a part of that. I
think they should know what he meant to the people; what he still
means to people. In New York, they loved him. I want the kids to
be able to feel some of that. And I don't want to make him a
monument, but I want them to share in his legacy.[62]

Legendary Yankee broadcaster Mel Allen stepped to the microphone
back of home plate to announce in his golden southern twang, "Welcome
to the 41st annual Old-Timers Day. We have a new format this year — one
that will match the stars of the '60s against the stars of the '70s. The likes
of Mickey and Whitey against the likes of Bucky Dent and Jim Hunter."
Catfish ended up introduced a dramatic last in honor of his induction that
summer to the Baseball Hall of Fame. He came out teary-eyed after the
display that followed.

Some player introductions were rattled off, then the organist played
"Auld Lang Syne." Allen's voice carried soft and calm as he requested a
moment of silence for "members of the Yankee family we have lost." Without mention of names, a video unfolded on the center field screen, a frame-
by-frame glimpse of Munson's career. A hit slapped to right field. Thurman
colliding with the catcher.... And on the receiving end. Triumphantly, he
pulled himself up, the ball cradled tightly in his stony palm. The picture
moved on to a shot of Diane and the kids in their private box behind home
plate. The crowd erupted in a growing ovation that cut off Allen's oration.

It would be a different story the second time around when on August
2, 1999, Diane was invited to throw out the first pitch at Yankee Stadium
on the 20th anniversary of her husband's death. Tracy, Kelly, and Michael
decided to stay in Canton this time, but Diane couldn't pass up the opportunity to brave her first 4:02 P.M. on the second of August not spent "in
private." The kids could not understand the change. "They think I'm a

glutton for punishment," she told Ursula Reel of the *New York Post.* "We are not a public family. But I thought it was appropriate for me to show the fans how much I appreciate their love and support.... If I didn't feel Thurman's spirit here, I wouldn't come."[63]

If his spirit wasn't visibly present, it was evident in the wall of number 15 jerseys outside the stadium and the gritty catcher who emulated Munson: 28-year-old backstop Jorge Posada had never seen Munson play, nor was he in the country to do so. But the Puerto Rican youngster had heard stories of Munson from his father throughout his childhood and wore the number 15 until reaching the Yankees. He continues to remember. Before every home game, Posada leaves his locker, which bears a quotation of Munson's, and travels to the center field monument that bears Munson's number 15. He taps it in memorial and heads to the field that his hero cannot take anymore.

New York, New York. Aside from Canton, it was the only city that truly knew Munson and the only one that truly remembers him today. Diane spoke to this pair of truths:

> New York knew him and knew the heart of a man.... For the rascal that Thurman could be at times, he was a good and gentle man, and people here could see that.
>
> I'm so amazed that when I go to Thurman's grave there are still flowers and baseballs put there for him. They are always from New Yorkers.[64]

Other memorials still live in Canton. Like father, like son: Michael Munson embarked in 1996 on a brief baseball career. The 21-year-old began in the Yankee organization with their Rookie League club, where he turned in a solid .300 average. Yet Mike lasted for only one game — not even an at-bat — with Class A affiliate Greensboro in '97. That's where son differed from father. Mike broke off from the loyal Yankees and latched on for 11 dismal games with the Indians' affiliate in Canton, Ohio, where he played at Thurman Munson Memorial Stadium.

Later in the summer of 1999, the Society for American Baseball Research — a comprehensive union of global baseball enthusiasts—conducted a poll of its 7,000 members concerning the top 100 ballplayers of the twentieth century. A total of 83,558 gross votes were cast. Among those nominated were Lee May, Ken Singleton, Dizzy Trout, Larry Doyle, Sal Bando, Cecil Cooper, Billy Pierce, Sherry Magee, and Chili Davis. Among former Yankee teammates on the list were Jimmy Wynn, Felipe Alou, Jackson, Lyle, and Nettles. Thurm failed to garner a single vote. There were times back a couple decades earlier when he wondered whether in 10 or 15 years young players would speak of Willie Randolph as having broken in "when Munson was still around."[65] Not many people remembered, and the ease with which they forgot Munson's name is his ultimate tragedy.

APPENDIX: CAREER STATISTICS OF THURMAN MUNSON

Minor and Major Leagues

Year	Club	G	AB	R	H	2B	3B	HR	RBI	BB	SO	SB	CS	Avg.	OBP	Slg.	PO	A	E	PB	F%
1968	Bing.	71	226	28	68	12	3	6	37	36	27	4	6	.301	.469	.540	327	53	9	5	.977
1969	Syra.	28	102	13	37	9	1	2	17	13	11	1	1	.363	.435	.529	81	13	6	1	.940
1969	NY	26	86	6	22	1	2	1	9	10	10	0	1	.256	.333	.349	119	18	2	5	.986
1970	NY	132	453	59	137	25	4	6	53	57	56	5	7	.302	.389	.415	631	80	8	10	.989
1971	NY	125	451	71	113	15	4	10	42	52	65	6	5	.251	.337	.368	547	67	1	9	.998
1972	NY	140	511	54	143	16	3	7	46	47	58	6	7	.280	.344	.364	575	71	15	9	.977
1973	NY	147	519	80	156	29	4	20	74	48	64	4	6	.301	.364	.487	673	80	12	10	.984
1974	NY	144	517	64	135	19	2	13	60	44	66	2	0	.261	.320	.381	743	75	22	6	.974
1975	NY	157	597	83	190	24	3	12	102	45	51	3	2	.318	.372	.429	725	95	23	9	.973
1976	NY	152	616	79	186	27	1	17	105	29	37	14	11	.302	.343	.432	546	78	14	12	.978
1977	NY	149	595	85	183	28	5	18	100	39	55	5	6	.308	.308	.352	657	73	12	10	.984
1978	NY	154	617	73	183	27	1	6	71	35	70	2	3	.297	.337	.373	698	61	11	8	.986
1979	NY	97	382	42	110	18	3	3	39	32	37	1	2	.288	.343	.374	428	44	10	5	.979

Major League Totals

G	AB	R	H	2B	3B	HR	RBI	BB	SO	SB	CS	Avg.	OBP	Slg.	PO	A	E	PB	F%
1423	5344	696	1558	229	32	113	691	438	569	54	50	.292	.350	.410	6342	742	130	93	.982

American League Championship Series

Year	Club	G	AB	R	H	2B	3B	HR	RBI	BB	SO	SB	CS	Avg.	OBP	Slg.	PO	A	E	PB	F%
1976	v. KC	5	23	3	10	2	0	0	3	0	1	0	1	.435	.435	.522	18	6	2	1	.923
1977	v. KC	5	21	3	6	1	0	1	5	0	2	0	0	.286	.273	.476	25	4	0	0	1.000
1978	v. KC	4	18	2	5	1	0	1	2	0	0	0	0	.278	.278	.500	22	4	0	1	1.000
Totals		14	62	8	21	4	0	2	10	0	3	0	1	.339	.333	.500	64	14	2	2	.975

World Series

Year	Club	G	AB	R	H	2B	3B	HR	RBI	BB	SO	SB	CS	Avg.	OBP	Slg.	PO	A	E	PB	F%
1976	v. Cin.	4	17	2	9	0	0	0	2	0	1	1	0	.529	.529	.529	21	7	0	0	1.000
1977	v. LA	6	25	4	8	2	0	1	3	2	8	0	0	.320	.370	.600	40	5	0	1	1.000
1978	v. LA	6	25	5	8	3	0	0	7	3	7	1	0	.320	.393	.560	33	5	0	0	1.000
Totals		16	67	11	25	5	0	1	12	5	16	1	0	.373	.417	.567	94	17	0	1	1.000

All-Star Games

Year	City	G	AB	R	H	2B	3B	HR	RBI	BB	SO	SB	CS	Avg.	OBP	Slg.	PO	A	E	PB	F%
1971	Det.	1	0	0	0	0	0	0	0	0	0	0	0	.000	.000	.000	1	0	0	0	1.000
1973	KC	1	2	0	0	0	0	0	0	0	1	0	0	.000	.000	.000	5	1	0	0	1.000
1974	Pitt.	1	3	1	1	1	0	0	0	0	0	0	0	.333	.333	.667	7	0	1	0	.875
1975	Mil.	1	2	0	1	0	0	0	0	0	0	0	0	.500	1.000	.500	1	1	0	0	1.000
1976	Phila.	1	2	0	0	0	0	0	0	0	0	0	0	.000	.000	.000	4	0	0	0	1.000
1977	NY	1	1	0	0	0	0	0	0	0	1	1	0	.000	.000	.000	0	0	0	0	.000
1978	SD	(selected for the team but unable to play due to injury)																			
Totals		6	10	1	2	1	0	0	0	0	2	0	0	.200	.273	.300	18	2	1	1	.952

NOTES

Preface

1. Don Johnson, ed., *Hummers, Knucklers, and Slow Curves* (Urbana, IL: University of Illinois Press, 1991), p. 109.
2. David Nemec and Pete Palmer, *1001 Fascinating Baseball Facts* (Lincolnwood, IL: Publications International, Ltd., 1994), p. 320.

Chapter 1. Munson v. State of Mind

1. Thurman Munson with Marty Appel, *Thurman Munson* (New York: Coward, McCann & Geoghegan, 1979), p. 163.
2. *Ibid.*
3. *Ibid.*
4. Sparky Lyle and Peter Golenbock, *The Bronx Zoo* (New York: Dell Publishing Co., Inc., 1979), p.110.
5. *Springfield* (Mass.) *Union,* August 3, 1979.
6. *Ibid.*
7. *Ibid.*
8. *Ibid.*
9. *Ibid.*
10. Whitey Herzog and Kevin Horrigan, *White Rat* (New York: Harper & Row, Publishers, 1987), p.104.
11. Bill Gutman, *At Bat: Carew, Garvey, Munson, Brock* (New York: Grosset & Dunlap, Publishers, 1978), p.113.
12. Gutman, *At Bat*, p. 93.
13. Wil A. Linkugel and Edward J. Pappas, *They Tasted Glory: Among the Missing at the Baseball Hall of Fame* (Jefferson, NC: McFarland & Company, Inc., Publishers, 1998), p. 85.
14. Lyle and Golenbock, *The Bronx Zoo*, p. 287.
15. *Springfield Union,* August 3, 1979.

16. *Ibid.*
17. Lou Piniella and Maury Allen, *Sweet Lou* (New York: Bantam Books, 1987), p. 183.

Chapter 2. Education of the Ohio Son

1. Bill Gutman, *At Bat: Carew, Garvey, Munson, Brock* (New York: Grosset & Dunlap, Publishers, 1978), p. 96.
2. *Ibid.*
3. Jim "Catfish" Hunter and Armen Keteyian, *Catfish: My Life in Baseball* (New York: The Berkeley Publishing Group, 1989), p. 206.
4. Gutman, *At Bat*, p. 96.
5. *New York Daily News*, November 25, 1970.
6. Gutman, *At Bat*, p. 98.
7. July 1999 author correspondence with Tim Lewis.
8. *Ibid.*
9. Gutman, *At Bat*, p. 102.
10. Gutman, *At Bat*, p. 104.
11. Wil A. Linkugel and Edward J. Pappas, *They Tasted Glory: Among the Missing at the Baseball Hall of Fame* (Jefferson, NC: McFarland & Company, Inc., Publishers, 1998), p. 85.
12. Gutman, *At Bat*, p. 101.
13. Gutman, *At Bat*, p. 101–102.
14. Gutman, *At Bat*, p. 102.
15. Gutman, *At Bat*, p. 113.
16. *Ibid.*
17. Robert O. Fishel, ed., *1971 New York Yankees Yearbook* (New York: New York Yankees, 1971), p. 7.
18. Thurman Munson with Marty Appel, *Thurman Munson* (New York: Coward, McCann & Geoghegan, 1979), p. 40.
19. Munson with Appel, *Thurman Munson*, p. 42.
20. Sparky Lyle and Peter Golenbock, *The Bronx Zoo* (New York: Dell Publishing Co., Inc., 1979), p. 276.
21. Munson with Appel, *Thurman Munson*, p. 44.
22. *Springfield* (Mass.) *Union*, September 3, 1969.
23. Gutman, *At Bat*, p. 106.
24. *Ibid.*
25. *Springfield* (Mass.) *Sunday Republican*, September 21, 1969.
26. David Nemec and Pete Palmer, *1001 Fascinating Baseball Facts* (Lincolnwood, IL: Publications International, Ltd., 1994), p. 74.

Chapter 3. Freshman in the Old School

1. Bill Gutman, *At Bat: Carew, Garvey, Munson, Brock* (New York: Grosset & Dunlap, Publishers, 1978), p.104.

2. Thurman Munson with Marty Appel, *Thurman Munson* (New York: Coward, McCann & Geoghegan, 1979), p. 55.

3. Bill "Spaceman" Lee with Dick Lally, *The Wrong Stuff* (New York: Penguin Books, 1985), p. 51.

4. Gutman, *At Bat*, p. 105.

5. *Ibid.*

6. Munson with Appel, *Thurman Munson*, p.56.

7. Robert O. Fishel, ed., *1971 New York Yankees Yearbook* (New York: New York Yankees, 1971), p. 30.

8. Fishel, ed., *1971 New York Yankees Yearbook*, p.17.

9. Munson with Appel, *Thurman Munson*, p. 56.

10. *Springfield* (Mass.) *Union*, June 22, 1970.

11. *Springfield Union*, June 26, 1970.

12. *Ibid.*

13. *Ibid.*

14. *Springfield Union*, July 7, 1970.

15. *Ibid.*

16. Fishel, *ed.*, *1971 New York Yankees Yearbook*, p. 17.

17. Munson with Appel, *Thurman Munson*, p. 59.

18. *New York Daily News,* November 25, 1970.

19. *Ibid.*

Chapter 4. Paying Dues

1. *Springfield* (Mass.) *Union*, April 6, 1971.

2. Robert O. Fishel, ed., *1971 New York Yankees Yearbook* (New York: New York Yankees, 1971), p. 17.

3. *Springfield Union*, April 8, 1970.

4. Thurman Munson with Marty Appel, *Thurman Munson* (New York: Coward, McCann & Geoghegan, 1979), p. 63.

5. David Nemec and Pete Palmer, *1001 Fascinating Baseball Facts* (Lincolnwood, IL: Publications International, Ltd., 1994), p. 195.

6. Munson with Appel, *Thurman Munson*, p. 64.

7. Rod Carew with Ira Berkow, *Carew* (New York: Simon & Schuster, 1979), p. 81.

8. *Springfield Union*, July 27, 1971.

9. Munson with Appel, *Thurman Munson*, p. 67.

10. *Springfield Union*, May 23, 1972.

11. *New York Times,* July 16, 1972.

12. *Springfield Union*, April 1, 1972.

13. *Ibid.*

14. *Ibid.*

15. *Springfield Union*, April 3, 1972.

16. *Springfield Union*, April 14, 1972.

17. Bill Gutman, *At Bat: Carew, Garvey, Munson, Brock* (New York: Grosset & Dunlap, Publishers, 1978), p. 109.

18. *Ibid.*

19. Gutman, *At Bat*, p. 117.

20. Danny Perry, ed., *Baseball's Finest* (North Dighton, MA: J.G. Press, 1990), p. 69.

21. Gutman, *At Bat*, p. 117.

22. *Springfield* (Mass.) *Sunday Republican*, April 23, 1972.

23. *Springfield Sunday Republican*, July 2, 1972.

24. *Springfield Union*, July 27, 1972.

25. Munson with Appel, *Thurman Munson*, p. 71.

26. *Springfield Union*, September 4, 1972.

27. *Springfield Union*, September 8, 1972.

Chapter 5. Object of New York Affliction

1. Thurman Munson with Marty Appel, *Thurman Munson* (New York: Coward, McCann & Geoghegan, 1979), p. 77.

2. Peter Golenbock, *Wild, High and Tight* (New York: St. Martin's Press, 1994), p. 241.

3. Graig Nettles and Peter Golenbock, *Balls* (New York: Pocket Books, 1985), p.1.

4. Golenbock, *Wild, High and Tight*, p. 259.

5. *Springfield* (Mass.) *Sunday Republican*, April 8, 1973.

6. *Springfield* (Mass.) *Union*, April 9, 1973.

7. Golenbock, *Wild, High and Tight*, p. 223.

8. Golenbock, *Wild, High and Tight*, p. 224.

9. Lou Piniella and Maury Allen, *Sweet Lou* (New York: Bantam Books, 1987), p. 92.

10. Golenbock, *Wild, High and Tight*, p. 224.

11. *Ibid.*

12. Sparky Lyle and Peter Golenbock, *The Bronx Zoo* (New York: Dell Publishing Co., Inc., 1979), p. 176.

13. Nettles and Golenbock, *Balls*, p. 55.

14. Nettles and Golenbock, *Balls*, p. 53.

15. *Springfield Union*, August 2, 1973.

16. Bill Gutman, *At Bat: Carew, Garvey, Munson, Brock* (New York: Grosset & Dunlap, Publishers, 1978), p. 111.

17. *Springfield Union*, August 2, 1973.

18. *Ibid.*

19. *Ibid.*

20. *Ibid.*

21. Gutman, *At Bat*, p. 111.

22. *Ibid.*

23. *Springfield Union,* August 3, 1973.

24. Jim "Catfish" Hunter and Armen Keteyian, *Catfish: My Life in Baseball* (New York: The Berkeley Publishing Group, 1989), p. 205.

25. Piniella and Allen, *Sweet Lou,* p. 137.

26. Bill Libby, *The Reggie Jackson Story* (New York: Lothrop, Lee and Sheppard and Co., 1979), p. 126.

27. Danny Perry, ed., *Baseball's Finest* (North Dighton, MA: J.G. Press, 1990), p. 66.

28. Nettles and Golenbock, *Balls,* p. 56.

29. *Ibid.*

30. *Springfield Union,* October 1, 1973.

31. Nettles and Golenbock, *Balls,* p. 56.

Chapter 6. Eastern Circuit Race

1. Dick Williams and Bill Plaschke, *No More Mr. Nice Guy* (San Diego: Harcourt Brace Jovanovich, Publishers, 1990), p. 168.

2. Lou Piniella and Maury Allen, *Sweet Lou* (New York: Bantam Books, 1987), p. 93.

3. Piniella and Allen, *Sweet Lou,* p. 88.

4. Piniella and Allen, *Sweet Lou,* p. 89.

5. Thurman Munson with Marty Appel, *Thurman Munson* (New York: Coward, McCann & Geoghegan, 1979), p. 80.

6. Bill Gutman, *At Bat: Carew, Garvey, Munson, Brock* (New York: Grosset & Dunlap, Publishers, 1978), p. 119.

7. Munson with Appel, *Thurman Munson,* p. 92.

8. Gutman, *At Bat,* p. 114.

9. Graig Nettles and Peter Golenbock, *Balls* (New York: Pocket Books, 1985), p. 62.

10. Sparky Lyle and Peter Golenbock, *The Bronx Zoo* (New York: Dell Publishing Co., Inc., 1979), p. 42.

11. Munson with Appel, *Thurman Munson,* p. 102.

12. Piniella and Allen, *Sweet Lou,* p. 107.

13. Jim "Catfish" Hunter and Armen Keteyian, *Catfish: My Life in Baseball* (New York: The Berkeley Publishing Group, 1989), p. 205.

14. Marvin Miller, *A Whole Different Ball Game* (New York: Simon & Schuster, 1991), p. 104.

15. Lyle and Golenbock, *The Bronx Zoo,* p. 37.

16. Lyle and Golenbock, *The Bronx Zoo,* p. 38.

17. *Springfield* (Mass.) *Sunday Republican,* September 21, 1969.

18. Munson with Appel, *Thurman Munson,* p. 110.

19. Hunter and Keteyian, *Catfish: My Life in Baseball,* p. 144.

20. Hunter and Keteyian, *Catfish: My Life in Baseball,* p. 145.

21. Hunter and Keteyian, *Catfish: My Life in Baseball,* p. 206.

22. *Springfield* (Mass.) *Union*, August 3, 1979.

23. Peter Golenbock, *Wild, High and Tight* (New York: St. Martin's Press, 1994), p. 249.

24. Golenbock, *Wild, High and Tight*, p. 245.

25. Golenbock, *Wild, High and Tight*, p. 246.

26. Billy Martin with Peter Golenbock, *Number One* (New York: Dell Publishing Co., Inc., 1980), p.17.

27. Wil A. Linkugel and Edward J. Pappas, *They Tasted Glory: Among the Missing at the Baseball Hall of Fame* (Jefferson, NC: McFarland & Company, Inc., Publishers, 1998), p. 86.

Chapter 7. The Experience Woke Up

1. Bill Gutman, *At Bat: Carew, Garvey, Munson, Brock* (New York: Grosset & Dunlap, Publishers, 1978), p. 119.

2. Peter Golenbock, *Wild, High and Tight* (New York: St. Martin's Press, 1994), p. 251.

3. Thurman Munson with Marty Appel, *Thurman Munson* (New York: Coward, McCann & Geoghegan, 1979), p. 130.

4. Munson with Appel, *Thurman Munson*, p. 128.

5. *Ibid.*

6. Munson with Appel, *Thurman Munson*, p. 129.

7. Golenbock, *Wild, High and Tight*, p. 251.

8. Munson with Appel, *Thurman Munson*, p. 9.

9. Dick Schaap, *Steinbrenner!* (New York: G.P. Putnam's Sons, 1982), p. 168.

10. Golenbock, *Wild, High and Tight*, p. 257.

11. Golenbock, *Wild, High and Tight*, p. 255.

12. Golenbock, *Wild, High and Tight*, p. 258.

13. Lou Piniella and Maury Allen, *Sweet Lou* (New York: Bantam Books, 1987), p. 115.

14. Golenbock, *Wild, High and Tight*, p. 259.

15. Golenbock, *Wild, High and Tight*, p. 256.

16. Jim "Catfish" Hunter and Armen Keteyian, *Catfish: My Life in Baseball* (New York: The Berkeley Publishing Group, 1989), p. 152.

17. Billy Martin with Peter Golenbock, *Number One* (New York: Dell Publishing Co., Inc., 1980), p. 33.

18. Mickey Morabito and Larry Wahl, ed., *1980 New York Yankees Yearbook* (New York: New York Yankees, 1980), p. s26.

19. *Ibid.*

20. *Ibid.*

21. Martin and Golenbock, *Number One*, p. 34.

22. *Springfield* (Mass.) *Union*, August 3, 1979.

23. Munson with Appel, *Thurman Munson*, p. 141.

24. Golenbock, *Wild, High and Tight*, p. 256.

25. Martin and Golenbock, *Number One*, p. 35.

26. Hunter and Keteyian, *Catfish: My Life in Baseball*, p. 152.

27. Joel H. Cohen, *Jim Palmer: Great Comeback Competitor* (New York: G.P. Putnam's Sons, 1978), p. 170.

28. Cohen, *Jim Palmer: Great Comeback Competitor*, p. 178.

29. Cohen, *Jim Palmer: Great Comeback Competitor*, p. 177.

30. *Ibid.*

31. Cohen, Jim Palmer: *Great Comeback Competitor*, p. 178.

32. Piniella and Allen, *Sweet Lou*, p. 126.

33. Martin and Golenbock, *Number One*, p. 40.

34. Piniella and Allen, *Sweet Lou*, p. 127.

35. Graig Nettles and Peter Golenbock, *Balls* (New York: Pocket Books, 1985), p. 102.

36. Piniella and Allen, *Sweet Lou*, p. 127.

37. Munson with Appel, *Thurman Munson*, p. 155.

38. Piniella and Allen, *Sweet Lou*, p. 128.

39. *Ibid.*

40. Shatzkin, Mike, ed., *The Ballplayers* (New York: Arbor House, William Morrow, 1990), p. 426.

41. Martin and Golenbock, *Number One*, p. 43.

42. Wil A. Linkugel and Edward J. Pappas, *They Tasted Glory: Among the Missing at the Baseball Hall of Fame* (Jefferson, NC: McFarland & Company, Inc., Publishers, 1998), p. 86.

43. Szen, David, *1986 New York Yankees Yearbook* (New York: Yankees Magazine, 1986), p. 165.

44. Munson with Appel, *Thurman Munson*, p. 165.

45. Golenbock, *Wild, High and Tight*, p. 265.

46. Schaap, *Steinbrenner!*, p. 172.

47. *Ibid.*

Chapter 8. Thorn in the Pride

1. Lou Piniella and Maury Allen, *Sweet Lou* (New York: Bantam Books, 1987), p. 133.

2. Dick Schaap, *Steinbrenner!* (New York: G.P. Putnam's Sons, 1982), p. 173.

3. Sparky Lyle and Peter Golenbock, *The Bronx Zoo* (New York: Dell Publishing Co., Inc., 1979), p. 206.

4. Schaap, *Steinbrenner!*, p. 176.

5. Ron Guidry and Peter Golenbock, *Guidry* (Englewood Cliffs, NJ: Prentice Hall, Inc., 1980), p. 125.

6. Lyle and Golenbock, *The Bronx Zoo*, p. 77.

7. Bill Libby, *The Reggie Jackson Story* (New York: Lothrop, Lee and Sheppard and Co., 1979), p. 130.

8. *Ibid.*

9. Thurman Munson with Marty Appel, *Thurman Munson* (New York: Coward, McCann & Geoghegan, 1979), p. 167.

10. Munson with Appel, *Thurman Munson*, p. 168.

11. Jim "Catfish" Hunter and Armen Keteyian, *Catfish: My Life in Baseball* (New York: The Berkeley Publishing Group, 1989), p. 157.

12. Peter Golenbock, *Wild, High and Tight* (New York: St. Martin's Press, 1994), p. 276.

13. Reggie Jackson with Mike Lupica, *Reggie* (New York: Ballantine Books, 1985), p. 153.

14. Piniella and Allen, *Sweet Lou*, p. 141.

15. Piniella and Allen, *Sweet Lou*, p. 137.

16. Golenbock, *Wild, High and Tight*, p. 271.

17. Libby, *The Reggie Jackson Story*, p. 130.

18. Billy Martin with Peter Golenbock, *Number One* (New York: Dell Publishing Co., Inc., 1980), p. 87.

19. Lyle and Golenbock, *The Bronx Zoo*, p. 47.

20. Libby, *The Reggie Jackson Story*, p. 138.

21. Jackson with Lupica, *Reggie*, p. 251-2.

22. Jackson with Lupica, *Reggie*, Critics' Review p. 4.

23. Martin and Golenbock, *Number One*, p. 32.

24. Jackson with Lupica, *Reggie*, p. 179.

25. Hunter and Keteyian, *Catfish: My Life in Baseball*, p. 156-7.

26. Jackson with Lupica, *Reggie*, p. 43.

27. Lyle and Golenbcok, *The Bronx Zoo*, p. 68.

28. Golenbock, *Wild, High and Tight*, p. 276.

29. *Ibid.*

30. Guidry and Golenbock, *Guidry*, p. 97.

31. Martin and Golenbock, *Number One*, p. 106.

32. Jackson with Lupica, *Reggie*, p. 146.

33. Schaap, *Steinbrenner!*, p. 185.

34. Martin and Golenbock, *Number One*, p. 108.

35. Schaap, *Steinbrenner!*, p. 184.

36. Schaap, *Steinbrenner!*, p. 184-5.

37. Schaap, *Steinbrenner!*, p. 185-6.

38. Jackson with Lupica, *Reggie*, p. 141.

39. *Ibid.*

40. Jackson with Lupica, *Reggie*, p. 143.

41. Jackson with Lupica, *Reggie*, p. 144.

42. Jackson with Lupica, *Reggie*, p. 150.

43. Jackson with Lupica, *Reggie*, p. 144.

44. Piniella and Allen, *Sweet Lou*, p. 138.

45. Munson with Appel, *Thurman Munson*, p. 171-2.

46. Golenbock, *Wild, High and Tight*, p. 271.

47. Golenbock, *Wild, High and Tight*, p. 272.

48. Munson with Appel, *Thurman Munson*, p. 172.
49. Golenbock, *Wild, High and Tight*, p. 272.
50. Jackson with Lupica, *Reggie*, p. 150.
51. Golenbock, *Wild, High and Tight*, p. 278.
52. Golenbock, *Wild, High and Tight*, p. 279.
53. *Ibid.*
54. Jackson with Lupica, *Reggie*, p. 155.
55. *Ibid.*
56. Munson with Appel, *Thurman Munson*, p. 172.
57. Jackson with Lupica, *Reggie*, p. 155.
58. Munson with Appel, *Thurman Munson*, p. 173.
59. Jackson with Lupica, *Reggie*, p. 156.
60. Jackson with Lupica, *Reggie*, p. 156-7.
61. Golenbock, *Wild, High and Tight*, p. 280.
62. Martin and Golenbock, *Number One*, p.113.
63. Golenbock, *Wild, High and Tight*, p. 280.
64. Martin and Golenbock, *Number One*, p. 113.
65. Jackson with Lupica, *Reggie*, p. 157.
66. Jackson with Lupica, *Reggie*, p. 158.
67. Golenbock, *Wild, High and Tight*, p. 280.
68. Libby, *The Reggie Jackson Story*, p. 137.
69. *Ibid.*
70. Golenbock, *Wild, High and Tight*, p. 281.
71. Jackson with Lupica, *Reggie*, p. 169.
72. Jackson with Lupica, *Reggie*, p. 171.
73. Martin and Golenbock, *Number One*, p. 122.
74. Munson with Appel, *Thurman Munson*, p. 177.
75. Golenbock, *Wild, High and Tight*, p. 287.
76. Golenbock, *Wild, High and Tight*, p. 288.
77. Munson with Appel, *Thurman Munson*, p. 178.
78. Piniella and Allen, *Sweet Lou*, p. 98.
79. *Ibid.*
80. Golenbock, *Wild, High and Tight*, p. 288.
81. Piniella and Allen, *Sweet Lou*, p. 99.
82. Martin and Golenbock, *Number One*, p. 125-6.
83. Piniella and Allen, *Sweet Lou*, p. 99.
84. Munson with Appel, *Thurman Munson*, p. 178-9.
85. Munson with Appel, *Thurman Munson*, p. 179.
86. Golenbock, *Wild, High and Tight*, p. 289.
87. Golenbock, *Wild, High and Tight*, p. 290.
88. *Ibid.*
89. Martin and Golenbock, *Number One*, p. 128.
90. Danny Perry, ed., *Baseball's Finest* (North Dighton, MA: J.G. Press, 1990), p. 67.

91. Perry, ed., *Baseball's Finest*, p. 67-8.

92. Hunter and Keteyian, *Catfish: My Life in Baseball*, p. 153.

93. Golenbock, *Wild, High and Tight*, p. 292.

94. Martin and Golenbock, *Number One*, p. 129.

95. Golenbock, *Wild, High and Tight*, p. 292.

96. Munson with Appel, *Thurman Munson*, p. 184.

97. Martin and Golenbock, *Number One*, p. 129-30.

98. Lyle and Golenbock, *The Bronx Zoo*, p. 52.

99. Jackson with Lupica, *Reggie*, p. 182.

100. Jackson with Lupica, *Reggie*, p. 183.

101. Jackson with Lupica, *Reggie*, p. 183-4.

102. Jackson with Lupica, *Reggie*, p. 185.

103. Jackson with Lupica, *Reggie*, p. 186.

104. Bill Gutman, *At Bat: Carew, Garvey, Munson, Brock* (New York: Grosset & Dunlap, Publishers, 1978), p. 130.

105. *Ibid.*

106. Guidry and Golenbock, *Guidry*, p. 101.

107. Piniella and Allen, *Sweet Lou*, p. 146-7.

108. Gutman, *At Bat*, p. 131.

109. Lyle and Golenbock, *The Bronx Zoo*, p. 13.

110. Golenbock, *Wild, High and Tight*, p. 296.

111. Lyle and Golenbock, *The Bronx Zoo*, p. 13.

112. Steve Garvey with Skip Rozin, *Garvey* (New York: Times Books, 1986), p. 113.

113. Munson with Appel, *Thurman Munson*, p. 191.

114. Golenbock, *Wild, High and Tight*, p. 297.

115. Tommy Lasorda and David Fisher, *The Artful Dodger* (New York: Avon Books, 1985), p. 261.

116. Gutman, *At Bat*, p. 133.

117. Jackson with Lupica, *Reggie*, p. 194.

118. Jackson with Lupica, *Reggie*, p. 249.

119. Jackson with Lupica, *Reggie*, p. 197.

Chapter 9. Keepers of the Flame

1. Roger Angell, *Late Innings* (New York: Ballantine Books, 1982), p. 47.

2. Bill Gutman, *At Bat: Carew, Garvey, Munson, Brock* (New York: Grosset & Dunlap, Publishers, 1978), p. 136.

3. Sparky Lyle and Peter Golenbock, *The Bronx Zoo* (New York: Dell Publishing Co., Inc., 1979), p. 33.

4. Wil A. Linkugel and Edward J. Pappas, *They Tasted Glory: Among the Missing at the Baseball Hall of Fame* (Jefferson, NC: McFarland & Company, Inc., Publishers, 1998), p. 83.

5. Thurman Munson with Marty Appel, *Thurman Munson* (New York: Coward, McCann & Geoghegan, 1979), p. 128-9.

6. Gutman, *At Bat,* p. 136.

7. Billy Martin and Peter Golenbock, *Number One* (New York: Dell Publishers, 1980), p. 216.

8. Lou Piniella and Maury Allen, *Sweet Lou* (New York: Bantam Books, 1987), p. 189.

9. Reggie Jackson with Mike Lupica, *Reggie* (New York: Ballantine Books, 1985), p. 245.

10. Jim "Catfish" Hunter and Armen Keteyian, *Catfish: My Life in Baseball* (New York: The Berkeley Publishing Group, 1989), p. 189.

11. Peter Golenbock, *Wild, High and Tight* (New York: St. Martin's Press, 1994), p. 299.

12. Lyle and Golenbock, *The Bronx Zoo,* p. 51.

13. Lyle and Golenbock, *The Bronx Zoo,* p. 70.

14. Bill Libby, *The Reggie Jackson Story* (New York: Lothrop, Lee and Sheppard and Co., 1979), p. 122.

15. Lyle and Golenbock, *The Bronx Zoo,* p. 71.

16. Lyle and Golenbock, *The Bronx Zoo,* p. 77.

17. Lyle and Golenbock, *The Bronx Zoo,* p. 72.

18. *Ibid.*

19. Lyle and Golenbock, *The Bronx Zoo,* p. 74.

20. Lyle and Golenbock, *The Bronx Zoo,* p. 75.

21. Lyle and Golenbock, *The Bronx Zoo,* p. 80.

22. Lyle and Golenbock, *The Bronx Zoo,* p. 82.

23. Lyle and Golenbock, *The Bronx Zoo,* p. 112.

24. Martin and Golenbock, *Number One,* p. 217.

25. Martin and Golenbock, *Number One,* p. 218.

26. Lyle and Golenbock, *The Bronx Zoo,* p. 114.

27. Hunter and Keteyian, *Catfish: My Life in Baseball,* p. 174.

28. *Springfield* (Mass.) *Union,* August 3, 1979.

29. Munson with Appel, *Thurman Munson,* p. 199.

30. Munson with Appel, *Thurman Munson,* p. 198.

31. Martin and Golenbock, *Number One,* p. 225.

32. Guidry and Golenbock, *Guidry,* p. 121.

33. *Ibid.*

34. *Ibid.*

35. Lyle and Golenbock, *The Bronx Zoo,* p. 171-2.

36. Lyle and Golenbock, *The Bronx Zoo,* p. 181.

37. Lyle and Golenbock, *The Bronx Zoo,* p. 198.

38. Lyle and Golenbock, *The Bronx Zoo,* p. 199.

39. Jackson with Lupica, *Reggie,* p. 200.

40. Lyle and Golenbock, *The Bronx Zoo,* p. 208.

41. Lyle and Golenbock, *The Bronx Zoo,* p. 203.

42. Jackson with Lupica, *Reggie*, p. 207.

43. *Ibid.*

44. Jackson with Lupica, *Reggie*, p. 208.

45. Martin and Golenbock, *Number One*, p. 236.

46. *Ibid.*

47. Martin and Golenbock, *Number One*, p. 237.

48. Munson with Appel, *Thurman Munson*, p. 200.

49. Golenbock, *Wild, High and Tight*, p. 308.

50. Martin and Golenbock, *Number One*, p. 237.

51. Lyle and Golenbock, *The Bronx Zoo*, p. 216.

52. *Ibid.*

53. *Ibid.*

54. Martin and Golenbock, *Number One*, p. 239.

55. Golenbock, *Wild, High and Tight*, p. 308.

56. Golenbock, *Wild, High and Tight*, p. 309.

57. Golenbock, *Wild, High and Tight*, p. 309-10.

58. Golenbock, *Wild, High and Tight*, p. 312.

59. Golenbock, *Wild, High and Tight*, p. 313.

60. Jackson with Lupica, *Reggie*, p. 216.

61. Golenbock, *Wild, High and Tight*, p. 313.

62. Jackson with Lupica, *Reggie*, p. 216.

63. *Ibid.*

64. Jackson with Lupica, *Reggie*, p. 219.

65. Jackson with Lupica, *Reggie*, p. 216.

66. Lyle and Golenbock, *The Bronx Zoo*, p. 223.

67. Golenbock, *Wild, High and Tight*, p. 304.

68. Golenbock, *Wild, High and Tight*, p. 314.

69. Golenbock, *Wild, High and Tight*, p. 315.

70. *Ibid.*

71. Piniella and Allen, *Sweet Lou*, p. 163.

72. *Ibid.*

73. Bill "Spaceman" Lee with Dick Lally, *The Wrong Stuff* (New York: Penguin Books, 1985), p. 186.

74. Lee with Lally, *The Wrong Stuff*, p. 187.

75. Jackson with Lupica, *Reggie*, p. 219.

76. Lee with Lally, *The Wrong Stuff*, p. 183.

77. Munson with Appel, *Thurman Munson*, p. 202.

78. Piniella and Allen, *Sweet Lou*, p. 165.

79. Piniella and Allen, *Sweet Lou*, p. 164-5.

80. Mickey Morabito and Larry Wahl, eds., *1980 New York Yankees Yearbook* (New York: New York Yankees, 1980), p. s26.

81. Peter Gammons, *Beyond the Sixth Game* (Boston: Houghton Mifflin Company, 1985), p.251-2.

82. Gammons, *Beyond the Sixth Game*, p. 154.

83. Piniella and Allen, *Sweet Lou*, p. 170.

84. Lyle and Golenbock, *The Bronx Zoo*, p. 295.

85. Jackson with Lupica, *Reggie*, p. 224.

86. Piniella and Allen, *Sweet Lou*, p. 170.

87. Carl Yastrzemski and Gerald Eskenazi, *Yaz* (New York: Doubleday, 1990), p.274.

88. Piniella and Allen, *Sweet Lou*, p. 170.

89. Jackson with Lupica, *Reggie*, p. 225.

90. Piniella and Allen, *Sweet Lou*, p. 171.

91. Gammons, *Beyond the Sixth Game*, p. 159.

92. Gammons, *Beyond the Sixth Game*, p. 160.

93. Yastrzemski and Eskenazi, *Yaz*, p. 275.

94. Gammons, *Beyond the Sixth Game*, p. 160.

95. *Ibid.*

96. Gammons, *Beyond the Sixth Game*, p. 161.

97. Linkugel and Pappas, *They Tasted Glory*, p. 83.

98. Jackson with Lupica, *Reggie*, p. 230.

99. Lyle and Golenbock, *The Bronx Zoo*, p. 58-9.

100. Jackson with Lupica, *Reggie*, p. 230.

101. Jackson with Lupica, *Reggie*, p. 232.

102. Tommy John with Dan Valenti, *T.J.* (New York: Bantam Books, 1992), p. 227.

103. Piniella and Allen, *Sweet Lou*, p. 175.

104. Hunter and Keteyian, *Catfish: My Life in Baseball*, p. 181.

105. *Ibid.*

106. *Ibid.*

107. John with Valenti, *T.J.*, p. 227.

108. David Nemec and Pete Palmer, *1001 Fascinating Baseball Facts* (Lincolnwood, IL: Publications International, Ltd., 1994), p. 293.

Chapter 10.　Early Descent

1. *Springfield* (Mass.) *Union*, August 3, 1979.

2. Richard Tellis, *Once Around the Bases* (Chicago: Triumph Books, 1998), p. 317-8.

3. Tommy John with Dan Valenti, *T.J.* (New York: Bantam Books, 1992), p. 244.

4. Reggie Jackson with Mike Lupica, *Reggie* (New York: Ballantine Books, 1985), p. 237.

5. John with Valenti, *T.J.*, p. 246.

6. Graig Nettles and Peter Golenbock, *Balls* (New York: Pocket Books, 1985), p. 232.

7. Billy Martin and Peter Golenbock, *Number One* (New York: Dell Publishers, 1980), p. 322-3.

8. John with Valenti, *T.J.*, p.249.

9. Sparky Lyle and Peter Golenbock, *The Bronx Zoo* (New York: Dell Publishing Co., Inc., 1979), p. 99.

10. Lou Piniella and Maury Allen, *Sweet Lou* (New York: Bantam Books, 1987), p. 184.

11. Peter Golenbock, *Wild, High and Tight* (New York: St. Martin's Press, 1994), p. 324.

12. Reggie Jackson with Mike Lupica, *Reggie* (New York: Ballantine Books, 1985), p. 236.

13. Golenbock, *Wild, High and Tight*, p. 324.

14. Jackson with Lupica, *Reggie*, p. 239.

15. *Ibid.*

16. Jackson with Lupica, *Reggie*, p. 240.

17. Martin and Golenbock, *Number One*, p. 326.

18. Golenbock, *Wild, High and Tight*, p. 326.

19. Martin and Golenbock, *Number One*, p. 326.

20. Golenbock, *Wild, High and Tight*, p. 326.

21. David Nemec and Pete Palmer, *1001 Fascinating Baseball Facts* (Lincolnwood, IL: Publications International, Ltd., 1994), p. 81.

22. Martin and Golenbock, *Number One*, p. 324.

23. Piniella and Allen, *Sweet Lou*, p. 184-5.

24. Martin and Golenbock, *Number One*, p. 332-3.

25. Jackson with Lupica, *Reggie*, p. 248.

26. Jackson with Lupica, *Reggie*, p. 245.

27. Jackson with Lupica, *Reggie*, p. 245-6.

28. Martin and Golenbock, *Number One*, p. 332.

29. Martin and Golenbock, *Number One*, p. 333.

30. *Ibid.*

31. Martin and Golenbock, *Number One*, p. 334.

32. Piniella and Allen, *Sweet Lou*, p. 190.

33. Piniella and Allen, *Sweet Lou*, p. 191.

34. John Thorn and Pete Palmer, *Total Baseball* (New York: Warner Books, Inc., 1989), p. 545.

35. Piniella and Allen, *Sweet Lou*, p. 185-6.

36. Piniella and Allen, *Sweet Lou*, p. 186.

37. Jackson with Lupica, *Reggie*, p. 247.

38. Jackson with Lupica, *Reggie*, p. 248.

39. *Springfield Union*, August 3, 1979.

40. *Ibid.*

41. Piniella and Allen, *Sweet Lou*, p. 189.

42. Piniella and Allen, *Sweet Lou*, p. 188-9.

43. Hunter and Keteyian, *Catfish: My Life in Baseball*, p. 189.

44. Guidry and Golenbock, *Guidry* (Englewood Cliffs, NJ: Prentice Hall, 1980), p. 137.

45. Piniella and Allen, *Sweet Lou*, p. 190.

46. *Springfield Union*, August 3, 1979.

47. *Ibid.*

48. *Ibid.*

49. Piniella and Allen, *Sweet Lou*, p. 191.

50. *Springfield Union*, August 3, 1979.

51. *Ibid.*

52. *Ibid.*

53. Danny Perry, ed., *Baseball's Finest* (North Dighton, MA: J.G. Press, 1990), p. 69.

54. Piniella and Allen, *Sweet Lou*, p. 193.

55. *Ibid.*

56. Guidry and Golenbock, *Guidry*, p. 139.

57. Guidry and Golenbock, *Guidry*, p. 137.

58. Martin and Golenbock, *Number One*, p. 331-2.

59. John with Valenti, *T.J.*, p. 249.

60. *Staten Island Advance*, July 30, 1999.

61. *Ibid.*

62. Hunter and Keteyian, *Catfish: My Life in Baseball*, p. 207.

63. *New York Post*, August 2, 1999.

64. *Ibid.*

65. Thurman Munson with Marty Appel, *Thurman Munson* (New York: Coward, McCann & Geoghegan, 1979), p. 146.

BIBLIOGRAPHY

Newspapers and Periodicals

Baseball Digest
New York Daily News
New York Times
Sporting News
Springfield (Mass.) *Sunday Republican*
Springfield (Mass.) *Union*

Books and Articles

Anderson, Sparky, with Dan Ewald. *Sparky!* Prentice Hall, New York, 1990.

Angell, Roger. *Late Innings: A Baseball Companion.* Ballantine, New York, 1982.

Biesel, David, et al., eds. *The Baseball Encyclopedia.* Macmillan, New York, 1974.

Bjarkman, Peter C., ed. *Encyclopedia of Major League Baseball: American League.* Carroll and Graf Sports, New York, 1993.

Carew, Rod, with Ira Berkow. *Carew.* Simon & Schuster, New York, 1979.

Cohen, Joel H. *Jim Palmer: Great Comeback Competitor.* G. P. Putnam's Sons, New York, 1978.

Fishel, Robert O., ed. *1971 New York Yankees Yearbook.* New York Yankees, New York, 1971.

Gammons, Peter. *Beyond the Sixth Game.* Houghton Mifflin, Boston, 1985.

Garvey, Steve, with Skip Rozin. *Garvey.* Times Books, New York, 1986.

Golenbock, Peter. *Wild, High and Tight: The Life and Death of Billy Martin.* St. Martin's, New York, 1994.

Guidry, Ron, and Peter Golenbock. *Guidry.* Prentice Hall, Englewood Cliffs, N.J., 1980.

Gutman, Bill. *At Bat: Carew, Garvey, Munson, Brock.* Grosset & Dunlap, New York, 1978.

Herzog, Whitey, and Kevin Horrigan. *White Rat: A Life in Baseball.* Harper & Row, New York, 1987.

Hunter, Jim "Catfish," and Armen Keteyian. *Catfish: My Life in Baseball.* Berkeley Publishing, New York, 1989.

Jackson, Reggie, with Mike Lupica. *Reggie.* Ballantine, New York, 1985.

John, Tommy, with Dan Valenti. *T. J.: My 26 Years in Baseball.* Bantam, New York, 1992.

Johnson, Don, ed. *Hummers, Knucklers, and Slow Curves.* University of Illinois Press, Urbana, Ill., 1990.

Lasorda, Tommy, and David Fisher. *The Artful Dodger.* Avon, New York, 1985.

Lee, Bill "Spaceman," with Dick Lally. *The Wrong Stuff.* Penguin, New York, 1985.

Libby, Bill. *The Reggie Jackson Story.* Lothrop, Lee and Sheppard, New York, 1979.

Linkugel, Wil A., and Edward J. Pappas. *They Tasted Glory: Among the Missing at the Baseball Hall of Fame.* McFarland, Jefferson, N.C., 1998.

Lyle, Sparky, and Peter Golenbock. *The Bronx Zoo.* Dell, New York, 1979.

Martin, Billy, with Peter Golenbock. *Number One.* Dell, New York, 1980.

McLain, Denny, with Dave Diles. *Nobody's Perfect.* Dial, New York, 1975.

Miller, Marvin. *A Whole Different Ball Game.* Simon & Schuster, New York, 1991.

Morabito, Mickey, and Larry Wahl, eds. *1980 New York Yankees Yearbook.* New York Yankees, New York, 1980.

Munson, Thurman, with Marty Appel. *Thurman Munson.* Coward, McCann & Geoghegan, New York, 1979.

Nemec, David. "The Four Dynasties," *1985 New York Yankees Yearbook.*

_____ and Pete Palmer. *1001 Fascinating Baseball Facts.* Publications International, Lincolnwood, Ill., 1994.

_____, et al. *Twentieth Century Baseball Chronicle.* Publications International, Lincolnwood, Ill., 1993.

Nettles, Graig, and Peter Golenbock. *Balls.* Pocket Books, New York, 1985.

Perry, Danny, ed. *Baseball's Finest: The Greats, the Flakes, the Weird, and the Wonderful.* J. G. Press, North Dighton, Mass., 1990.

Piniella, Lou, and Maury Allen. *Sweet Lou.* Bantam, New York, 1987.

Schaap, Dick. *Steinbrenner!* G. P. Putnam's Sons, New York, 1982.

Shatzkin, Mike, ed. *The Ballplayers.* Arbor House, William Morrow, New York, 1990.

Szen, David. *1986 New York Yankees Yearbook.* Yankees Magazine, New York, 1986.

Tellis, Richard. *Once Around the Bases: Bittersweet Memories of Only One Game in the Majors.* Triumph, Chicago, 1998.

Thorn, John, and Pete Palmer. *Total Baseball.* Warner, New York, 1989.

Ward, Geoffrey C., and Ken Burns. *Baseball: An Illustrated History.* Alfred A. Knopf, New York, 1994.

Weaver, Earl, with Berry Stainbeck. *It's What You Learn After You Know It All That Counts.* Doubleday, Garden City, N.Y., 1982.

Williams, Dick, and Bill Plaschke. *No More Mr. Nice Guy: A Life of Hardball.* Harcourt Brace Jovanovich, San Diego, 1990.

Yastrzemski, Carl, and Gerald Eskenazi. *Yaz: Baseball, the Wall, and Me.* Doubleday, Garden City, N.Y., 1990.

INDEX

Splittorf, Paul 122, 164–5
Sport 142–3
Springfield, Massachusetts 63, 226
Stanley, Bob 201–2
Stanley, Fred 78, 100, 110, 127, 136, 145, 164
Steinbrenner, George 6, 68–73, 79, 86, 89–92, 99–101, 106–10, 112, 116, 118, 120, 124–5, 131–2, 134–6, 139, 141, 148–160, 164, 172–5, 182, 185–6, 188–95, 197–8, 203, 207–8, 210–1, 213–6, 220, 224–7, 229, 232
Stengel, Casey 19, 45, 101, 124, 227
Stottlemyre, Mel 24, 30, 32, 41, 57–9, 86–7
Syracuse, New York 26–7, 31

Tallis, Cedric 190, 225, 227
Tepedino, Frank 22, 41
Thomasson, Gary 183
Thurman Munson: An Autobiography 12, 182
Tiant, Luis 71, 88, 120, 208
Tidrow, Dick 67, 86–7, 99, 110, 116, 123, 129, 137, 157, 159, 163, 166, 175, 180, 198, 208, 212–3
Torrez, Mike 139–40, 147, 156–7, 159, 162, 165, 167–8, 170, 175, 195, 200
Tresh, Tom 27–8, 37

Upshaw, Cecil 86

Veeck, Bill 189
Virdon, Bill 6, 22, 83–4, 87–9, 93–4, 97, 99–100

Ward, Robert 142–3
Weaver, Earl 48, 53, 65, 117, 119, 141, 177
Welch, Bob 205, 207
White, Bill 23, 170
White, Roy 39, 41–3, 50, 97, 99, 113, 119, 122, 126–7, 132, 138, 140, 149–50, 163, 165–6, 182, 186, 195–6, 200, 204–5, 208, 220
A Whole Different Ball Game 93
Williams, Dick 82–3, 118, 154
Wolff, Bob 5–6, 181, 226
Woodling, Gene 12, 19–20, 22, 30
Woods, Ron 26, 33, 40, 42
Wright, Harry 125
The Wrong Stuff 38
Wynn, Jimmy 147–8, 235

Yankee Stadium 85, 111–2
Yastrzemski, Carl 63, 75, 114, 147, 196–7, 200–3
Yeats, William Butler 72
Young, Cy 13, 94

Zimmer, Don 114, 184, 194, 200–1